An unknown flower in a strange land
speaks to the poet:
'Are we not of the same soil, my lover?'

Rabindranath Tagore

SHADES OF DIFFERENCE

SELECTED WORKS OF RABINDRANATH TAGORE

with

Audio Visual Material

Tagore & His World

Edited by

RADHA CHAKRAVARTY

SOCIAL SCIENCE PRESS

9.9 MEDIA

Published by

Esha Béteille
Social Science Press
69 Jor Bagh, New Delhi 110 003

Distributed by
Orient Blackswan Private Limited
Bangalore Bhopal Bhubaneshwar Chandigarh
Chennai Ernakulam Guwahati Hyderabad Jaipur
Kolkata Lucknow Mumbai New Delhi Noida Patna
www.orientblackswan.com

ISBN 978-93-83166-084

Set in Goudy Old Style 11/13
Typeset by Eleven Arts, Delhi 110 035

Printed by
Summit Advertising
2, DLF (Part), Industrial Area,
Moti Nagar, New Delhi 110 015

To Ma and Baba–
for opening the windows of my mind

CONTENTS

SHORT STORIES

PLAYS

PROSE

POEMS

Rabindranath Tagore. 1886

Portrait of Rabindranath Tagore by Gaganendranath Tagore

CONTRIBUTORS

Fakrul Alam is an academic, a literary critic, essayist and editor as well as a translator from Bengali. He is Professor of English at the University of Dhaka. He was a member of the jury of the Commonwealth Writer's Prize for 2003 (Eurasia region) and adjudicator for the DSC South Asian Prize for Literature in 2011. He received the SAARC Literature Award 2012 and the Bangla Academy Puroshkar for Translation in 2013. Forthcoming works include *Gitanjali: New Translations of the Nobel-Prize winning Poems* and *An Ocean of Sorrow*, a translation of *Bishad Sindhu* by Mir Masharraf Hussain. His publications include *Rabindranath Tagore and National Identity Formation in Bangladesh: Essays and Reviews* (Dhaka Bangla Academy, 2013); *Imperial Entanglements and Literature in English; South Asian Writers in English* (Writers ink, 2007); *Jibanananda Das: Selected Poems* (The University Press Ltd, 1999); *Bharati Mukherjee* (Twayne Publishers, 1995); and *Daniel Defoe: Colonial Propagandist* (University of Dhaka Publications, 1989). He has co-edited *The Essential Tagore* (Bellknap Press, 2011) and translated Sheikh Mujibur Rahman's *Unfinished Memoirs* (Penguin Books, 2012).

Nirmalkanti Bhattacharjee is former Director of the National Book Trust and former editor of the Sahitya Akademi's journal *Indian Literature*. Currently, he is Editorial Director of Niyogi Books. He has published three volumes of translation from Bengali into English that include the fiction of Mahasweta Devi, Sunil Gangopadhyay and Sirshendu Mukhopadhyay. He has also co-translated U R Ananthamurthy's short story collection into Bengali and co-edited a collection of stories of displacement from Assam under the title, *Barbed Wire Fence* (Niyogi Books, 2012). He is the winner of the prestigious IBBY international award for translation, 2012.

Aruna Chakravarti was Principal of Janki Devi Memorial College, University of Delhi, for ten years. She is also a well known academic, creative writer and translator and has contributed widely to national and international journals and anthologies. Three of her thirteen published books are in the field of creative writing. Two novels, *The Inheritors* (Penguin 2004) and *Jorasanko* (Harper Collins 2013), have been widely acclaimed by critics. The former was shortlisted for the Commonwealth Writers Prize and the latter is a best selling novel. The third is a volume of short stories, *Secret Spaces* (Zubaan 2010) Of her seven translations, her English rendering of Saratchandra Chattopadhya's *Srikanta* and Sunil Gangopadhyay's *Those Days* and *First Light*, published by Penguin Books India in 1993, 1997 and 2001 respectively, are considered among her best work. Her volume of translated stories from the masters of contemporary Bengali fiction entitled *The Way Home* (Penguin 2010) and a hundred lyrics of Rabindranath Tagore–*Tagore: Songs rendered into English*–(Vaitalik 1884) were also widely acclaimed as outstanding translations. The last has appeared in another avatar–*Songs of Tagore* (Niyogi Books 2012) with revisions and fresh inputs. Her last two works are *Primal Woman: Stories* (Harper Collins 2014), a translation of 15 stories by the master story teller Sunil Gangopadhyay, and *On the Wings of Music* which she has co-authored with Bollywood composer Shantanu Moitra. She has two academic works to her credit. A biography of Saratchandra Chattopadhyay, *Saratchandra: Rebel and Humanist* (National Book Trust 1985) and a work of literary criticism, *Empathy and Exile: The Novels of Ruth Prawer Jhabvala* (B.M. Publishing Corp. 1998). She is the recipient of several prestigious awards. Among them are the Vaitalik Award, the Sahitya Akademi Award and the Sarat Puraskar.

Radha Chakravarty is a writer, critic and translator. She has co-edited *The Essential Tagore* (Harvard & Visva-Bharati, 2011), nominated Book of the Year by Martha Nussbaum. She is the author of *Feminism and Contemporary Women Writers* (Routledge, 2008) and *Novelist Tagore: Gender and Modernity in Selected Texts* (Routledge, 2013). Her Tagore translations include *Gora* (Penguin, 2009), *Chokher Bali* (Random House, 2012), *Boyhood Days* (Hesperus & Penguin, 2007), *Farewell Song: Shesher Kabita* (Hesperus & Penguin, 2011) and *The Land of Cards: Stories, Poems and Plays for Children*(Penguin/ Puffin Classics). Other books in translation are Bankimchandra Chatterjee's *Kapalkundala* (Penguin, 2006), *In the Name of the Mother* by Mahasweta Devi (Seagull, 2004; nominated for the Crossword Translation Award), *Vermillion Clouds: Stories by Bengali Women* (Women Unlimited, 2010), and *Crossings: Stories from Bangladesh and*

India (Indialog, 2003). She has edited *Bodymaps: Stories by South Asian Women* (Zubaan, 2007) and co-edited *Writing Feminism: South Asian Voices* (UPL, 2010), *Writing Freedom: South Asian Voices* (UPL, 2010) and *Tagore, the Eternal Seeker: Footprints of a World Traveller* (ICWA, 2015). She is Professor of Comparative Literature and Translation Studies at Ambedkar University, Delhi.

Uma Dasgupta is a historian and Tagore biographer. She studied History at Presidency College, Calcutta, and did her doctorate in History at Oxford University. She retired as Professor in the Social Sciences Division of the Indian Statistical Institute. Her publications include *The Global Reception of Rabindranath Tagore 1913–2013* as ed. adv., OBS, 2015; *An Illustrated Life of Rabindranath Tagore*, (OUP, 2013); *Science and Modern India: An Institutional History, 1784–1947*, (Pearson Education, 2011); *Rabindranath Tagore: My Life in My Words*, (Penguin Books, 2010); *The Oxford India Tagore: Selected Writings on Education and Nationalism*, (OUP, 2009); *Rabindranath Tagore: A Biography*, (OUP, 2004); and *A Difficult Friendship: Letters of Edward Thompson and Rabindranath Tagore, 1913–1940*, (OUP, 2002). Forthcoming publications include: *Lonely Friendships of 'largeness and freedom': Charles Andrews, Mahatma Gandhi, Rabindranath Tagore: An Epistolary Account from Santiniketan's History, 1912–1940.*

Nandini Guha is Associate Professor, College of Vocational Studies, University of Delhi. She received the Katha Award for translating Bani Basu's novel *Dark Afternoons* (Katha, 2007). Other translations from Bangla to English include Taslima Nasreen's autobiography, *Wild Wind* (Srishti Publishers, 2006) and Anita Agnihotri's *Awakening*, (Zubaan, 2009). She has contributed to *Women in Concert* (Stree, Kolkata) and *The Essential Tagore* (Bellknap Press, 2011). Her translation of Professor Amalendu De's award winning historical treatise *In Search of Siraj's Son and Descendants* (Parul Prakashani, 2015), has been published recently. Awaiting publication is her translation of Bani Basu's novel *Swet Patharer Thhala.*

Ananda Lal is Professor of English, and Coordinator, Rabindranath Studies Centre and Tagore Cultural Centre, Jadavpur University, Kolkata. He directs Writers Workshop, the pioneering publisher of Indian writing in English. His books include the *Oxford Companion* *to Indian Theatre* (OUP, 2004) and *Rabindranath Tagore: Three Plays* (with new translations and the first full-length study in English of Tagorean drama) (OUP, 2001). His CD, *The Voice of Rabindranath Tagore*, compiled Tagore's own audio recordings. He has directed many theatre productions, including Tagore's *Arup Ratan* (as a multilingual musical) and *Tapati* (a site-specific performance). He is a scriptwriter, researcher, commentator, narrator and subtitler for film and television, much of this related to Tagore. He has lectured widely on Tagore in the USA, Canada, UK, Europe, Australia and, of course, India.

Subhransu Maitra is Superintendent (Publications) at Netaji Subhas Open University, Calcutta. He has worked in Public Relations, advertising and business journalism, and taught English at a Calcutta college. He is a translator of Bengali fiction, poetry and critical prose into English. Works in translation include *Gaandharva Poems* of Sankha Ghosh (Paschimbanga Bangla Akademi, 2004), *Wrong Number and other Stories* of Mahasweta Devi (Seagull), *Here & Beyond* (Yapanchitra Books), an anthology of Bengali short stories written by women, Tagore's letters to Mrinalini Devi, a Tagore collection (Publication Department, Visva-Bharati), *Education as Freedom* (Niyogi Books), and *Endless Night and Eternal Sunrise: Jibanananda's World* (Ekush Shatak, 2009).

Arunava Sinha translates classic, modern and contemporary Bengali fiction and nonfiction into English. Over thirty of his translations have been published so far. Twice the winner of the Crossword translation award, for Sankar's *Chowringhee* (2007) and Anita Agnihotri's *Seventeen* (2011), respectively, he has also been shortlisted for The Independent Foreign Fiction prize (2009) for his translation of *Chowringhee*. Besides India, his translations have been published in the UK and the US in English, and in several European and Asian countries through further translation. He was born and grew up in Kolkata, and lives and writes in New Delhi.

Rabindranath Tagore at the age of five

Samindranath Tagore, youngest son of Rabindranath Tagore, was a child prodigy who had blossomed into a playwright. He died in 1907 at the age of 11.

A MANY COLOURED WORLD

RABINDRANATH TAGORE AND THE DYNAMICS OF DIFFERENCE

> Sameness and difference, both must be taken into account. Without difference, the world cannot survive at all. All human beings are indeed equal, yet all human beings are different. . . . Similarly, between two independent cultures, there is the common element of human nature, but there is also difference. That disparity, indeed, is the saving grace. . . . If the temperature everywhere became uniform, the wind would not blow, the river would not flow, our spirit would not survive. . . . [Rabindranath Tagore, 'The Music of the Bauls'].

Life in its infinite variety provides the wellspring of inspiration for Rabindranath Tagore (1861–1941). His multifaceted genius revels in the shades of difference that define and animate our universe. Yet beneath this joy in plenitude runs a powerful cross-current: the longing for oneness, harmony and connectivity. The dialectical relationship between sameness and difference, unity and diversity, remains a vital driving force in the entire range of Tagore's writings. That crucial dynamic is the subject of this book. Tagore of course was neither a politician nor a sociologist. He did not produce a systematic philosophical theory. Yet, in his life and thought, he embraced a phenomenal range of ideas, ranging across fields as wide apart as religion, science, politics, social thought, philosophy, education, ecology, history, myth, literature, fine arts, popular culture, classical traditions, local custom, international relations and ethics. This very ability to think across the boundaries between disciplines demonstrates his awareness of the tension between difference and the possibility of transcending it. His writings, lectures, letters, dramatic works, musical compositions and paintings provide a fertile ground for exploring this productive tension.

The idea of difference is today fashionable in theoretical discussions. But 'difference' per se is not a term imbued with political or aesthetic significance, for in some theoretical frameworks, it can signify plurality without value. Tagore's intuitions and judgements, however, are never value-neutral. His recognition of heterogeneity and insistence on inclusivity do not imply an absence of ethical, moral, social, political and aesthetic discrimination. For instance, in his dialogue with Romain Rolland in 1930, even as he speaks of 'balance and harmony' and the need for cooperation between different cultures, Tagore also asserts: 'Truth cannot afford to be tolerant where it faces positive evil; it is like sunlight, which makes the existence of evil germs impossible' *(Shades of Difference: 252)*. This is typical of Tagore's approach. The cross-hatched patterns of difference represented in his works become meaningful only if we pay attention to questions of value. What does the text endorse in each instance, and what, by implication, does it negate or problematize? How does the process of writing become a way of negotiating conceptual or ideological conflict? These conflicts, too, are not staged in a vacuum. In re-reading Tagore, it is vital to contextualize, and to understand him as a man of his times, although he was also in many ways ahead of his times.

Nor is Tagore's thinking simplistic. While constantly alive to the heterogeneity of the world around him, he refuses to reduce things to rigid binaries. In place of black and white categorizations, we discover in his works fine-tuned shades of difference, a whole spectrum of possibilities. His thinking does not always seem consistent; in fact, he seems to revel in contraries. Patrick Hogan observes: 'He seems to shift continually between opposites. . . . Thus, he was the champion of the national movement. . . . But he was also the staunchest enemy of nationalism. . . . He was a patriarch and a critic of feminism. But he was also relentless in his attacks on the mistreatment of women. . . . He was well known for advocating the incorporation of European learning into Indian education. At the same time, he vociferously denounced what he viewed as the carceral structures and routines of European schools' (Hogan and Pandit: 9). Often, the Tagore text also dissolves apparent oppositions to present altered configurations that introduce new forms of conflict a renewed search for resolutions. What lends vibrancy to Rabindranath's writings is the desire for harmony that propels this quest, rather than the achievement of a static state of equilibrium. The process is dynamic, for rather than presenting foregone conclusions, his works provide the arena where the drama of contrary elements plays itself out, often arriving at precarious, provisional insights that do not have the cold finality of absolute truths.

Tagore's fascination with difference has much to do with the contradictions in his own personality. Some of these stem from his exposure to contrary influences in early life. Tagore asserts that he was born at the confluence of three great movements in Bengal: the drive for social reform, the renaissance in literature and the arts, and the nationalist upsurge. Rabindranath's family members were at the forefront of the movement for social reform during the years when Tagore was a child and an adolescent. His sister Swarnakumari Devi went to school and later became a prominent littérateur; his elder brother invited social controversy by bringing his wife out of 'purdah' or seclusion. Yet, as Tagore tells us in his memoirs *Reminiscences* and *Boyhood Days*, his earliest memories are of a home where most of the women lived in seclusion and child marriage was the norm for girls. In his own writings, the same ambivalence would surface in his intense preoccupation with the position of women in a changing society.

The Tagores belonged to the privileged class of zamindars or land-owners, yet Rabindranath writes with deep sympathy and understanding about the lives of the deprived. Accustomed to a life of privilege at their Kolkata home in Jorasanko, he underwent a life-changing experience when dispatched to mind the family estates in rural East Bengal during the 1890s. There, living on a boat on

Shilaidaha Kuthibari, in the Tagore family estate in East Bengal

The Padma river and the boat

the river Padma, he came into contact with the poor peasantry, and his social conscience was awakened. His writings, especially the stories he wrote during this period, express his sympathy for the underprivileged sections in society. The Sriniketan experiment in rural reconstruction probably owes much to this early phase in Tagore's life. Contact with the rural world also deepened Tagore's awareness of nature, and added a new dimension to his love for the landscape. The nature/culture relationship, generally treated as a binary fundamental to Western thought, acquired for Tagore a new complexity that no simple dualism could contain.

The young Rabindranath was brought up in a household that followed eclectic cultural practices, drawing elements from indigenous as well as European traditions. He was thus acutely aware of differences between cultures, but also receptive to a range of influences from traditions that did not always dovetail neatly. His emergence as a painter owed a great deal to his exposure to trends in diverse traditions of art, although he created a visual idiom uniquely his own.

Tagore's early life was frequently touched by the shadow of death. In his memoirs, he recounts the death of his mother, an event whose implications he did not fully understand at the time. He also talks of the devastating effect of the death of another person who remains unnamed, but is probably his sister-in-law Kadambari Devi, whose suicide left him permanently scarred. Paradoxically, this brush with death and loss was also the experience that taught him the value of life: 'Death had created the distance that is required for one to see the world whole, and to see it in all its beauty. From my position of detachment, I gazed at the image of the world etched against the vast backdrop of death, and realized that it was exquisitely beautiful'.[1]

The intimate relationship between life and death becomes one of the profoundest strains in Tagore's writings. The story 'Living and Dead' draws upon this paradox with incisive irony.

An inveterate traveller, Tagore journeyed across continents in search of connections with the peoples and places of the world. His contact with other cultures broadened his horizons and made him unusually sensitive to the need to reach out to our social and cultural 'others'. In *Gitanjali* this sensitivity would articulate itself through the dialectic between difference and unity:

> *Thou hast made me known to friends whom I knew not. Thou hast given me seats in homes not my own. Thou hast brought the distant near and made a brother of the stranger. . . .*
>
> *When one knows thee, then alien there is none, then no door is shut. Oh, grant me my prayer that I may never lose the bliss of the touch of the one in the play of many.* (*Gitanjali*: Poem 63)

Tagore's travels travels also influenced the complexity of his approach to the relationship of East and West. A stringent critic of British imperialism and what he regarded as Western materialism, he remained, nonetheless, a great admirer of English literature, Western music, and other aspects of European culture. Unlike Gandhi, he embraced the ideas of modern science, and saw contact between East and West as vital to the renewal of Indian society, which had become moribund and mired in obsolete practices. In a letter to C.F. Andrews (London, 1920), Tagore affirms the value of co-operation between different cultures rather than a forced homogeneity: '. . . let India stand for the co-operation of all peoples of the world' (*Shades of Difference*: 223). He goes against the prevailing spirit of non-cooperation promoted by Indian nationalists under Gandhi's leadership, arguing instead for a more nuanced approach to the East-West relationship:

> India has ever declared that Unity is Truth, and separateness is *maya*. This unity is not a zero; it is that which comprehends all, and therefore can never be reached through the path of negation. Our present struggle to alienate our heart and mind from the West is an attempt at spiritual suicide. . . . For it is the mind of Man, in the East and West, which is ever approaching Truth in her

> different aspects from different angles of vision. . . . Let us be rid of all false pride and rejoice at any lamp being lit in any corner of the world, knowing that it is a part of the common illumination of our house. (*Shades of Difference*: 223)

Tagore's writings disrupt the conventional opposition between backward-looking 'tradition' and a progressive 'modernity'. These terms, for him, are not absolute but relative, for their significance alters with changing contexts, and their importance diminishes when seen in relation to what he describes as the eternal, or the 'ever-new'. He distinguishes between modernity in the West and the need for modernization in India and other countries trapped under the colonial yoke. The West, he predicts, will go into decline, and the sun of the future will rise in the East.

Rabindranath Tagore. 1900

For a person born into privilege, Tagore's empathy with those at the margins of society provides a remarkable testimony to his capacity for crossing socially defined boundaries. Gayatri Chakravarty Spivak draws our attention to 'Apoman', a poem Tagore wrote after reading Kshitimohan Sen's translations of Kabir. Here, Tagore refers to 'human rights' (*manusher adhikar*) and predicts: '. . . my unfortunate country, you will have to be equal in disgrace to each and every one of those you have disgraced millennially' (Spivak: 19). Spivak takes this to mean: 'the one you fling down will bind you down there' (ibid.). This idea is already present in *Gitanjali*, and recurs at significant moments through Tagore's writings. In the epigrammatic *Stray Birds*, for instance, we hear the note of prophecy:

> *Man's history is waiting in patience for the triumph of the insulted man.* (*Shades of Difference*: 271)

In his writings, Tagore engages with diverse forms of prejudice and discrimination, based on differences of class, caste, gender, language, community and nationality. He raises his voice against social injustices and imbalances of power, making a plea for a more tolerant and harmonious world.

The position of women in society, for instance, remains a deep and persistent concern in Tagore's writings. They express his firm belief that for India to come into its own as a nation, it is necessary to acknowledge the place of women within the life of the nation. Alongside his preoccupation with the emancipation of women, Tagore is also concerned about the discourse of masculinity, which posits a set of norms by which men are to be judged. In the novel *Ghare Baire* (*The Home and the World*), this is one of the major issues explored through the triangular relationship between Nikhil, Bimala and Sandip. 'The Wife's Letter' is a story that records the rebellion of a wife against the shackles placed upon her freedom and individuality by a patriarchal society. The narrative also suggests the possibility of same-sex love.

The dance drama *Chitrangada* questions the stability of gendered identities and powerfully foregrounds the issue of women's claim to subjectivity and desire. Tagore's English version of the play, titled *Chitra* (1914), is included in this volume. Here, the legend from the *Mahabharata* about Arjuna's romantic encounter with the 'un-feminine' warrior princess Chitrangada ends with Chitra's proud assertion of her own uniqueness, which cannot be contained by any gender stereotype:

> *I am Chitra. No goddess to be worshipped, nor yet the object of common pity to be brushed aside like a moth with indifference. If you deign to keep me by your side in the path of anger and daring, if you allow me to share the great duties of your life, then you will know my true self. (Shades of Difference: 93)*

Interestingly, Tagore often adopts the female voice, especially in his devotional poems, love songs, and short stories. Virginia Woolf claims that true great minds, at the moment of creative expression, are androgynous; but in Tagore's works, the use of the female voice deliberately tests the limits of gender identities and asserts the need to think beyond them. Difference here becomes a call to imagine a stage beyond difference.

Although Tagore's treatment of gender issues is radical in many ways, his approach to women remains ambivalent, and not always consistent. In 1931, he writes to Hemantabala Devi about gender difference and the need for balance between masculine and feminine elements within each individual, and also within the world at large:

> Remember, all of us are in a sense Ardhanarishwar, the deity who is half male, half female.... Had the world been divided between

> pure women and pure men, the two elements could never unite. Hence, though there is no difficulty in mutual understanding, it is also possible to sustain our distinctive qualities within our respective spheres. In other words, the male is predominant and the female subordinate in the composition of masculine character, while in feminine character, the reverse is true. That is what generally happens, else it would be hard for balance to prevail in this world. *(Shades of Difference: 226)*

Gora *in Kannada, directed by Prakash Belawadi*

Here, a seemingly traditional essentializing of 'male' and 'female' elements is destabilized by the assertion that each gender includes elements of the other. In the essay 'Woman' (1936), Tagore speaks in conventional terms about woman as beloved and mother, but also makes a strong statement about the need to educate women in order to liberate their minds. Talking of the changing role of women in society, he hails them as the harbingers of a new world:

> If the call of the new age is knocking at their doors, I urge women not to allow their conservative minds to cling passionately to the age-old unhealthy rubbish–let them liberate their hearts, brighten their intellect and devote themselves to the cultivation of wisdom. They must remember that indiscriminate and blind conservatism is completely at odds with creativity. The new age of creativity lies ahead. (*Shades of Difference*: 205)

Clearly, for Tagore, the 'woman question' is not an isolated problem, but an issue to be considered in relation to larger social problems. This is only one instance of the way in which multiple forms of difference can intersect in a single literary text. The story 'Trespass' (*Anadhikar Prabesh*), for example, sets up a series of axes along which difference can be understood: pure/impure, high-caste/low-caste, human/animal, male/female, adult/child, and sacred/profane. The story's powerful ending disrupts the stability of these hierarchical divisions, in the protagonist's impulsive move to protect the 'other'.

Identity, when understood as a space where diverse socially-constructed subject-positions intersect, emerges as the product of a complex set of hierarchies. Tagore's novel *Gora* addresses the limits of this notion of identity-as-difference through its eponymous protagonist, an Irish orphan brought up by Indian foster-parents, who wrongly assumes that he is a high-caste Brahmin. The narrative of Gora's growth to self-knowledge is set within the larger narrative of a society in ferment, a nascent nation that must rise above petty identity politics in order to find strength in the underlying unity of all its diverse peoples. Only by losing the markers of conventional identity based on caste, class, religion and nationality, can Gora in the end declare himself a true Indian, '*bharatvarshiya*'.[2]

Tagore's egalitarian impulse finds expression in his opposition to communal strife, and his espousal of a tolerant religious ethic. This finds its inspiration in various sources, including not only his upbringing in a Brahmo household and his reading of the *Upanishads*, but also the mystical thought of Kabir, and the Bauls of Bengal. Tagore's translations of Kabir and the poem 'Kabir and the Woman' express this secular vision. Although he differed from the Bauls in many aspects of his thinking, and has been sometimes accused of misinterpreting Kabir, Tagore found elements in their work that strengthened his own humanist, syncretic approach to religion and society. About the mystics of medieval India, Tagore says: 'The Infinite cannot be comprehended through mere knowledge.... The god of the maramiyas is a very different god; He is the Lord of the Heart'.[3] Christ and the Buddha also emerge as inspirational figures in Tagore's writings, especially for bringing religion to the common man. In the evolution of Tagore's views on religion, it is possible to see a progression towards a faith centred on Man rather than God. To express his sense of the connection between the personal and the universal, Tagore creates the concepts of Jeebondebata, his personal god, and Viswadebata, the Lord of the Universe. In a lecture delivered at Santiniketan in 1921, he says: 'There is a certain space where God is entirely mine; in that space, there is just Him and me.... However, there is yet another point at which my personality merges with the universal. Jeebondebata resides within me but also goes beyond me, towards that indivisible, infinite, inexpressible joy represented by Viswadebata (the Lord of the Universe)' (Sen 2014: 153).

In *Gitanjali*, the poet abjures the elitism of Brahminical temple-rituals, and affirms his faith in a God who lives among the downtrodden toilers of this earth:

> *Leave this chanting and singing and telling of beads! Whom dost thou worship in this lonely dark corner of a temple with doors all shut? Open thine eyes and see thy God is not before thee!*
>
> *He is there where the tiller is tilling the hard ground and where the pathmaker is breaking stones. He is with them in sun and in shower, and his garment is covered with dust. Put of thy holy mantle and even like him come down on the dusty soil!* (*Shades of Difference*: 276)

The dignity of labour affirmed here is significant in its displacement of caste and class hierarchies. Tagore's discomfort with the exploitative aspects of the zamindari system, and his concern for the plight of the poor peasantry surfaces in many of his texts, including the novel *Ghare Baire* and the poem *Dui Bigha Jami*. Changing class relations in an emergent society figure prominently in the novel *Jogajog* (*Relationships*). In the essay 'The Cooperative Principle' (*Samabayniti*, c. 1928), he argues for the self-empowerment of the poor: 'It is the poor who bear the responsibility of freeing a society that has been trampled upon by the wealthy. It is for them to restore peace and harmony in society' (*Shades of Difference*: 181).[4]

At every level, from the localized politics of the zamindari system to national issues such as the struggle for freedom from British rule, to an international awareness of the need for contact between cultures, Tagore engages with forms of difference without succumbing to simple dualisms. His ideas on nationhood provide a graphic example of this. The difference between patriotism and nationalism is a grey area; critical opinion remains divided about Tagore's understanding of these separate but overlapping terms. According to Ashis Nandy, 'Tagore rejected the idea of nationalism but practised anti-imperialist politics all his life . . . at a time when nationalism, patriotism and anti-imperialism were a single concept for most Indians' (Nandy: 80). Dutta and Robinson argue that Tagore endorses the idea of self-respect, while rejecting patriotism (Dutta and Robinson: xx), but Amartya Mukhopadhyay insists that in the social sciences, patriotism is not a pejorative term. In contrast to nationalism, he says, patriotism represents a 'sentiment of attachment' as opposed to an 'ideology of national superiority', social allegiances rather than paternalism, and a natural feeling rather than an aggressive idealism.[5]

Tagore makes it clear in 'What is a Nation?' (1902) and later, in *Nationalism* (1917), that he perceives the nation as a limited ideal, derived from what he describes as the Western cult of materialism and aggressive self-aggrandizement. The slow but sure rise of the idea of 'one nation', spread across the world by imperialist politics, strikes him with dread. He blames the process on industrialization, utilitarianism, and the exploitation of nature by humans.[6] Tagore was convinced, though, that the situation would ultimately boomerang on the oppressors. In 'A Cry for Peace', for instance, he predicts the rise of the weaker nations who will defy the Western League of dominant nations.

Humanism, for Tagore, has greater value than nationalism, though he sees the two as interconnected. In 'Society and State' (*Swadeshi Samaj*, 1904), he declares: 'This we must know that every nation is part of humanity and each must answer the question: "What have you to give to man, what new ways have you discovered for his happiness?" As soon as a nation loses the vital strength for such discovery, it becomes a dead weight, like a paralyzed limb on the body of the universal man. Merely to exist is no glory.'[7]

As a counterpoint to this, Tagore posits the idea of 'society'. The nation emerges as more or less synonymous with the state, representing 'the organised self-interest of a whole people, where it is least human and least spiritual' (Tagore, 1991: 55). On the other hand, society is 'an end in itself', for it has 'no ulterior purpose' (Tagore, 1991: 55). Michael Collins calls it Tagore's 'contrast concept', because it offers an alternative to the idea of the nation. Swadeshi samaj, according to Tagore, 'is a spontaneous self expression of man as a social being. It is a natural regulation of human relationships, so that men can develop ideals of life in cooperation with one another'. Here, social relations 'are not mechanical and impersonal but based on love and cooperation'. In the essay 'Tagore's Non-Nation', Partha Chatterjee describes this as 'an attractive moral counterpoint for the intellectual critique of modernity' (Chatterjee: 126).[8]

With a sense of foreboding, Tagore seems to sense the rising tide of revolution that is likely to result from the forms of oppression at work in his world. In *Creative Unity* (c. 1927) he says: 'The people who grow accustomed to wield absolute power over others are apt to forget that by so doing they generate an unseen force which some day rends that power into pieces. The dumb fury of the downtrodden finds its awful support from the universal law of moral balance. . . . This has been proved in history over and over again, and stormy forces arising from the revolt of insulted humanity are openly gathering in the air at the present time.' The play *Raktakarabi* (1924) presents a dramatized version of the same idea. It shows us the power of the human spirit to revolt against tyranny and to challenge the supremacy of the machine.[9]

Tagore's dystopian view of divisive politics and oppressive hierarchies paradoxically provides the trigger for his utopian vision of a harmonious world. In *Gitanjali*, he articulates his desire in terms that succinctly express this tension between contraries:

> *Where the mind is without fear and the head is held high;*
>
> *Where knowledge is free;*
>
> *Where the world has not been broken up into fragments by narrow domestic walls . . .*
>
> *Into that heaven of freedom, my Father, let my country awake.*

The visionary dimension is evident also in Tagore's educational experiments. A school dropout who could never conform to the conventional patterns of the education system of his time, Tagore founded a school in Santiniketan in 1901, with the aim of exploring alternative approaches to learning, closer to nature and to indigenous traditions. 'The Parrot's Training' uses the fictional mode to present a succinct satirical indictment of the educational systems of the time for their attempt to stifle the freedom of the human spirit. To this system, Tagore's university, Visva-Bharati was meant to be a resounding rejoinder. Founded in 1918, Visva-Bharati was formally inaugurated in 1921. Here, he attempted to combine a rooted approach with one that was truly international. Rabindranath envisioned an alternative pattern of education that would be holistic and creative, with a view to nurturing the freedom of the mind. Education would be imparted in an environment close to nature and in harmony with the universe, and it would be modelled on a syncretic combination of the finest resources from across the world. Indian tradition would be combined with modern scientific knowledge, and languages and fine arts would be an essential part of the curriculum. The project for rural reconstruction, centred at Sriniketan, emerged alongside, as an attempt to generate social awareness and improve the lives of the socially marginalized inhabitants of the Bolpur area.

The motto of Visva-Bharati, *Yatra visvam bhavatyekanidam*—'Where the world makes its home in a single nest'—encapsulates this spirit. In his essay 'The Centre of Indian Culture', Tagore affirms: 'On each race is laid the duty to keep alight its own lamp of mind as its part in the illumination of the world. To break the lamp of any people is to deprive it of its rightful place in the world festival' (Tagore 1999: 482). The essay 'An Eastern University' develops the idea of dissemination of knowledge via local, regional and international levels: 'What is needed . . . is for the East to collect its own scattered lamps and offer them to the enlightenment of the world'. (*Shades of Difference*: 162)

Education, for Tagore, also represents a space where the perceived opposition between science and religion may be dismantled, and the spirit of religious tolerance nurtured through a broadening of mental horizons. In 'The Way to Unity' (July 1923), Tagore argues that each community must be allowed to develop along its own lines. He insists that communication between cultures can promote harmony, and feels that proper education should be promoted by all communities as a way of developing and liberating the mind.

Tagore's dialogue with Einstein (in Kaputh, on 14 July 1930) expresses Tagore's humanist interpretation of science and religion:

> The infinite personality of Man comprehends the Universe. . . . [T]he truth of the Universe is human truth. I have taken a scientific fact to illustrate this. Matter is composed of protons and electrons, with gaps between them; but matter may seem to be solid. Similarly humanity is composed of individuals, yet they have their inter-connection of human relationship, which gives living solidarity to man's world. The entire universe is linked up with us in a similar manner, it is a human universe. (*Shades of Difference*: 257)

To bridge the gap between the imperfections of our own world and the perfection of the ideal realm, Tagore develops the concept of the Supreme Man. He declares to Einstein:

> We realize the Supreme Man who has no individual limitations through our limitations. Science is concerned with that which is not confined to individuals; it is the impersonal human world of truths. Religion realizes these truths and links them up with our deeper needs; our individual consciousness of truth gains universal significance. Religion applies values to truth, and we know truth as good through our own harmony with it.

Tagore's conversation about science and religion demonstrates his ability to think beyond binaries even while retaining a fine-tuned awareness of difference. This transcendence of simple dualisms becomes apparent also in his rejection of the nature/culture divide, an idea central to many traditions of Western thought. Amit Chaudhuri rightly points out that Tagore sees nature as the very locus of culture, rather than its antithesis: 'for Tagore, nature is *the* site of civilization, refinement, and of certain ideals of the secular enlightenment, such as the ideal of living in harmony with the world' (Chaudhuri: 100). Tagore's educational experiment in Santiniketan is premised on a recognition of nature as the cradle of intellectual growth.

Tagore's love for nature springs from a profound apprehension of the link between man, environment and the universe. In a letter to Indira Devi written from Shilaidaha, Tagore expresses in a lyrical vein his profound ecological consciousness:

> This earth, like someone I have loved long, through many births, remains ever-new to me; the two of us share a very deep and extensive acquaintance. I can well remember that many ages ago, when the youthful earth had freshly emerged from her immersion in the sea to offer homage to the young sun of that era, I had blossomed into foliage as a tree in the new soil of this earth, in a primal life-urge that came from who knows where (*Chhinnapatrabali*, *Shades of Difference*: 217).

'The Divinity of the Forest' (*Aranyadevata*, 1938) presents a prophetic view of the environmental issues that we confront today, as we find ourselves grappling with an endangered planet: 'Man receives the bounty of nature greedily but not content with what he has received so easily he sets out to ravage nature mercilessly. That is why mankind now seems bent on turning earth into a desert' (*Shades of Difference*: 207).

Tagore's love for nature testifies to a passionate attachment to life and to the physical world, an urge that sometimes runs contrary to his spiritual longing for union with the divine. Some of his finest writings emerge from the pull of these contrary impulses. The artist's longing for withdrawal into contemplative solitude comes up against the awareness of his role in the world, for Tagore also feels intensely his living bond with the world around him. These tensions are framed within an overarching vision that encompasses the here and the hereafter in a single broad sweep. In this all-inclusive vision, even the humblest forms of existence acquire a special significance.

> *The same stream of life that runs through my veins night and day runs through the world and dances in rhythmic measures.*
>
> *It is the same life that shoots in joy through the dust of the earth in numberless blades of grass and breaks into tumultuous waves of leaves and flowers.*
>
> *It is the same life that is rocked in the ocean-cradle of birth and of death, in ebb and in flow.*
>
> *I feel my limbs are made glorious by the touch of this world of life. And my pride is from the life-throb of ages dancing in my blood this moment.* (*Gitanjali*. *Shades of Difference*: 262)

Tagore sees the eternal manifest in the transient, and celebrates the presence of abstract truths in the very dimensions of concrete reality.

Nowhere is this more apparent than in Tagore's representations of the body. In the sphere of dance, he sees the principles of beauty and rhythm played out in the movements of the body. Training in dance was an important part of the curriculum, especially for girls, in Santiniketan, for it provided a way of overcoming the inhibitions associated with the female body in traditional patriarchal discourse. Tagore's paintings reveal his recognition of the body as a vital aspect of human identity and self-expression. His writings, too, present the body as an important signifier. In the play *Natir Puja* (1926) for instance, the climactic scene affirms the centrality of the body in the act of devotion, as the court dancer expresses her spiritual surrender to the Buddha through the very ritual of dance itself: '*Bandana mor bhangite ar sangite biraje*' (my prayer resides in gesture and song).[10] In *Gitanjali*, although the poems are fraught with spiritual longing, the poet rejects asceticism for a vibrant entanglement with the material world.

> *Deliverance is not for me in renunciation. I feel the embrace of freedom in a thousand bonds of delight.*
>
> *Thou ever pourest for me the fresh draught of thy wine of various colours and fragrance, filling this earthen vessel to the brim.*
>
> (*Gitanjali. Shades of Difference*: 263)

The senses are not negated, but celebrated as a way of apprehending reality:

> *No, I will never shut the doors of my senses. The delights of sight and hearing and touch will bear thy delight.*
>
> *Yes, all my illusions will burn into illumination of joy, and all my desires ripen into fruits of love.*
>
> (*Gitanjali. Shades of Difference*: 263)

Novels such as *Chokher Bali* and *Chaturanga* assert the importance of recognizing woman as a desiring subject, and not merely as the object of male fantasy.

Language, like body language, provides Tagore with a dynamic field for the drama of difference. Alive to the rhythms of colloquial speech, Tagore was the first to introduce *chalitbhasha* or colloquial Bengali into the domain of literature, displacing the monopoly of *sadhubhasha* or chaste, formal Bengali. In 'Rhythm' (*Chhanda*), he affirms the importance of this move, drawing our attention to the suppleness and flexibility of the spoken idiom. 'The ground of colloquial Bengali is not even. . . . [I]t has its own play of undulations, like the waves of the ocean. . . . [I]n the treasure-chest of colloquial Bengali, . . . there is an accumulation of words from Sanskrit, Persian, English, and various other languages. . . . This broad-mindedness of colloquial language is a supreme value in our literature'. (*Shades of Difference*: 186)

Tagore frames the marginalization of colloquial Bengali within the larger context of the division between 'high' and 'popular' culture. He asserts: This Prakrit, or colloquial Bengali, has found its natural expression in women's nursery rhymes, Baul songs, and in the verses of Ramaprasad. But because it has not gained respect in classical Bengali, it has not been able to tell the world all about itself, and the full extent of its power remains unknown. . . . Its sense of identity is being eroded. . . .' Women, Bauls and Ramaprasad belong in the sociocultural space outside the mainstream. By aligning himself with their forms of expression, Tagore blurs the boundary between 'high' and 'low' culture.

Interestingly, his description of the status of colloquial Bengali uses a gendered trope that draws upon the public/private dichotomy of a patriarchal society: 'The lively, natural resonance of colloquial Bengali verse, when it encountered Sanskritized Bengali—what we call formal Bengali—found itself confined within four walls like a woman in purdah, kept within the zenana, the secluded quarters reserved for women.' In contrast, classical Bengali is presented in masculinized terms, associated with the law, order and social hierarchy of the public domain: 'classical Bengali is an artificial language; there, external rules reign supreme, while the laws of its own nature are often circumscribed. . . . In a public meeting, there is a place, an asana, assigned to each member. . . . [W]ith an eye to prestige, one must freeze the laws of human nature to fit the fixed laws of civilization.' Tagore's account of the dominant language seems to anticipate, though in a different context, some of Lacan's formulations about language, the Law of the Father, and the Symbolic realm.

Tagore, however, does not sustain this binary for long. Instead, he suggests an inclusive approach for the creative writer, who should be free to access a spectrum of resources upon which to draw, depending upon the specific demands of the work at hand. Rather than supporting the either/or approach through a simple reversal of the power axis, he argues for the value of a vital duality in place of a dull sameness: 'in the flowing stream of these two languages, if the rhythmic forms have taken divergent courses, then I am not at all in favour of objecting to this and blending everything into a uniform oneness by smearing purifying cow-dung over it. *Dwau kartavyau*, I say: we have a double duty. For, in matters of rhythm, my tongue is tempted by this very duality of taste.'

The politics of language also figure in Tagore's dialogue with H.G. Wells in 1930. Wells claims that 'we are reaching out for a new world-wide human order which refuses to be localized', and speaks of the likelihood that '[o]ne common language will probably be forced upon mankind whether we like it or not'. Tagore responds that even in the presence of a common international language, different national languages will not lose their force: 'this common language would probably not exclude national languages. In a characteristic generic boundary-crossing, he uses a musical analogy to describe the domain of words: 'Music of different nations has a common psychological foundation, and yet that does not mean that national music should not exist. The same thing is, in my opinion, probably true for literature.' (*Shades of Difference*: 248)

This ability to think across the differences between genres of writing, as well as those that separate diverse creative mediums is one of the extraordinary qualities of Tagore's entire oeuvre. In his written texts, he often incorporates poems in his fiction, converts songs into poems, and translates poems into prose. At other times, he combines different performative modes; his dance-dramas, for instance, combine theatre, music and dance in a seamless blend. Central to this process is the idea of translation. For Tagore, as for his most insightful interpreters, translation is not just a linguistic process, but also performative act that blurs the dividing lines between different languages, cultures, creative genres and audiences. It involves an awareness of difference, but also of potential communication and connectivity.

Perhaps the most unique examples of this inter-generic creativity are to be found in Tagore's doodles. Although he had early training in art and had intermittently dabbled in the visual arts throughout his life, it was late in life that Tagore blossomed into a painter of international repute. While his paintings themselves constitute a genre that is impossible to classify despite its many similarities to other traditions both Indian and Western, it is in the doodles that we find the supreme expression of Tagore's creative bent for cross-generic experiments. In these spontaneous scribbles, erased words and lines of handwritten manuscripts metamorphose into lines of miraculous drawing, so that the page simultaneously presents two creative works, one verbal, and the other visual. The two co-exist on the page, depend on each other in intimate relationship, but also assert their difference from each other. It is as if Tagore's genius overflowed beyond the limits of the written word and spilled over into the page in another, more mysterious form of self-expression.

Tagore with Victoria Ocampo at opening of his painting exhibition in Paris, 1930

This is what he tries to communicate to Romain Rolland in their famous conversation: 'Words are too conscious; lines are not. Ideas have their form and colour, which wait for their incarnation in pictorial art. Just now painting has become a mania with me. My morning began with songs and poems; now, in the evening of my life, my mind is filled with forms and colours.' (*Shades of Difference*: 256)

Although Tagore's thought and creativity continued to evolve throughout his life, certain core concerns remain central to his writings: freedom, equality, politics, education, rural reconstruction, culture, ecology, science, religion, forms of domination and marginalization, collaboration between cultures, tolerance, creativity and philosophy. On many counts, Tagore emerges as a prescient thinker. In the following conversation with H.G. Wells (June 1930), for instance, he seems to anticipate the controversies that surround the contemporary phenomenon of globalization:

> Tagore: The tendency in modern civilization is to make the world uniform. Calcutta, Bombay, Hong Kong, and other cities are more or less alike, wearing big masks which represent no country in particular.
>
> Wells: Yet don't you think that this very fact is an indication that we are reaching out for a new world-wide human order which refuses to be localized?
>
> Tagore: Our individual physiognomy need not be the same. Let the mind be universal. The individual should not be sacrificed. (*Shades of Difference*: 248)

This ability to hold heterogeneity and unity within the same range of vision is typical of Tagore's thought. He understands that perception is a matter of perspective. Anticipating the future age of explorations in outer space, he speculates about the presence of other worlds, and imagines the universe as a grand harmony of differences:

> How can we assert that at this very moment there do not exist countless similar worlds all around us, each imperceptible to all the others? What the minds there apprehend, know and perceive, according to their respective forms of consciousness, is utterly unknowable for us. Through the play of different minds, like the instruments in a great symphony, the outpourings of different worlds are simultaneously emerging, rolling forth towards an infinite unknown. (*In Persia*, *Shades of Difference*: 245)

Difference persists as a constant in Tagore's universe. Contradictions do not disappear, and antitheses are not neatly resolved. Patrick Hogan argues perceptively that 'Tagore's apparent contradictions are not contradictions at all, but the consistent pursuit of an anti-dogmatic, empathetic universalism in a world that is itself constantly changing and full of contradictions' (Hogan and Pandit: 11). The truth is actually more complex than this; Tagore's worldview is more profound than the mere pursuit of an anti-establishment stance might suggest. While he was always against dogma and blind faith, Tagore was also constantly trying to refine his value-structures in ways that would express a vision of unity without obliterating difference. To read Tagore is to immerse oneself in that dynamic. It has been a challenge, but also an exhilarating learning experience, working on *Shades of Difference*, the book and the Audio Visual Material. I wish to thank Esha Béteille for encouraging me to conceptualize and develop this dual project. A number of people offered me their valuable advice, including Sibaji Bandyopadhyay, Manabi Majumdar, Rosinka Chaudhuri, Dwaipayan Bhattacharya and Nirmalkanti Bhattacharjee. Without the effort put in by the entire team at Social Science Press—especially Chandana Dey, Radha Béteille, Ankita Sharma, Arup Giri and Neelima Rao—the book would not have been possible.

We are especially indebted to Sushanta Dattagupta, Upacharya, Visva-Bharati without whose help the Audio Visual Material would not have been possible. I am also overwhelmed by the generosity of all those who have helped us with material and permissions, especially Tapati Mukherjee (Director Rabindra Bhavan, Visva-

Bharati), Kumar Shahani, Mrinalini Sarabhai, Mallika Sarabhai, Rani Ray, Prakash Belawadi, Manoj Murali Nair and Madhuboni Chatterjee, Lubna Marium, Nayeema Ali, the Bengal Foundation (Bangladesh), the Shanghai Municipal Archives, Gustavo Canzobre, Francesca Cassio and Sanjog Sharan. I thank the contributors who have done the new translations in this text, and above all, I wish to acknowledge my debt to my family for their unwavering support.

The book presents a selection of Tagore's writings in several genres, including fiction, essays, travelogues, poems, plays and letters. New translations by diverse hands are included here, along with many of Tagore's own writings in English, and some of his works in translation. The illustrations in the book remind us that Tagore's multifaceted genius encompasses much more than the written word.

Tagore and his World, the Audio Visual Material that accompanies this volume, is an integral part of our project, for it attempts to present Tagore's creative engagement with the forms of difference within the larger context of his life and legacy. Through photographs, paintings, music and video, our endeavour is to offer a more comprehensive idea of Tagore's life and times, and also the extent of his creative range and influence. Arranged in separate sections that deal with Tagore's life, his travels and encounters with diverse places and personalities, his experiments in music, dance, theatre and the visual arts, and his dream university at Santiniketan, the Audio Visual Material provides significant audio-visual coordinates for the writings compiled in the book. It gives us a sense of Tagore as a man of his own times, but also reminds us that his creations live on through contemporary adaptations that speak to us in the language of the world we live in today. It alerts us to the difficulty of trying to label and define Tagore, for faced with the vastness and versatility of his achievement, we realize that attempts to pin down the 'real Rabindranath' in a one-dimensional definition are doomed to failure. In the infinite variety of his works and their changing reception through the years, the shades of difference are too many, and far too subtle.

Radha Chakravarty

NOTES

1. Rabindranath Tagore, *Jibansmriti* (1912), translated by Radha Chakravarty, *The Essential Tagore*: 48. See the section on 'Life' in the Audio Visual Material, for a brief pictorial biography
2. See the 'Performances' section of the Audio Visual Material for images from Prakash Belawadi's Kannada adaptation of *Gora*.
3. Rabindranath Tagore, 'The Mystics of Medieval India', trans. Amiya P. Sen, in Sen, ed., 81–82. Originally published in Bengali as Introduction to 'Dadu' by Kshitimohan Sen, in *Prabasi* (c. 1925).
4. Translated by Fakrul Alam.
5. Mukhopadhyay (147) cites Roger Scruton, *A Dictionary of Political Thought* (London.: Pan and Macmillan, 1982) 315–6.
6. Amartya Mukhopadhyay points out that Tagore's intuition anticipates Foucault's prediction, in *The Order of Things* (1970), that "the history of the order imposed on things would be . . . a history of the same" (Mukhopadhyay: 145).
7. Trans. Nirmalkanti Bhattacharjee. (*Shades of Difference*: 132–39)
8. Chatterjee contrasts Tagore's concept of Swadesh with Gandhi's idea of Swaraj. He argues that Tagore distanced himself from modern technologies of power, which had somewhat compromised the Gandhian ideal.
9. An excerpt from Madhuboni Chatterjee's stage adaptation of *Raktakarabi* (*Red Oleander*) is included in the Audio Visual Material that accompanies this book.
10. Translation mine. The English version of Tagore's poem *Pujarini*, which he later developed into the play *Natir Puja*, is included in this book (*Shades of Difference*: 274–75), and the Audio Visual Material contains clips from the stage adaptation *Hey Ananta Punya* produced by Shadhona (Bangladesh).

Tagore did not believe in adding titles to his pictures. The captions accompanying the paintings reproduced in this book are not Tagore's own, but descriptive phrases used by art critics when referring to these works.

REFERENCES

Alam, Fakrul and Radha Chakravarty, eds. *The Essential Tagore*. Cambridge, Mass.: Harvard University/ Belknap Press, 2011.

Chakravarty, Radha ed. *Shades of Difference: Selected Works of Rabindranath Tagore with Audio Visual Material, Tagore & His World*. New Delhi: Social Science Press, 2015.

Chatterjee, Partha. *Lineages of Political Society: Studies in Postcolonial Democracy*. Ranikhet: Permanent Black, 2011.

Chaudhuri, Amit. *On Tagore: Reading the Poet Today*. New Delhi: Viking/ Penguin India, 2012.

Collins, Michael. 'Rabindranath Tagore and Nationalism: An Interpretation'. *Heidelberg Papers in South Asian and Comparative Politics*, Working Paper 42. Oct. 2008, p.7. http://archiv.ub.uni-heidelberg.de/volltextserver/8844/1/HPSACP_COLLINS.pdf

Das, Sisir Kumar, ed. *The English Writings of Rabindranath Tagore* Vol. II. New Delhi: Sahitya Akademi, 1999.

Ghosh, Nityapriya, ed. *The English Writings of Rabindranath Tagore* Vol. IV. New Delhi: Sahitya Akademi, 2007.

Hogan, Patrick Colm, and Lalita Pandit, eds. *Rabindranath Tagore: Universality and Tradition*. Madison: Fairleigh Dickinson University Press, 2003.

Mukhopadhyay, Amartya. 'Bhinnata of Nations'. *Tagore: At Home in the World*. Ed. Sanjukta Dasgupta and Chinmoy Guha. New Delhi: Sage, 2013. 125–51.

Nandy, Ashis. *The Illegitimacy of Nationalism: Rabindranath Tagore and the Politics of Self*. Delhi: OUP, 1994.

Sen, Amiya P., ed. and trs., *Religion and Rabindranath Tagore: Select Discourses, Addresses, and Letters in Translation*. New Delhi: Oxford University Press, 2014.

Spivak, Gayatri Chakravorty. 'Ethics and Politics in Tagore, Coetzee, and Certain Scenes of Teaching'. *Diacritics*, 32. 3–4 (Fall/Winter 2002) 17–31.

Tagore, Rabindranath. *Nationalism*. 1917. Repr. London: Papermac, 1991.

____. *Creative Unity*. c. 1927

____. *Gitanjali*. 1912. Repr. New Delhi and Kolkata: UBS & Visva-Bharati, 2003.

____. *Selected Letters of Rabindranath Tagore*. Ed. Krishna Dutta and Andrew Robinson. Cambridge: Cambridge University Press, 1997.

SHORT STORIES

Tasher Desh
performed by Dancers' Guild, Kolkata

A FANTASTIC TALE

Far out in the ocean lies an island.* There, the only inhabitants are cards: Kings, Queens, Aces and Knaves. From Twos and Threes to Nines and Tens, there are many more families residing in households there, but they are not high-born.

Aces, Kings and Knaves: these are the three major castes; the Nines and Tens are indigenous people, unfit to dine with the high-born.

But their discipline is amazing. Each member's value and prestige has been determined ages ago, and there is no question of the slightest deviation, not even by a hair's breadth. All of them go about their respective duties as prescribed—down the generations, they merely follow the tracks of their ancestors.

What those duties are, it is hard for a foreigner to understand. One might suddenly mistake them for games. Simply following rules, coming and going according to rules, rising and falling according to rules. An unseen hand controls them, and so they move.

Their faces show no change of expression. Forever, the same expression is imprinted on them. Like the blank stare of a portrait. Since times immemorial, from the caps on their heads to the shoes on their feet, they have remained exactly the same.

Nobody ever has to think, or to use their judgement; all of them walk about with a lifeless, silent tread; when it is time to fall, they collapse noiselessly, and with an unperturbed countenance, they lie flat on their backs gazing up at the sky.

They have no hope, no desire, no fear—none of them. No effort to take a new path, no laughter, no tears, no suspicion, no doubt. Within the hearts of these picture-like figures, there is no sign of the restless anguish of a living creature, akin to the desperate fluttering of a bird in a cage.

*The play *Tasher Desh* (c.1933) is based on this story.

Yet once upon a time, within these cages, living beings had resided. Then, the cages would sway and from within them, the sound of wings and birdsong could be heard, arousing memories of deep forests and the vast sky. Now, in the cages, one can only feel a sense of confinement and the presence of iron bars arranged in precise order. Whether the birds have flown or died, or remain in a state of living death, who can say?

What extraordinary stillness and peace. Utter relaxation and contentment. Out in the streets and at home, everything is proper and orderly. No noise, no conflict, no eagerness, no enthusiasm, just routine, everyday, small tasks and small breaks for rest.

The sea, with is ceaseless monotonous sound, patting the shore with a thousand foam-white, tender palms, has kept the entire island wrapped in a sleepy stupor. The sky, like the outspread blue wings of a mother-bird, protects the peace of the environment, right up to the furthest horizons. In the far distance, like a deep blue line, the trace of a foreign land can be seen. From there, the struggle and clamour of anger and jealousy can't cross the ocean to reach this shore.

2

On that faraway shore, in that foreign land, lives a prince, the son of a Duorani, a queen who has fallen out of favour. With his banished mother, he spends his childhood by the seashore, lost in his own world.

Sitting in solitude, all by himself, he weaves in his imagination the net of a vast desire. Casting that net into the great beyond, gathering in his fantasy all the masses of mystery in the universe, he draws them in, to his own door. His restless spirit roves continuously beyond the range of those blue, horizon-blocking mountains close to the horizon at the edge of the sea. It wants to discover where the pakshiraj, the winged horse, may be found, or the jewel on the snake's hood, or the parijat, flower of paradise, or the magic rods of gold and silver. Or where, beyond the seven seas and thirteen rivers, in the inaccessible ogre's castle, a divinely beautiful dream princess lies asleep.

The prince goes to the pathshala, the local school, to study. There, at the end of their lessons, he hears the merchant's son talk about different lands, and the kotwal's son tell tales of those legendary figures, Tal and Betal.

The rain comes pouring down, clouds darken the sky. At the doorstep, sitting beside his mother, the prince gazes at the sea and says:

'Ma, tell me a story about a land that's very far away.'

The mother would tell a long-drawn-out story, heard in childhood, a wonderful story about a wonderful land. Listening to that narrative amidst the sound of pouring rain, the prince's heart would grow melancholy.

One day, the merchant's son came to the prince and said: 'So I am done with my studies, my friend; now I will set out on a tour of other lands. I have come to take your leave.'

'I'll go with you', declared the prince.

'Will you leave me alone, then?' demanded the kotwal's son. 'I too will be your companion.'

The prince went to his unhappy mother and informed her: 'Ma, I am going to travel. This time, I will return with a solution to your sufferings.'

The three friends set forth.

3

At sea, the merchant had a dozen boats ready. The three friends climbed aboard. The southerly breeze filled out their sails, and the boats raced ahead, like the prince's heartfelt desires.

They acquired a boatload of conch-shells at the Conch-shell island, a boat-load of sandalwood at Sandalwood island, and a boat-load of coral at Coral island.

After that, over the next four years, when four more boats had been loaded with ivory, musk, cloves and nutmeg, there was a sudden devastating storm.

All the boats sank. Just one boat flung the three friends onto an island, and then shattered into fragments.

On this island, the Aces, Kings, Queens and Knaves of cards lived according to the law, and the Tens and Nines also passed their time bowing and scraping at their feet, as the law prescribed.

4

In the land of cards, there had been no trouble, all this time. This was the first time that the seeds of complication were sown.

Now, after all this while, a matter for debate arose: these three men who had suddenly come up from the sea one evening, in what category where they to be placed?

First, what was their caste—ace, king, knave, or nines-and-tens?

Second, what was their subcaste—Spades, Clubs, Hearts, or Diamonds?

Until all this was settled, it was difficult to have any kind of interaction with them. Whose food they could accept, in whose company they could live, and among them, as per different rights, who could sleep with his head towards the north-west, south-west or north-east, and who must sleep standing up, none of these things could be determined.

In this kingdom, never before this had there been such a major cause for anxiety.

But the three famished friends had not the slightest concern for all these grave matters. How they could get some food by some means, was all that mattered to them. When they found everyone hesitating about offering them food and hospitality, and saw the Aces summon a huge gathering to seek out a legal solution, they began to devour whatever eatables they could lay their hands on.

Such conduct astounded even Two and Three.

'Dear Two', Three remarked, 'these people have no discrimination whatsoever!'

'Friend Three', Two responded, 'I can clearly observe that they rank even lower than us in the caste hierarchy.'

Having fed themselves, the three friends felt calmer. Now they noticed that the inhabitants of this place were of a new variety. As if they had no roots, anywhere in the world. As if someone had grasped them by the tiki, the tuft of long hair on their crown, and uprooted them. They seemed to lurch about in a sort of trance, having relinquished all contact with the world. All their actions seemed to be controlled by some invisible hand. Just like dolls on strings, in a puppet show. Hence nobody's face bore any expression, any emotion; all of them went about in a regular, orderly way, looking extremely grave. Yet it was an amazing spectacle, altogether.

Looking all around and observing this living lifelessness with all its pompous gravity, the prince raised his face to the sky and burst into a guffaw. In the public highway of the land of Cards, devoid of all noise and hubbub, this loud, spontaneous, heartfelt mirth sounded very strange. Everyone here was so extremely correct, so neat, so antiquated, so grave, that humour baulked at its own sudden eruption of unruly clamour, faded away, and was snuffed out altogether. The movement of people all around appeared twice as quiet and solemn as before.

The merchant's son and the kotwal's son grew desperate.

'Friend', they said to the prince, 'we don't want to stay in this joyless place, not even another hour. Spend a couple of days here, and we will have to touch ourselves to see if we are still alive.'

'No, my friends', responded the prince. 'I feel curious. These people look like human beings. I need to shake them up, to see if there is even a drop of living spirit in them.'

5

And so some time passed. But these three young men from elsewhere could not be contained by any rules. When and where it was appropriate to rise, sit, turn aside, lie face down, lie face up, shake one's head, or turn somersaults, they did not care at all; rather, they would observe everything sarcastically, and laugh. It was beyond their comprehension that in all these rule-bound, endless acrobatics, there resided an erudite gravity.

One day, the Aces, Kings and Knaves came to the prince, kotal and merchant and asked in hollow voices, with bland, grave expressions: 'Why don't you follow the rules?'

'It is our desire', replied the three friends.

Like sleepwalkers, the three leaders asked, in voices as hollow as empty handis: 'Desire! Who is that fellow?'

What desire was, they did not comprehend on that occasion. But gradually, they came to understand. Everyday they began to notice that instead of moving in a particular way, it was also possible to move differently. If one thing was possible, so was another. From foreign climes, three living examples came and demonstrated to them that rules alone did not set the limits for all human freedom.

In this way, the Cards began to feel indistinctly the influence of a ruling force called Desire.

No sooner had they experienced that feeling, than the entire kingdom of cards began to feel gently shaken, from top to bottom. It was slow, like the wakefulness that courses slowly through the many coils of a giant, sleeping python.

6

The Queens, expressionless figures, had not spared a glance for anybody up until now, going about their business unperturbed. Now, on a spring afternoon, one of them suddenly fluttered her deep, dark lashes like a flash of lightning, and cast a besotted sidelong glance at the prince. Startled, the prince exclaimed: 'What's this? I had taken them for lifeless statues—but it is not so! This is a woman, I now realize!'

Calling the kotwal's son and merchant's son aside, he said: 'Friends, there is an immense grace that resides in her. That sidelong glance of from her dark eyes, lit up with a new emotion, made me feel that I had witnessed the first sunrise on the first dawn of a newly created world. Today, our long, patient wait here seems worthwhile.'

With great curiosity, the two friends teased him: 'Is that so, indeed, O friend?'

The hapless Queen of Hearts now began to daily forget the rules. From moment to moment, she deviated from the rules that prescribed where she was supposed to be at given times of day. Imagine, for instance, that when she was supposed to stand in line, next to the Knave, she would suddenly take her place beside the prince. In a calm, sober tone, the Knave would say: 'Queen, you have made a mistake'. At this, the naturally rosy cheeks of the Queen of Hearts would grow even rosier, and she would lower her unblinking, tranquil gaze.

'There is no mistake', the prince would respond. 'From today, it is I who am the Knave.'

What unprecedented loveliness, what unimaginable grace showered forth, from the newly awakened female heart! What exquisite restlessness in her gait, what heartfelt turbulence in her gaze! What a fragrant, exuberant devotion her whole being seemed to exude, as if from a fountain!

In their attempt to focus with extreme concentration on correcting the errors of this new offender, everybody now began to make mistakes. The Ace forgot about his eternal prestige, there no longer remained any difference between King and Knave, and even the Tens and Nines began to behave oddly.

In this ancient isle, the call of the cuckoo had been often heard in spring, but that season, its call had a sound never heard before. Since times immemorial, the sea had sung in the same monotonous babble; but all these days, it had been singing the same tune, announcing the undimmed glory of the pure rule of law. Now, suddenly, like world-pervading restless waves of youth, stirred by the southerly breeze, it began to struggle to express the unfathomable depths of its yearning, in light and shade, through gesture and language.

7

Were these the same Aces, the same Kings, the same Knaves, as before? Where had it gone, that complacent, plump, rounded facial expression? Some gazed skywards, some lolled by the seashore, some could not sleep at night, while some lost all interest in food.

Some faces expressed envy, some love, some desperation, some doubt. Somewhere there was laughter, somewhere tears, and in other places, music. All of them had begun to pay attention to themselves, and to others. All were comparing themselves with others.

The Ace was thinking, 'The King may not be a bad-looking lad, but he has no grace. My movements have such a distinctive quality, that they cannot but attract the attention of certain people.'

The King was thinking, 'The Ace is constantly strutting about arrogantly. He thinks the Queens are broken-hearted at the very sight of him.' So saying, he gazed at his own face in the mirror, with a faint sneer.

All the Queens in the land were dressed to the nines, and observing each other, they would remark: 'Ah, this is to die for. Why must this vain woman dress so flagrantly, I ask? Her airs make me want to die of shame.' With these words, they would redouble their efforts to augment their looks and demeanour.

Again, on occasion, a pair of male friends, or a pair of female companions would carry on secret conversations in private, lost in each other's embrace. Sometimes laughing, sometimes weeping, sometimes angry, sometimes sulking, sometimes trying to win each other over.

The young men would rest their backs against tree-trunks, in shady forests by the wayside relaxing indolently with their legs outstretched over the heaps of dry leaves. Young women in blue, traversing that shaded path, lost in their own thoughts, would reach that spot, lower their heads, drop their gaze and walk away, as if they had now spotted anyone, as if they had not come there to be seen by anyone.

Observing this, some crazy youths would audaciously advance and come up close, but find themselves unable to summon up a single suitable speech. Awkwardly, they would stop short, the opportunity would be lost, and the woman, too, would gradually grow remote, like a moment from the past.

Overhead, birds would call, the breeze would blow away people's sari anchals and their hair, the leaves would rustle and murmur, and the ceaseless effusion of the sound of the sea would sway the unexpressed desires of the heart with redoubled force.

One spring, three youths from foreign climes came and raised such a fierce storm in what was once a dried-up channel.

8

The prince observed that the entire land was caught between high-tide and ebb-tide. No words, just the exchange of glances; just a step forward, then two steps back; just shoring up one's heart's desires, building a house of sand, then making it collapse. As if everyone was languishing in a corner, sacrificing themselves in their own fire, daily dwindling away, and growing inarticulate. Only the eyes glowed, and swayed by the turbulence of repressed speech, their lips trembled like leaves shivering in the wind.

Calling everyone together, the prince demanded: 'Bring your flutes. Bring on the horn and the drums. Rejoice, celebrate with music. The Queen of Hearts will choose her mate, in the ritual swayamvar ceremony.'

At once, Ten and Nine began to blow into their flutes, while Two and Three took up the horn and the bugle. In this sudden, tumultuous wave of rejoicing, the silent exchange of glances was disrupted.

During the festivities, as men and women mingled, what an effusion of words there was, and of laughter, and jollity. What mysterious ways of expressing one's deepest feelings, what pretended scepticism, what trivial gossip, to the tune of exuberant mirth. What began to happen among these people was similar to the diverse ways in which swayings and entanglements take place among the branches, leaves, vines and trees when the wind starts up in the depths of the forest.

Amidst such hubbub and festivity, from the beginning of the day, the flute began to play the ragini sahana in exquisite melodious tones. It awakened depth within rejoicing, yearning within union, beauty within the aspect of the universe, heartache within every heart. Those who had never loved in earnest now fell in love, those who had been in love now grew melancholy in their joy.

The Queen of Hearts, dressed in red, had spent the entire day concealed in a shady grove. The remote strains of sahana reached her ears as well, and her eyelids had grown heavy. Suddenly, at one point, she opened her eyes and found the Prince sitting before her, gazing at her face. Trembling, she at once sank to the ground, covering her face with both hands.

Pacing the seashore alone all day, the Prince ruminated about that terror-stricken glance and that bashful collapse.

9

At night, by the light of a hundred thousand lamps, in the fragrance of garlands, to the strains of the flute, at a gathering of a smiling row of ornamented, elaborately attired young men, a young girl came slowly, with trembling steps, carrying a garland, and stood before the Prince, her head bowed. The garland failed to reach the chosen neck, nor could she raise her eyes to the chosen countenance. The Prince then bowed his head, and the garland slipped down, onto his neck. The assembly, silent as a painting, suddenly burst into an effusion of joy.

With great pomp and ceremony, all of them escorted the wedded couple to the throne and ensconced them there. Together, they anointed the Prince and made him King.

10

From across the sea, the long-suffering Duorani arrived at her son's new kingdom on a golden boat.

The crowd of pictures had suddenly become human. Now, there was no longer the unbroken peace and unchanging gravity of yore. The flow of worldly life, with its joys and sorrows, rage and envy, risks and assets, filled the new kingdom of this young monarch. Now, some were good, some evil, some were happy, some were sad. Now, all had become human beings. Now, instead of every member remaining gentle and submissive according to unshakable rules, each of them, according to their individual will, could be good or evil.

(*Ekta Ashare Galpa*, c. 1892)
Translated by Radha Chakravarty

Rabindranath Tagore. Pen and ink and pastel on paper. 22 February 1935. Lahore

THE LIVING AND THE DEAD

1

The young widow, Kadambini, who lived in the household of the zamindar of Ranihaat had no parents, siblings or direct kin of any kind, for they had all died, one by one.* She had no one she could truly call her own, in the family in which she had been wed, neither husband nor child. The apple of her eye was her brother-in-law Saradashankar Babu's youngest son. His mother having contracted a long and complicated illness immediately after his birth, the care and nurture of the new born had fallen on his widowed aunt Kadambini. A foster mother's love is, perhaps, stronger and more unconditional than a biological mother's for she has no claim on the child. Society is willing to give her responsibility but not authority. She has no rights other than the right to love. But love cannot take the place of a legal document. It cannot be proved in a court of

* Rabindranath Tagore recounts that late one night, standing in the veranda, he suddenly felt he was not himself, that there was a rupture between his past and present selves. He resisted a wild impulse to see what might happen if he should tiptoe to his sleeping wife Mrinalini Devi, to tell her that the man she saw before her was not her husband. That night, he conceived the idea for the story 'Living and Dead', imagining a character wandering distraught at the realization that everyone else also believed she was not herself, but someone else. [Source: Maitreyi Devi, *Mangpute Rabindranath* (Bengali), p. 182, cited in *Rabindra Rachanabali Vol. 9*, Sulabh Sanskaran; Kolkata: Visva-Bharati, 1987, p. 686.]

law. Consequently, a bond thus formed is vulnerable and subject to assault. Having nothing else to feed on, except itself, it grows more bountiful and unstinting day by day.

Having showered all the love and longing pent up in her desolate soul, on the child in her care, Kadambini died suddenly on a wild rainy night of Sravan. Her heart stopped beating without any warning. Life went on uninterrupted around her. Nothing changed for anyone. Only the clock ticking in the young widow's tender breast fell silent. Fearing that delay might result in the police finding out and asking uncomfortable questions, Saradashankar Babu sent for four Brahmins and instructed them to carry the body to the burning ghat and cremate it that same night.

The burning ghat of Ranihaat was situated at quite some distance from the village. A river had flowed past it many years ago but now it was almost gone. The only relic of its existence was a pond which had been carved out of it before it went completely dry. This stagnant pool was revered by the locals as the once fast flowing Ganga and its waters were deemed holy. A banyan tree grew beside it and beneath its spreading branches a small hut had been built as a resting place for pall-bearers. Nothing else could be seen for miles.

The four Brahmins put down their load and sat in the hut waiting for the wood to arrive. Hours passed but no one came. Weary of the long vigil they decided that two of them, Nitai and Gurucharan, would go back and find out the cause for the delay. The other two, Bidhu and Banamali, would remain where they were, guarding the dead.

It was a dark monsoon night with clouds massed so tightly across the sky that not a star was visible. The two men sat silent for a long time. One of them had a lamp and a box of matches knotted at one end of his uduni. But he couldn't light it—the air was so damp. Presently the lantern they had brought along flickered and went out. Now they were in complete darkness.

'Bhai re!' Banamali exclaimed, 'A few puffs of smoke would make the time pass more quickly. We should have brought a hookah and some tobacco. But in the hustle of leaving we quite forgot. . . .'

'True,' Bidhu agreed instantly. 'It would have made a world of difference. Shall I run home and bring them? I'll be back in a jiffy.' Banamali realized that Bidhu was planning to escape. 'Indeed!' he exclaimed sarcastically, 'You run off home and I sit here, all alone, with the corpse for company. Nothing doing!'

The two men sat in sullen silence their backs to one another. Curses aimed at the other two rose to their lips but remained unuttered. Both were convinced that Nitai and Gurucharan had made no effort to track down the men who were to bring the wood. Instead they were sitting somewhere, in cosy comfort, smoking and chatting. The silence, broken occasionally by the chirping of crickets and croaking of frogs from the pond, became more acute with every passing minute.

Suddenly the cot on which the body lay creaked and moved as though the corpse was changing its position. Bidhu and Banamali rose trembling to their feet. And now a long shuddering sigh came wafting over the air. 'Ram! Ram! Ram! Ram!' The two men shrieked in terror and ran out of the hut in the direction of the village.

After running three miles or so they saw a light, which looked as though it came from a lantern, moving towards them. In a few minutes Nitai and Gurucharan came into view. Bidhu and Banamali were right in their assumption that the former had done nothing other than whiling away a couple of hours puffing at their hookahs. They hadn't made any enquiries about the wood but they had a story ready. A tree had been felled, they said, and was being split into logs. The work was almost done and the men would be arriving any minute now. Far from being apologetic at their prolonged absence they took the other two to task. What did they mean by abandoning their duty and leaving the corpse unattended? Bidhu and Banamali described what they had seen and heard but the other two laughed their story away. A heated argument followed, the former stoutly defending the testimony of their eyes and ears and the latter insisting it was a figment of their imagination. Finally, it was decided that all four would go back to the hut and keep a close watch. But, entering it, they got a shock. The cot was empty. The corpse had disappeared.

The four stared at one another, their jaws dropping in dismay. Could a jackal have dragged the body away? But the covering cloth was missing too! Searching every inch of the hut they came to the entrance. And there, etched in the wet earth, were freshly made foot prints. Small and light, they were clearly a woman's.

Breathless with shock, their lips white and twitching, the four men considered their position. Saradashankar Babu was a hard task master. Going to him with the truth would bode them nothing but ill. He would never believe their story. What should they do? After a good deal of argument and counter argument they arrived at a consensus. They would go back to the village and tell the zamindar that the work of cremation had been completed.

The men who were to bring the wood arrived at dawn to be told that, weary of the delay, the pall-bearers had cremated the body using the wood of which there was a sufficient stock in the hut. No one doubted the veracity of their claim. Why would they? A dead body is hardly a valuable commodity which anyone would care to steal or whisk away.

2

Everyone knows that sometimes a person only appears to be dead. In reality, life lurks within the body waiting for an opportunity to reassert itself. That was what happened to Kadambini. She hadn't died. For some unknown reason the workings of her organs had been suspended for a while. . . .

On coming back to life, she found herself lying on a strange bed in a strange room. She looked around with puzzled eyes. This wasn't the place in which she usually slept. And why was the darkness so intense? 'Didi,' she called softly. No answer. She sat up slowly. And now the events of the night came drifting into her memory. That sudden spasm of pain in her chest! The sense of suffocation. The inability to breathe. The sight of her sister-in-law warming her son's milk on some embers in a corner of the room. 'Didi,' she had called out. 'Give Khoka to me. Let me hold him to my breast. I feel. . . I feel so strange.' Even as she had said those words everything had gone dark and she had fallen crashing on the bed. As though an ink pot had toppled over on the book of her life. Smudging its contents. Wiping them out. Had Khoka called out to her in his high sweet voice? *Kakima!* Had that most precious, most beloved of calls entered her ears before she embarked on her journey towards death? Had it sustained her on the way? She couldn't remember.

At first she thought she was in the other world. This was perhaps the way it was. Eternal dark and eternal desolation! Nothing to see or hear. Nothing to do. Only to sit in patience, as she was doing, waiting. . . .

Suddenly a rush of air, cold and moist, came from the open door and passed over her limbs. It smelled of rain; of wet earth. And, at the same time, the harsh croaking of frogs came to her ears. These were monsoon sounds and smells. All the monsoons she had seen in her short life came flooding into her memory. She felt the touch of the earth. It was close to her and she was still part of it.

And now a burst of lightning illumined the sky. In a flash she saw the banyan tree, the pond and the line of palms beyond it. She recognized the place. She had come here, several times, on auspicious days and bathed in the holy waters of what was, once, the fast flowing Ganga. She had looked at the corpses being brought to the burning ghat with fearful eyes. Death had seemed such an alarming, such a terrifying reality.

She rose gingerly to her feet. Her first impulse was to go home. But, almost immediately, a thought struck her. 'I'm not alive,' she muttered to herself, 'I'm dead. They'll never let me in. Bad luck will fall on the house if I cross the threshold. I must remember that I've been banished from the land of the living. I'm, now, my own ghost.'

If it weren't so, what was she doing in this burning ghat? So far away from the securely guarded and protected women's wing of Saradashankar Babu's mansion? Where were the men who had brought her here? Why hadn't they performed the funeral rites and burned her body? Her last memory was that of falling on the bed in her sister-in-law's brightly lit apartments. The next was waking up in this dark, desolate forest surrounded by the dead. Alone; all alone. 'I don't belong with the living', she spoke the words aloud, 'Nor with the dead.' There was wonder in her voice. 'I'm . . . I'm a monstrous, a terrifying entity! A harbinger of evil. I'm . . . I'm my own ghost.'

Even as the thought struck her a load lifted from her chest. She felt strangely light; almost weightless. As though released from the shackles of iron laws that had trapped women and held them captive since the making of the Universe. A sense of power, now unleashed, surged through her veins. She tasted freedom for the first time. Unbounded, unstinted, limitless freedom! She could go where she liked. Do what she liked. Borne on the wings of this intense yet undefined and hitherto unknown emotion she went gliding out of the hut into the forest. Like a sudden burst of wind in a static stratosphere she darted in and out of the shadows of trees, her feet swift and sure. Not a tinge of shame, fear, doubt or anxiety touched her.

Leaving the burning ghat behind she walked for miles, crossing field after field, meadow after meadow. Dodging pits and holes and wading through puddles of rain water. And then . . . as night began to wane and the first bird call came to her ears in the light of a grey dawn, her feet began to falter, her limbs to weaken. The village lay ahead. She could see the silhouettes of the bamboo clumps that bounded it.

And now a sudden fear assailed her. She had no notion of what her relationship was with the living now; how they would view her. Pushing her way through the dense foliage of the burning ghat, stumbling over furrows of jute and paddy fields and striding across stretches of wasteland, she had been in her own world. In the deep darkness of a monsoon night she had known no fear. Nature and night had enveloped and protected her. But day was dawning now and she was approaching the land of the living. Her heart thudded painfully.

As humans are afraid of ghosts, ghosts are afraid of humans. They dwell on either side of the river of death and gaze on each other with fearful eyes. . . .

3

Had ordinary people seen Kadambini, as she appeared at the time, they would have stared at her as at a lunatic. And little boys would have run away and thrown stones at her from a distance. Her sari was torn and mud-splattered and her eyes wild and ringed with dark shadows. Shock and bewilderment were etched in every line of her face. Fortunately, an elderly gentleman was the first to see her.

'Ma', he addressed her politely, 'What are you doing here, all by yourself, at this unearthly hour? You are obviously a daughter-in-law of a wealthy, distinguished family. Where are you going?'

Kadambini lifted her face to the stranger's and gazed on it with vacant eyes. The fact that she was being spoken to by a living human being, that she still appeared to be a woman from a good family, filled her with awe and wonder. 'Come Ma', the gentleman looked at her with kindness in his eyes, 'Tell me where you live. I'll take you home.'

Home! Where was that? Saradashankar Babu's mansion in Ranihaat? There was no question of going back there. As for a parental home—she hadn't had one ever since she could remember.

Suddenly she thought of her childhood friend Jogmaya. They had been separated for many years but hadn't forgotten each other. Frequent letters were exchanged in which each professed her love in impassioned words and complained of the other's indifference. If Kadambini loved her friend as much as she did her, Jogmaya grumbled in every letter, wouldn't she have made an effort to come and see her? Once at the very least? And when that happened Jogmaya wouldn't let go of her ever again. They would live together as sisters for the rest of their lives. 'I live in Nishchindipur', Kadambini muttered, her eyes on the ground, 'In Sripaticharan Babu's house.' The gentleman was going to Kolkata. Though Nishchindipur didn't fall on the way he knew where it was. Taking a considerable detour he left Kadambini in Jogmaya's house.

The reunion was a joyful one even though the two friends didn't recognize one another at first. Gradually, as they started detecting traces of features and expressions remembered from childhood, their happiness was complete. 'O Ma!' Jogmaya exclaimed, 'How fortunate I am! I never dreamed a day would come when I would actually have you under my roof! But tell me sister, how are you here? Didn't your in-laws object to your coming?' Kadambini was silent for a while. Then, lifting her eyes to her friend's face, she said softly, 'Don't ask me any questions about my in-laws. Keep me as a servant in a corner of your house. I'll do all your work.'

'O Ma!' Jogmaya was shocked at her words. 'Why should you live as a servant? You're my best friend. You're my. . . .' In the middle of Jogmaya's effusions the master of the house walked in. Kadambini gazed on his face steadily for a while then left the room with slow, measured steps. She didn't cover her head as she had always done at the sight of an unknown male. Nor did she betray any sign of reticence or embarrassment at his presence. Afraid that her husband would be critical of Kadambini's conduct Jogmaya started defending her with several emotionally charged arguments. But, as it turned out, the defence was unnecessary. Sripati Babu was neither annoyed at Kadambini's sudden appearance in his house nor surprised by her behaviour. In fact, his ready endorsement of everything Jogmaya was saying in her friend's favour, left her surprised and somewhat miffed.

Kadambini found shelter in Jogmaya's house but the bonds of childhood love, preserved over years of separation, snapped as soon as the two came face to face. A wall stood between them. The wall of death. Unsure and diffident, conscious of the chasm that lay between her and other humans, Kadambini couldn't communicate freely and spontaneously with her friend. She gazed on Jogmaya's face, from time to time, her eyes wary, her thoughts far away. As though she was reminding herself that Jogmaya inhabited another world. A distant world where she would never find a place. 'She's a living, breathing entity!' Kadambini thought, 'and I am an empty shadow. She lives securely in the present whereas I float on the wings of eternity.'

Jogmaya found her behaviour strangely out of sync with her expectations. She couldn't understand it. It disturbed and unsettled her. Women hate mysteries. For that which is alien, ill defined and nebulous might be bragged about, written about, even pontificated on. But it cannot be lived with on a day to day basis. Which is why women prefer to get into a denial mode when it comes to the inexplicable. Outright rejection is one way of dealing with it. Changing its contours and giving it the shape of a known stereotype is another. And when neither of the two is possible they flare up in righteous indignation. The more baffled she was by Kadambini's behaviour the more incensed Jogmaya became. 'Why do I have to put up with this woman?' she thought resentfully, 'Who knows how long she plans to stay!'

But it wasn't only a question of giving a destitute woman shelter for an indefinite period of time. Her friend's mental condition shocked and alarmed Jogmaya. For Kadambini lived in dread of herself. Those who are afraid of ghosts keep looking behind them and feel reassured when they find nothing. For they fear that which they cannot see. Kadambini's fear did not lie outside herself. It lay within. Sometimes the silence of a long, lonely afternoon would be shattered by Kadambini's shrieks. Piercing shrieks that shook the whole household. And, at dusk, seeing her own shadow by the light of a lamp she would quiver like a leaf in a storm. What was worse, she was communicating her fears to everyone else. Servants and maids were seeing ghosts everywhere. So was Jogmaya.

One night Kadambini rose from her bed and came and stood at Jogmaya's door. It was past midnight. 'Didi!' she cried sobbing bitterly. 'Don't keep me alone so far away, I beg of you. Let me stay close to you.' Jogmaya sat up in bed trembling with fear and fury. If she had her way she would have thrown Kadambini out of the house that very moment. But Sripati Babu's intervention prevailed and Kadambini was allowed to sleep in the adjoining room.

Next day a message arrived for Sripati from the women's wing. The mistress wished to see him. He was surprised at the summons for the hour was an unusual one. 'What sort of a man are you?' Jogmaya turned on him aggressively the moment he stood before her. 'A woman leaves her own home and comes to live in yours. A month passes and she doesn't utter a word about going back. Yet you do nothing! Just tell me, in plain words, what is on your mind. You men are all the same. Totally untrustworthy!'

The truth is that the male of the species has a weakness for the female. Particularly when she is beautiful and helpless. Protective instincts are aroused. And other instincts as well. Sripati's solemn assurances, his readiness to swear on his wife's head that there was nothing in his heart beyond pity for Kadambini's plight, cut no ice with Jogamya. For it was evident to her that there was more. Much more. It was true that the young widow often took hold of Sripati's thoughts. 'Poor woman!' he mused from time to time. 'A helpless orphan and a childless widow! Who knows what cruelties she has been subjected to in the house of her in-laws! Is it surprising that she has run away from them? She is my wife's friend and has taken shelter under my roof. Can I drive her away?' Reasoning thus he had refrained from contacting her in-laws or even asking her any questions. He didn't want to cause her more pain than she was suffering already. But now that his wife was pointing out the impracticality, the lack of worldly wisdom in giving an unknown woman shelter without making the most basic enquiries, he was inclined to agree with her. There was something strange about Kadambini. There was no doubt about that. And it was also true that she was disturbing the household. He took a decision. He would find out why she had left her in-laws' house. Writing a letter was not a good idea. He would visit Ranihaat in person and talk to Saradashankar Babu.

After Sripati's departure Jogmaya sent for Kadambini. 'It's time you went home sister', she said. 'It's been a long time and people are talking.' Kadambini raised her eyes to her friend's face. 'What do I have to do with people?' she asked. Jogmaya was taken aback. 'You may not care for what people say', she answered sullenly, 'but we do. How long can we keep you with us? Your place is in your in-laws' house.'

'Where is the house of my in-laws?'

'Aa maran!' Jogmaya muttered to herself, 'What will the mad woman say next?' A shiver ran down her spine. And now Kadambini fixed her eyes on Jogmaya's and held them with a compelling gaze. 'Am I one of you?' she asked softly, 'Do I belong to your world? You laugh and weep; love and hate. You have each other. But I . . . I have no one. All I can do is gaze at you from afar. You are human. I'm a shadow. You are afraid of me. I'm a blot on your lives of joy and laughter. And I . . . I fear you too. For the old bonds are broken and I've no notion of what we are to one another. I don't know why God keeps me here amongst you. But since he has denied me another space I hover around you still. What else can I do?'

Jogmaya felt the blood curdling in her veins. Her face and limbs grew stiff and heavy. She understood something of what Kadambini was trying to say. But not all. She wanted to answer, to ask a question, but the words froze in her throat. She rose and walked quietly out of the room.

4

Sripati returned from Ranihaat around ten o clock. It was a wild stormy night with rain falling so hard and fast that it threatened to wash the earth away. Nothing could be heard except the screeching of the wind and the pelting of the rain on this seemingly endless night. 'What happened?' Jogmaya asked her husband. 'It's a long story', Sripati answered grimly. 'I'll tell you later.' Changing his clothes, he had his meal and, after a few puffs from his albola, he prepared to go to sleep. His face and manner appeared anxious and disturbed.

Jogmaya had contained her curiosity long enough. She could do so no longer. 'What did they say?' she cried bursting into the room, 'Tell me.' Sripati sat up in bed. 'It seems you've made a mistake', he answered gravely. Jogmaya felt a jab of annoyance. A woman never makes a mistake, she thought, and even if she does, no man with any sense will point it out. Taking the blame on himself is the mark of a truly intelligent man. 'What do you mean by that?' she asked testily.

'The woman you've taken under your wing is not your friend Kadambini.'

Jogmaya flared up at this as well she might. What woman would stand for such drivel? And that, too, from a husband? 'Are you trying to tell me that I don't know my own friend?' she asked angrily, 'Do I need you to teach me how to recognize people? What kind of nonsensical talk is this?' Sripati made haste to explain that he wasn't trying to undermine his wife's memory or powers of discernment. He had proof on his side. Her friend Kadambini was dead. She had been dead for over a month.

'What are you saying?' Jogmaya didn't know whether to laugh or cry. 'You've committed a blunder. That's for sure. Who knows where you went and with whom you spoke! Why did you have to go in person? A letter would have sufficed. . . .' Now Sripati lost his temper. He had taken so much trouble to bring her authentic information and she was dismissing it as nonsense. He described to her in detail his visit to Ranihaat and his meeting with Saradashankar Babu. He gave her a clear account of the questions he had asked and the answers he had received. But Jogmaya wouldn't believe him. The two argued and contradicted each other half the night. Not because there was a conflict of views regarding what was to be done about Kadambini. She had to be asked to leave the house immediately. Husband and wife were in total agreement on that. Sripati, convinced that an imposter had wormed her way into his household, was inclined to be even harsher than Jogmaya. But neither was willing to lose the argument and be proved wrong. Hence, the prolonged war of words. 'This is too much!' Sripati exclaimed angrily, 'I heard it with my own ears, I keep telling you!'

'I don't believe it', Jogmaya's answered firmly, 'Can I deny the evidence of my own eyes?' Their voices rose in excitement. They quite forgot that Kadambini was sleeping in the next room.

'Tell me', Jogmaya asked her husband at last, 'When did Kadambini die? On which date?' She hoped to prove him wrong by producing a letter written after it. Sripati told her and the two made a quick calculation. Kadambini had come to their house on the day following the night she was supposed to have died. Jogmaya stared at her husband in shock and horror. Her heart began to thump in her chest. And now, for the first time, a cold eerie current passed slowly down Sripati's spine.

Suddenly the door flew open. A blast of moisture-laden air came in and snuffed out the flame of the lamp. Within seconds the impenetrable darkness of the outer world took possession of the room. Kadambini walked in through the open door and went right up to their bed. 'Sister', she said quietly, 'I *am* your friend Kadambini. But I'm not alive. I'm dead.' Jogmaya shrieked. Sripati's face turned ashen. He tried to speak but couldn't utter a word. 'But what have I done?' Kadambini went on in the same, soft, reasonable voice. 'What is my crime? Apart from the fact that I died?' Suddenly her voice changed. It rose in an anguished scream. 'O go!' She raised her head and cried out as though to her Maker. Her Maker who lay sleeping, indifferent to the plight of her whom He had created, on this dark monsoon night. 'O go!' She howled, her voice higher than the howling wind, 'If there is no place for me in this world and no place in the hereafter, where shall I go? Tell me! Where shall I go?' Leaving the near-fainting couple behind, Kadambini stumbled out of the room and out of the house, looking for a place she could call her own.

5

How Kadambini found her way to Ranihaat is a long story and difficult to tell. Suffice it to say that she did. Entering the village she didn't show her face to anyone. Seeking out an old abandoned temple, she hid herself through the daylight hours. Then, when the short dusk of a monsoon eve crept over the earth and the prospect of another stormy night made people hurry back to their homes, she ventured out of her hiding place and stepped on the path that led to the zamindar's mansion. Reaching the entrance, she pulled her veil down to her breast, her heart quaking with fear. But no one stopped her. Mistaking her for a serving maid the guards let her in. And now the rain came pelting down and the wind started blowing, keen as a knife.

The lady of the house, Saradashankar Babu's wife, was playing cards with her widowed sister-in-law. The maid was in the kitchen and Khoka, just recovering from a fever, was sleeping upstairs. Kadambini managed to evade everyone's eyes and slip into the room where the sick child lay. What she expected when she came into the house I cannot say. Perhaps she herself did not know. All she knew was that she had to see her darling once. Only once. Then she would . . . she didn't know what she would do after that.

She gazed on the child by the light of the lamp. He looked thin and frail and his fists were clenched on the sheet. Her heart swelled with love and longing. If only she could hold him to her breast and wipe out his suffering! Suddenly a thought struck her. 'Who looks after him now that I'm gone?' His mother was a sociable woman who loved cards and gossip. Ever since the child was born she had left him in Kadambini's care, and indulged herself in her chosen amusements. 'But now?' Kadambini looked at the sick boy sleeping all alone in the room and thought, 'Who looks after him now?'

'Kakima.' Khoka turned over on his side and murmured in his sleep, 'I want some water.' 'Aa ha re!' Tears rolled down Kadambini's cheeks. 'Oh my darling!' she cried, 'My lump of gold! You haven't forgotten me!' Rising swiftly she went to the pitcher of water that stood in a corner and poured some in a bowl. Then, clasping the child to her breast, she held it to his lips. Khoka, half asleep, drank the water from her hands as he had always done. But when she took his face in her hands and kissed it tenderly, he awoke. Opening his eyes he asked, 'Did you die Kakima?'

'Yes darling', Kadambini answered.

'But you've come back', Khoka smiled, 'Promise me you won't die again.'

Before she could answer she heard a scream and something fell clattering to the floor. Kadambini looked up. A maid stood at the door, her eyes wide and staring. The brass bowl of sago and milk she had brought for the child had fallen from her trembling hands. 'Ma go!' She screamed and fainted, falling in a heap to the floor. The mistress heard the commotion and, throwing down her cards, came running into the room. Seeing her son in Kadambini's arms, her face turned deathly white. She tried to run away but her feet were rooted to the ground. She tried to speak but couldn't utter a sound. Khoka saw all this and was frightened. 'Go away Kakima', he said fretfully.

Kadambini looked around her. She knew, now, without a doubt that nothing had changed. She had the same thoughts, the same feelings and emotions as when she was alive. The house was the same and so were the people in it. The love she felt for the child she had nurtured and his love for her hadn't changed a whit. She felt no disconnect with anyone, with anything. In her friend's house she had believed herself to be dead because the little girl she had been when she knew Jogmaya was, indeed, dead. But now, with Khoka in her arms, she knew she was alive. Vibrantly alive. Jogmaya's friend had died, but Khoka's Kakima lived. . . . 'Didi', she turned to her sister-in-law, 'why are you afraid of me? I'm the same Kadambini. Touch me and see. I'm just as I was.' At this the mistress, too, swooned away.

In the meantime Saradashankar's sister had rushed to him with the news. And now he came into the women's wing and entered the room where Kadambini sat with Khoka on her lap. 'Chhoto Bouma', he pleaded with folded hands, 'Satish is my only son and heir to the estate. Is it fair of you to covet him from the land of the dead? Ever since you died he has been ailing. Growing weaker and weaker. Every night he calls out for you in his sleep. Release him from the bonds of your love and let him live. Go back to the world to which you belong. We'll perform the funeral rites with due ceremony.'

Kadambini could bear it no longer. 'O go!' she uttered a piercing shriek, 'I'm not dead. How can I make you believe me? I'm as alive as any of you. Look at me. I'm alive!' Picking up the brass bowl she hit it forcefully against her brow. Again and again, till blood gushed down her face. 'Look!' she screamed, 'I'm alive!' Still screaming, she ran out of the room, down the stairs and out of the house. Reaching the pond in which the women bathed, she leaped into its dark swirling waters. From the room upstairs Saradashankar Babu heard the sound of a splash. . . .

The rain kept falling in incessant torrents the whole night. And through the next morning and afternoon. Dying, Kadambini proved to the world that she was not dead.

(*Jibita O Mrita*, c. 1894)
Translated by Aruna Chakravarti

Rabindranath Tagore. Face of an Elderly Woman. Coloured ink and watercolour on paper, c. 1932-33

TRESPASS

One day, early in the morning, standing on the roadside, a boy had laid a bet with another boy, regarding the execution of an extremely daring feat.* Whether he could pluck and bring a fragrant flower from the evergreen canopy made by the myrtle creeper covering the Thakurbari, was the challenge being discussed. One boy said, 'I can', and the other said, 'You will never be able to'.

Why the job sounded simple but was not easy to execute, obviously requires a little more elaboration.

Joykali Debi was the widow of the late Madhobchandra, a learned debater. She was the proprietress of the blessed Radhanath Temple. The Professor, who had been honoured with the title, Orator of Logic, had never even for a day been able to justify this title before his wife. In the opinion of some learned pundits, the title had been vindicated, as all the expertise in both logic and oratory had fallen to his wife's share. So in the role of her husband, he must surely have imbibed the fruits to the full.

* The writings of Raja Rammohan Roy inspired Karl Eric Hammergren, a young man from Sweden, to travel to Kolkata for social work in 1893. He died in 1894, and as per his wishes, was cremated in the Hindu fashion. This caused public outrage in the orthodox Hindu press. Rabindranath protested against such bigotry in an article titled 'Bidheshiya Atithi Ebang Deshiya Athithya' (Foreign guests and local hospitality). 'Trespass' was published in the same month, in the journal *Sadhana*.

Truth be told, it must be said that Joykali was not a person of many words. However, very often she was quite capable of silencing the most powerful voices by just uttering a couple of words, or even by saying nothing at all.

Joykali was a tall, strong, sharp-witted and acutely intelligent woman. After the death of her husband, their God-gifted property was in imminent danger of being ruined. However, the widow had managed not only to collect all their payments and dues; she had even recovered very old, wrongfully occupied land and cleared up all disputed matters. No one was able to deprive her of even one paisa of her legitimate inheritance.

Since there was a larger measure of male characteristics in this lady's nature, she had no true friends or companions. The women were afraid of her. Gossip, small talk or crocodile tears were unbearable to her. Even the men were afraid of her, because she was able with a kind of sharp, silent contempt-filled look to insult these immensely lazy country gentry. These men were perpetually gathered around the Chandi shrine, wasting their time in small talk. In fact her mockery was able to penetrate their gross inertia right through to their innermost beings.

This middle-aged widow had the extraordinary ability not only to strongly hate, but also to strongly express this hatred. In her judgement, those she found guilty, she was able by words or even silently, through her attitude and gestures, to completely scorch and disgrace.

Joykali's untiring hand was always visible in all the ritual ceremonies of the Palli, the local community and in every problem or celebration. Everywhere, she was able to effortlessly secure a position of honour for herself. Wherever she happened to be, she naturally assumed she was the most important person there. Of this never was there any doubt in her mind and nor was there any in the minds of those who were present.

Joykali Debi was very skilled in nursing the sick, but the patients feared her as if she were Yama, the God of Death. If they flouted the diet restrictions or other regulations in the slightest measure, the heat in her angry disposition caused the patient to feel even more traumatised than usual.

This tall, strict, arrogant widow would invariably dispense justice in the locality according to her own idea of the Almighty's harsh punitive laws. No one had the courage to either love her or neglect her. She was in contact with everyone in the locality, yet no one was as extremely isolated as Joykali Debi.

The widow was childless. Two orphaned nephews, her brother's sons, were being brought up in her house. No one could say that the boys, in the absence of a male guardian were lacking in disciplinary control, or that they were getting spoilt because of their Pishima's blind love for them. Between the two, the elder one had attained eighteen years of age. Once in a while, proposals of marriage came for him, but mentally he was quite indifferent about such matters. However, his Pishima did not for a day encourage any desires for marital bliss even if he were to have had them. Given the conduct of other women and newlyweds, Joykali did not have romantic notions about young love. In fact, the possibility of her nephew marrying and living the same lazy relaxed life, like that of other gentlemen, was abhorrent to her. She believed that the sight of them sitting at home, bloating up, being spoilt daily by adoring wives, was excessively despicable. She would categorically say, 'Pulin has to first earn his living, only after that will he bring a wife home.' This harsh pronouncement by Pishima rent the neighbours' hearts.

Above everything, the Thakurbari was Joykali's most well cared for treasure. Even a tiny mistake could not be made in the Deity's bedding, clothing, bathing and feeding. The Brahmin priest, in comparison, was more afraid of this one human being than he was of the two deities. Earlier there was a time when the deities did not get their full allotment of supplies. This was because the priest had another idol he worshipped in his hidden shrine; her name was Nistarini. Secretly ghee, clarified butter, milk, cottage cheese, flour and other offerings to the Gods, got divided between heaven and hell. However, nowadays under Joykali's rule, one hundred percent of all the offerings came to the share of the deities. The minor idols now had to search elsewhere for subsistence.

Under the care of the widow, the Thakurbari premises shone with cleanliness—there was not even a tiny straw to be seen anywhere. On one side, taking the support of a platform, a myrtle creeper had climbed up. The minute any of its dried leaves fell, Joykali picked them up and threw them outside. The widow couldn't stand it if there came any hindrance in the way of the neatness, cleanliness and purity of the Thakurbari. Earlier, the neighbourhood boys used to use this compound to enjoy an un-interrupted game of hide and seek. In addition from time to time, the kid-goats in the locality, would come and consume some portions of the myrtle bark as well. Now that opportunity did not exist. Except for festival days, the boys could not enter the compound. The baby goats were beaten back with sticks. Invoking their mothers' souls and bleating loudly in distress, they were forced to return from the gate itself.

Abominable people, even if they were close relatives, were not allowed to enter the holy portals. At one time, an aged, greedy, chicken-eating brother-in-law of Joykali, who was visiting relatives in the village, was about to enter the temple premises. Thanks to the swift and sharp disapproval expressed by Joykali, there had arisen the possibility of an estrangement between her own sister and herself. The widow was so overprotective, and over cautious regarding this holy place, that to ordinary people it appeared more like neurosis in her.

Everywhere else, Joykali was progressive and independent. Only before this temple, she had completely surrendered herself. To this deity, she was, in all earnest, mother, wife, servant–before the deity she was attentive, soft, tender, beautiful and completely humbled. This stone temple and the stone idol were the only means for the fulfilment of her hidden femininity. The idol was her husband, her son, in fact, her entire world.

From this background, the reader will appreciate the extraordinary courage of the boy, who had taken up the challenge of stealing a spike of flowers from the myrtle canopy in the temple compound. The boy was Joykali's younger nephew, Nalin. He knew his Pishima well, but in spite of this, had not been browbeaten by her dominating and controlling personality. Wherever there was danger, he was attracted to it, and where there were rules his mind was restless until he could violate them. Rumour had it, that in her youth, his Pishima's character had been very similar.

Joykali was at that moment in the prayer hall, telling her holy beads. Her gaze, a mixture of motherly love and devotion, was fixed on the deity.

The boy silently approached from the back and stood under the myrtle canopy. He saw that all the flowers on the lower branches had already been taken away for the Puja rituals. He, therefore, very slowly and carefully climbed on to the platform. He saw a couple of ready to bloom buds on the higher branches. In order to pluck them, he stretched out to reach for them. Just then, with the weight of his great effort, the dilapidated platform collapsed with a loud crash. The creeper it was supporting, and the boy, both fell together on the ground.

Joykali came rushing, only to witness the outcome of her nephew's antics. Forcefully, she held his arm and picked him up from the ground. He had been hurt quite badly, but that injury did not count as a punishment, because that was an accidental injury which had occurred in the midst of unexpected confusion. Therefore, on the fallen boy's injured body now rained repeatedly, Joykali's intended punishment of hard blows. Without shedding a tear, the boy silently bore the punishment. Then his Pishima dragged him to his room and shut him inside. He was forbidden dinner that evening.

The servant maid Mokkhoda, on hearing of the ban on his evening meal, pleaded in a plaintive tone and with tearful eyes, for the boy to be forgiven. Joykali's heart did not melt. There was no one in the household who would dare to secretly give the starving boy any food, without the knowledge of the Thakurani.

To repair the platform, the widow called some people, and once again sat down in the hall with her rosary in hand. Mokkhoda, after a while, came close and fearfully asked 'Thakurma, Kakababu is crying with hunger; should I bring some milk for him?'

'No', replied Joykali without any change of expression on her face. Mokkhoda retreated. From the room in the cottage not too far away, Nalin's pathetic cries gradually grew into a roar of anger. Finally, after a long time, though tired, his passionate cries of distress began to penetrate his bead-counting Pishima's engrossed ears from time to time.

Just when Nalin's cries were nearly exhausted and he had almost fallen silent, the sound of another plaintive cry began to be heard from close by. Mixed together with the fleeting far off cries of a human being, the two began to create quite a tumultuous uproar in the path in front of the temple.

Suddenly within the courtyard a footstep could be heard. Looking behind her, Joykali saw the scattered myrtle creeper stirring by itself on the ground.

'Nalin!' she called, in a wrathful voice.

No one answered. She assumed that the disobedient Nalin had somehow escaped from his lockup, and had once more come to annoy her.

Then pursing her lips very sternly, the widow descended to the compound.

She then came close to the creeper garden and again called–'Nalin!'

She got no reply. Lifting the branch, she found that an extremely dirty little pig had taken shelter amidst the thick leaves out of fear for its life.

This myrtle creeper, within these brick walls, was a small symbol of the holy gardens of Brindavan. It reminded one of the fragrance of the flowers and the scented breath of Lord Krishna's female followers. It was the creeper that aroused beautiful dreams of the pleasure grounds on the banks of the River Yamuna. Suddenly, this horrifying incident occurred in this dearly cared for holy ground that belonged to the widow. It took place in her own land of Lord Krishna, which she valued even more than her life.

The Brahmin priest came running with a stick in hand in order to chase it away.

Joykali immediately stepped forward to prevent him. She ran and locked the door of the temple from within.

Before long a heavily drunken group of doms, who looked after cremations, assembled at the entrance of the temple, and began to demand loudly for their sacrificial animal.

'You fellows, go back. Do not desecrate the purity of my temple,' called Joykali from behind the closed door.

The mob withdrew. That Joykali Thakurani would shelter an impure animal inside her blessed Radhanath Temple, was something they could not believe even though they had almost visibly perceived it happening before them.

This minor incident made the Great Almighty, lord of all living creatures, extremely happy no doubt, but it also must have caused the minor local deities, called the community, to grow quite agitated as well.

(*Anadhikar Prabesh*, c. 1894)
Translated by Nandini Guha

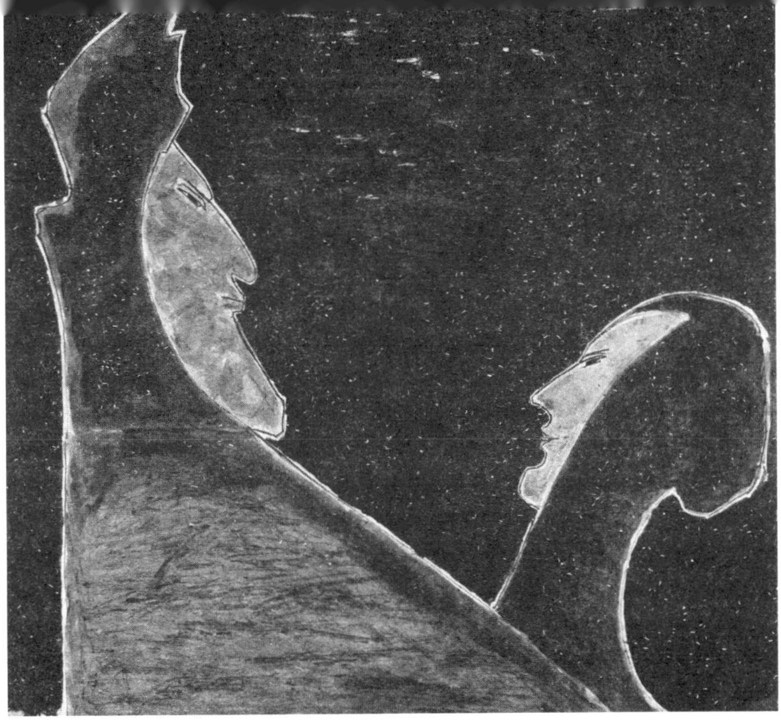

Rabindranath Tagore. A Couple Looking at Each Other. Coloured ink and pastel on paper, c. 1929-30

MISPLACED HOPE

Arriving in Darjeeling, I found the town enveloped in mist and rain.* I felt little inclination to go out, and even less of an inclination to stay indoors.

After breakfast at the hotel, I went out for a walk in thick boots, wrapped from head to foot in a mackintosh. It drizzled insistently, and the curtain of dense fog everywhere made it appear that the Creator was intent on obliterating the canvas of the world with an eraser.

Pacing up and down in solitude on the deserted Calcutta Road, I mused on the unbearable nature of the featureless kingdom of fog, for my heart yearned for a mother earth whose wealth of sounds and textures and form I wished to grasp once again with each of my five senses.

Suddenly I heard a woman weeping pitifully. In a household wracked by illnesses, the sound of sobbing would hardly have been unexpected, I doubt whether I would even have turned a hair, but in this infinite realm of clouds, she seemed to be the only person weeping in the now-obliterated universe—I could not dismiss this as insignificant.

* Tagore says that he invented 'Misplaced Hope' in Darjeeling, when Suniti Devi, the Maharani of Koochbihar, urged him to narrate a story while they were out walking together. [Source: Letter quoted in 'Patradhara' in the Sravan 1339 (c.1932) issue of *Prabasi*, p. 451; cited in *Rabindra Rachanabali* Vol. 11 (Sulabh Sanskaran; Kolkata: Visva-Bharati, c. 1990, p. 679).].

Following the sound, I went closer to its source to discover a woman in saffron, her golden yellow matted locks piled high on her head like a mountain-peak, seated on a rock by the side of the road, weeping softly; she was not grieving for a recent loss; many years of silent, repressed fatigue and weariness had burst forth in a torrent today, under the weight of the foggy bleakness.

This is excellent, I thought to myself; it has started just like a homespun story; in all my life, I had never harboured the hope of actually setting eyes on a weeping woman ascetic on a mountainside.

I could not discern her origins. 'Who are you, what is the matter?' I asked compassionately in Hindi.

There was no answer at first, she only cast a tearful glance at me, her eyes glistening through the mist.

'You need not be afraid of me', I continued. 'I am a gentleman.'

At this she laughed, saying in chaste Hindustani, 'It's been a long time since I've been afraid, nothing can embarrass me anymore. Once upon a time even my own brother had to seek permission to enter the ladies' chamber I lived in, *babuji*, but no curtain secludes me from the world today.'

I was irked; considering my deportment, entirely like a sahib's, why had this wretched woman unhesitatingly addressed me as *babuji*? I considered ending my novel this very instant and staging a swift, emphatic exit, emitting cigarette smoke like an English steam engine with its nose in the air. But curiosity triumphed eventually. Loftily I asked, tilting my head, 'May I be of help? Do you need anything?'

She looked steadily at me, then answered briefly after a few moments, 'I am the daughter of Nawab Ghulam Kader Khan of Badraon'.

What kingdom Badraon was located in, what kind of nawab Ghulam Kader Khan was, or what misery had forced his daughter to become a woman of religion and weep by the side of Calcutta Road in Darjeeling, was entirely beyond my knowledge or belief, but I decided not to ruin the atmosphere, for the story was turning out to be most fascinating.

Saluting her gravely at once, I said, 'Pardon me, Bibisahiba, I could not recognise you.'

There were a number of logical reasons for not recognising her, primary among them being that I had never seen her in my life. Moreover, the dense fog made it difficult even to identify one's own limbs.

Bibisahiba took no offence, and, gesturing with her right hand at an adjacent rock, she gave me permission in a satisfied tone. 'Please take a seat.'

I observed that the lady possessed the ability to issue orders. Receiving her approval for occupying the wet, moss-covered slab of rock, hard and uninviting, was an unexpected honour. The daughter of Ghulam Kader Khan of Badraon, Noor-un-neesa, aka Meher-un-neesa, aka Noor-Ulmulk had granted me the privilege of sitting on a low, slippery rock not far from herself. When I had left the hotel in my mackintosh, I had not even dreamed of such a sublime possibility.

The tale of a mysterious dialogue between a wayfaring couple amidst Himalayan peaks sounds like a freshly-completed poetic narrative hot off the author's pen. But although the sound of rushing torrents from distant, desolate mountain ranges and the exotic notes of music from Kalidasa's *Meghdootam* and *Kumarsambhava* might come alive in the reader's heart, we must all acknowledge that there are very few modern Bengalis in boots and mackintosh capable of retaining their full sense of self-importance while sharing a mud-spattered seat by the side of Calcutta Road with a Hindustani woman in rags. But the world was shrouded in a dense vapour that day, there was nothing anywhere to cause the slightest embarrassment; in the unending realm of mist there remained only the daughter of Ghulam Kader Ali Khan, Nawab of Badraon, and I, a freshly-bloomed Bengali Englishman. Like two pieces of debris from the universe after the apocalypse, we sat on our respective slabs of stone, an incongruous juxtaposition whose extreme irony was visible to no one but destiny.

'Who has done this to you, Bibisahiba?' I asked.

The princess of Badraon smote herself on the forehead. 'What do I know of who is instrumental in such acts?' she declared. 'Who has cloaked these enormous Himalayan mountains behind a flimsy veil of mist?'

I accepted this without any philosophical argument. 'True', I said. 'Who can claim to understand the mysteries of fate? We are mere insects.'

I would have debated the point without letting Bibisahiba off the hook so easily, but my linguistic skills would not have proved equal to the task. Whatever little Hindi I had mastered through interaction with doormen and bearers would have made it impossible for me to discuss destiny and free will cogently with the daughter of the Nawab of Badraon—or of any other place, for that matter—by the side of Calcutta Road.

'The astonishing saga of my life has drawn to a close this very day', announced Bibisahiba. 'If you so command, I shall narrate it to you.'

'But of course', I replied, flustered. 'Where's the question of commanding? If you deign to recount it, I shall be gratified to be your audience.'

Let no one imagine I used these precise words in Hindustani, for I had the desire but not the prowess. When Bibisahiba spoke, a sweet, temperate breeze seemed to waft over a soothing, verdant harvest with dew-soaked golden crests, such was the facile gentleness, the beauty, the untrammelled flow, of her words. And I could only respond in terse, direct fragments, like a barbarian. I had never acquired the well-rounded, uninterrupted, and natural grace of speech that she displayed; for the first time, while conversing with Bibisahiba, I sensed my shortcoming at every step.

She said, 'The blood of the emperors of Dilli coursed in my veins; it had become well-nigh impossible for my father to locate a suitable groom for my lineage to be preserved. A proposal had been sent by the Nawab of Lucknow, which my father was hesitating over, when a battle broke out between the sepoys and the British Raj over the business of biting bullets; Hindustan was darkened by the smoke from cannons.'

I had never heard Hindustani spoken in a woman's voice, especially in the voice of a lady of noble blood. Hearing it now made it obvious that this was the language of the aristocracy. The period to which this language belonged no longer existed; the railway, the telegraph, swarms of industrial workers, and the eclipse of the upper classes had made everything small and insignificant, without embellishments. No sooner did I hear the daughter of the nawab speak than a wonderful power made the imagined palace of the Mughal emperor materialise before my eyes through the impenetrable web of fog and mist there in the modern hill-station of Darjeeling built by the British. Large marble pillars soaring into the sky, long-tailed horses adorned with finely-woven fabric, canopies with golden fringes on the backs of elephants, citizens sporting multihued headgear, dressed in diverse apparel of silk, wool, and muslin, curved swords dangling at their waists, the tips of their embroidered shoes curling upwards. Long hours of leisure; long, flowing garments; and an abundance of courtesy.

'Our fort was situated by the Yamuna', the nawab's daughter told me. 'The general of our troops was a Hindu Brahmin. His name was Kesharlal.'

The woman seemed to pour all the melody in her feminine voice at once into her pronunciation of the name. Placing my walking stick on the ground, I stirred and sat up.

'Kesharlal was an upright Hindu. Every morning at dawn I would observe through the window of the ladies' chamber how he immersed himself up to his neck in the waters of the Yamuna, pivoting on his heels as he offered his prayers to the newly-risen sun with raised arms, the palms joined. Later, he would sit down on the steps of the ghat in his sodden clothes and count his beads before returning home, all the while singing devotional songs in the Bhairon raga in his clear, pleasant voice.

'I was a Muslim girl, but I had never been instructed about my own religion, nor was I aware of the methods of worship that it demanded; the bonds of our faith among the men had been loosened at the time by debauchery, drinking and tyranny, nor were its tenets pursued actively in the pleasure chambers in the inner sanctum.

'Possibly the Lord had given me a natural longing for a religious way of life. Or perhaps there was some other hidden reason, I cannot say. But at the sight of Kesharlal's prayers and rituals under the newly risen sun on the desolate ivory-coloured steps leading into the placid blue Yamuna every tranquil morning, my recently-awakened heart would be flooded with the indescribable sweetness of devotion.

'The Brahmin Kesharlal's regular, disciplined acts of self-cleansing made his fair, sprightly, ageless figure appear like a pure flame unsullied by smoke; the sacred aura of the Brahmin made the heart of this daughter of a Muslim defer to him with exquisite reverence.

'I had a Hindu maid, who would bow in respect to Kesharlal every day, touching his feet devotedly, a sight that aroused both joy and envy in me. On auspicious occasions and festivals she would serve a ritual feast to Brahmins to signal her faith. Helping her with money, I would ask her, "Are you not going to invite Kesharlal?" Biting her tongue to indicate the impropriety of such an act, she would answer, "Kesharlal thakur accepts neither hospitality nor alms."

'Thus unable to display any direct or indirect sign of my devotion to Kesharlal, my famished heart felt discontent.

'One of our forefathers had forcibly married a Brahmin woman, it was her sacred blood that I sensed in my veins there in the ladies' chamber, and imagining a connection with Kesharlal by virtue of this lineage offered me a modicum of satisfaction.

'From my Hindu maid, I used to hear the details of every single Hindu ritual, each of the wonderful stories about their gods and goddesses, the glorious history of the Ramayana and the Mahabharata. Listening to them there in the corner of my sanctum unveiled a wondrous image of the Hindu world to my mind's eye. Idols and statues, the sonorous sound of conch-shells, the temples with their spires cased in gold, the smoke rising from the incense, the fragrance of flowers mixed with sandalwood and perfume, the miraculous powers of yogis and sages, the superhuman greatness of the Brahmin, and the wondrous play of the gods and goddesses masquerading as human beings all combined to put within my reach a vast, primordial, remote and supernatural world of illusion; like a tiny bird cut off from its nest, my heart seemed to flutter from room to room within an enormous, ancient palace at dusk. The Hindu world was like a charming fairytale to the soul of the young girl that I was.

'That was when the battle broke out between the British and the sepoys. A revolutionary wave swept our little fort in Badraon too.

'"It is time to banish the beef-eating British from the land of the Aryas and resume the game of dice between Hindus and Muslims for the right to rule Hindustan", declared Kesharlal.

'My father Ghulam Kader Khan was a cautious man; referring to the British in terms of unflattering kinship, he said, "They are capable of performing impossible tasks; the people of Hindustan cannot overcome them. I do not intend to lose my little fort for the sake of uncertain expectations; I shall not fight the British."

'At a time when the blood of all Hindus and Muslims in Hindustan was boiling, this mercantile prudence on my father's part elicited condemnation from us all. Even my mothers, the begums, grew agitated.

'An armed Kesharlal arrived with troops. "If you do not join us, Nawab Sahib, we will incarcerate you and I shall take command of your fort", he told my father.

'"You need not go to such trouble", answered my father, "I am on your side".

"You must give us some money from the treasury", said Kesharlal.

My father did not offer very much, saying, "I shall provide it as needed".

'Tying up every single ornament I possessed, from head to toe, in a cloth bundle, I sent them to Kesharlal secretly through my Hindu maid. He accepted them. My unadorned limbs thrilled in delight at this.

'As Kesharlal prepared to scrub and clean the barrels of rusted guns and disused swords, one afternoon the Commissioner of the district, accompanied by British redcoats, entered our fort in a cloud of dust.

'My father Ghulam Kader Khan had surreptitiously passed on information about the rebellion to him.

'Such was Kesharlal's magical influence over the troops of Badraon that they prepared to join battle with their damaged guns and blunt swords and die if needed.

'My treacherous father's house seemed like hell to me. My heart was breaking with rage and sorrow and hatred, but not a single teardrop escaped my eyes. Disguising myself in my cowardly brother's clothes, I left the women's chambers. No one had the leisure to notice my departure.

'By then the cloud of dust and the gunpowder fumes, the cries of the soldiers and the sound of the guns, had stopped, and the land and water and skies were in the grip of the terrible calm of death. The sun had set after painting the waters of the Yamuna a bloody red, a near full moon hung in the evening sky.

'The battlefield was strewn with grotesque scenes of death. At another time my heart would have ached in compassion, but that day I wandered about like a person in a dream, searching for Kesharlal's whereabouts. This was the only objective in my life; all else appeared unreal.

'In the course of my search I discovered under the bright moonlight, late at night, the corpses of Kesharlal and his devoted servant Devkinandan, in the shade of a mango orchard on the bank of the Yamuna, not far from the battlefield. I realized that, grievously injured, the master had borne the servant—or the servant, the master—away from the battleground to the shelter of this spot and given him up into the arms of death.

'My very first act was to fulfil my pent up desire for expressing my devotion. Throwing myself at Kesharlal's feet, and releasing my hair which flowed down to my hips, I repeatedly wiped the dust off those feet and held his ice-cold toes against my heated brow. As soon as I kissed his feet, the tears I had held back all this time welled up.

'Kesharlal's body stirred, and hearing a sudden, stifled groan emerge from his lips, I released his feet in shock; "Water", I heard him say, his eyes still closed and his voice parched.

'At once I soaked the scarf around my shoulder in the water of the Yamuna and ran back. Wringing the water out of the scarf, I poured it drop by drop into Kesharlal's parted lips, and bandaged the severe wound that had destroyed his left eye with the torn-off end of my sodden garment.

'After I had fetched water several times from the Yamuna in this way and sprinkled it on his face and eyes, he regained consciousness gradually. "Do you wish for some more water?" I enquired. "Who are you?" asked Kesharlal. Unable to restrain myself, I said, "Your servant is your devotee. I am Nawab Ghulam Kader Khan's daughter." I had assumed that, death being imminent, he would depart with the knowledge of his disciple's identity; no one would be able to deprive me of this joy.

'As soon as he discovered my identity, Kesharlal roared like a lion, "Daughter of a traitor! Heretic! You have cut me off from my faith by offering water from a Muslim at the hour of my death." With these words he struck a mighty blow on my face with his right hand. I almost fainted; a veil of darkness descended before my eyes.

'I was sixteen then, having emerged from the women's chamber for the first time in my life; the fiery and lascivious sun in the external sky had not yet robbed me of the glow on my tender cheeks. The instant I entered the world outside I received my first greeting from it, from the god of my universe.'

My cigarette extinguished, I had been listening transfixed all this time. I did not know whether it was the story or the form of the music that I was listening to, but I hadn't said a word. Now I could hold myself back no longer. 'Beast!' I exclaimed suddenly.

'Who is the beast?' The nawab's daughter said. 'Can a beast in the throes of death refuse the water held to its lips?'

'That is true', I replied, subdued. 'He was a god.'

'What sort of god!' responded the nawab's daugher. 'Can a god reject the follower's devoted offering?'

'True', I answered, and fell silent.

'At first I was shattered', continued the nawab's daughter. 'I felt as though the universe had collapsed around me. Regaining consciousness in an instant, I offered my respects, from a distance, at the feet of the harsh, unbending, cruel, indifferent, pious Brahmin. To myself, I said, "You accept nothing, O Brahmin—the humble man's service, another's hospitality, the rich man's gift, the maiden's youth and the woman's love, none of it. You are unique, you are solitary, you are detached, you are distant, I do not even have the right to surrender to you!"

'I cannot say what Kesharlal thought when he saw the daughter of the nawab offering her respects with her forehead touching the ground, but there was no surprise or change of expression in his face. He gave me a single serene glance, then got to his feet slowly. Startled, I extended by arm to offer support, which he rejected in silence, and went up to the bank of the Yamuna with great effort. A ferry boat was moored at the spot, but there was neither anyone to row him across, nor anyone to be ferried. Climbing into the boat, Kesharlal untied it from the stake. The boat drifted midstream and then disappeared gradually. On that hushed night I wished, with all the burden of my soul and of my youth, with all the unacknowledged devotion in my heart, to join my palms in reverence towards this invisible boat, and like a flower fallen prematurely from its stem, give up my failed life to the tranquil waters of the Yamuna, joyous under the moonlight.

'But I could not. The moon in the sky, the dense, black line of forest by the Yamuna, the deep blue unwavering waters of the river, the turrets of our fort shining in the moonlight beyond the mango orchard, all sang the symphony of death in silent harmony; on that night the three soundless worlds of land, air and water, studded with the stars and planets, ordered me in unison to die. Only a single invisible, ramshackle boat floating along the tranquil Yamuna, with not a wave disturbing its surface, prised me away from the embracing arms of dignified, soothing, eternal and universally enchanting death to drag me along the path of life. Like one entranced by a dream I walked along the Yamuna, passing through reeds as well as sandy beaches, traversing land that was cleft and uneven in some places, and overgrown with trees, weeds and vines in others.'

The speaker stopped. I did not say a word, either.

After a long silence, the nawab's daughter continued. 'The events that unfolded thereafter were complex. I do not know how to explain them clearly. I was passing through a dense forest, I could no longer determine the path I had taken. How should I begin? Where should I end? What should I purge and what should I keep? How do I tell this tale clearly and directly so that nothing appears impossible or improbable or unnatural?

'But what I have learnt during my brief life is that nothing is impossible or beyond reach. To a girl brought up in the inner sanctum of the nawab's home, the world outside might seem inaccessible, but this is an imaginary notion; once you have stepped outside, there is always a road to take. It is not the royal path, but it is a path nevertheless; mankind has always taken this path–it is rocky and strange and unending, it branches out in different directions, it is made difficult by joys and sorrows and obstacles and hindrances, but it is a path.

'The details of the solitary nawab's daughter's journey along this path taken by everyday human beings will not make for pleasant hearing, nor do I feel any enthusiasm for recounting them. To put it briefly, many miseries and dangers and much humiliation had to be endured, but still life did not become unbearable. Like fireworks, the more I burnt, the more irresistible my pace became. All the time that I moved swiftly, I had no sensation of burning, but now that this flame of intense sorrow and extreme joy has been extinguished, depositing me in the dust on the roadside like an inanimate object, my journey is over, my story ends here.'

With these words, the nawab's daughter stopped. Mentally, I shook my head; by no means could the story end here. After a brief silence I said in broken Hindi, 'Pardon my insolence: if you could explain the end in greater detail, your servant would be relieved greatly of his anxiety.'

The nawab's daughter smiled. I realized that my broken Hindi had worked. Had I been able to conduct the conversation in chaste Hindi, her reserve would not have been lowered, but the fact that I knew very little of her mother tongue created a substantial gap, drawing a veil between us.

'I received news of Kesharlal frequently', she resumed, 'although I was unable to meet him despite my best efforts. Having joined Tantia Tope's group, he would strike without warning like lightning under the revolutionary sky, sometimes in the east, sometimes in the west, sometimes in the north-west or the south-east, and disappear instantly.

'I had disguised myself as an ascetic at the time in Kashi, where I addressed Swami Shivananda as my father and learnt Sanskrit from him. All the news from everywhere in India would gather at his feet; I would study Sanskrit devotedly and follow the news of the battles with dreadful anxiety.

'Gradually the British Raj ground out the flames of revolution in Hindustan under its feet. Suddenly, there was no more news of Kesharlal. The valiant figures from distant parts of the country who had become visible every now and then in the bloodied light of the apocalypse were eclipsed unexpectedly.

'I could hold myself back no longer. Abandoning the protection of my teacher, I became a wanderer again in the guise of a worshipper. I travelled through the roads, to places of pilgrimage, to temples and hermitages, but nowhere did I find any trace of Kesharlal. One or two people who were familiar with him said, "He has been killed, either in battle or by royal decree." My soul said, "Never, Kesharlal cannot die. This Brahmin, this flame that burns unbearably bright, has not yet found release; the fire in him is still blazing up to the skies in some remote spot readied for a holy fire ritual, awaiting my self-sacrifice."

'The Hindu scriptures say that knowledge and penance can turn a Shudra into a Brahmin, but they make no reference to whether a Muslim can become a Brahmin, the only reason being that there were no Muslims at the time. I knew that it would be a long while before I could be united with Kesharlal, for I would have to become a Brahmin first. One by one, thirty years passed. In my soul and in my appearance, in my behaviour and in my habits, I became a Brahmin in word and in deed; the blood of the Brahmin woman, my ancestor, flowed in my veins without impurity. Mentally establishing myself without reservation at the feet of the first Brahmin of my youth, the last Brahmin at the end of my life, the only Brahmin in my entire universe, I acquired a magnificent radiance.

'I had heard many accounts of Kesharlal's valour during the revolutionary battles, but none of them had been imprinted on my heart. The image I had seen of a solitary Kesharlal silently floating along in a tiny boat midstream on a placid Yamuna on a moonlit night was the one that had remained in my consciousness. Every day I would see the Brahmin rowing along the desolate currents day and night, towards an undefined mysterious destination, without a companion, without an attendant. He needed no one; a pure and self-absorbed man, he was complete in himself; the stars and moon and planets in the sky observed him in silence.

'Then I heard that Kesharlal had escaped from prison and had taken shelter in Nepal. I went to Nepal too. After a long sojourn there, I was informed that he had left Nepal long ago. No one knew where he had gone.

'Since then I have been wandering around the mountains. This is not a land of Hindus—Bhutias, Lepchas and others are heathens, their daily acts follow no principles; their gods, their prayers, their rituals are all different. I began to worry about the possibility of the slightest defilement of the sacred purity that I had acquired after years of penance and devotion. With great effort I proceeded to protect myself from all manner of impure contact. I knew that my boat was close to the shore now; the ultimate holy destination of my life was at hand.

'What more is there to say? The final chapter is brief. When the lamp goes out it needs only a single puff of breath. How do I elaborate on this?

'Thirty-eight years later, here in Darjeeling, I found Kesharlal this morning.'

When the speaker stopped here, I asked, bursting with curiosity, 'What did you see?'

The nawab's daughter said, 'I saw an aged Kesharlal living amidst the Bhutias with a Bhutia wife and the grandchildren she has engendered, harvesting corn in tattered clothes in their soiled courtyard'.

The story had ended; I thought it imperative to offer some consolation. 'How can someone who has had to live thirty-eight successive years in fear for his life in the company of people of other faiths possibly adhere to prescribed behaviour?'

'I understand that', said the nawab's daughter. 'But what about the illusion under which I had been living all these years? I did not know that the Brahminism which had conquered my adolescent heart was nothing but habit, nothing but practice. I had thought of it as dharma, as eternal, without beginning or end. If that were not so, why had I accepted the unbearable humiliation I had suffered from the Brahmin's right hand on that moonlight night in return for the adoration which resonated within my blossoming mind, body and soul? Why had I thought of it as a rite of initiation from my mentor and acknowledged it with bowed head and redoubled devotion? Ah, Brahmin, you have exchanged one set of practices for another; but how will I get my youth, my life, back in exchange for another?'

With these words, the woman rose to her feet, saying, 'Namaste, *babuji*'.

The very next moment she said, as though correcting herself, 'Salaam, Babu Sahib!' With this Muslim form of address, she seemed to bid her final farewell to the decayed, ruined Brahminism lying in the dust. Before I could say a word, she disappeared like a cloud in the grey fog gathered over the Himalayan peaks.

For a few brief moments I closed my eyes to see all these events taking place before my mind's eye. I saw the sixteen-year-old girl comfortably seated on her fabric cushion at the window by the bank of the river, I saw the intent figure of the female ascetic brimming over with devotion during the evening prayers at the temple, and then I saw, too, the form of the woman of advancing years, weighed down by her broken heart and her misery, shrouded in fog here on Calcutta Road in Darjeeling. The wondrous, ardent music rising from the conflicting flow of Muslim and Hindu blood within the veins of a tender young woman melted into the self-contained beauty of the Urdu language to reverberate in my mind.

Opening my eyes, I discovered that the clouds had lifted suddenly, with the unsullied sky glittering in the pleasant sunlight. Englishwomen in carriages and Englishmen on horseback were out for some fresh air, interspersed by one or two Bengalis casting amused glances at me from faces wrapped in mufflers.

I rose to my feet quickly. At the sight of this uncovered world lit up by the sun, the story wrapped in layers of fog no longer seemed real. I believe I must have mixed the fog over the mountains with the smoke from my cigarette to spin an imaginary tale. The Muslim Brahmin woman, the revolutionary, the fort by the Yamuna—perhaps none of them had ever existed.

(*Durasha*, c. 1898)
Translated by Arunava Sinha

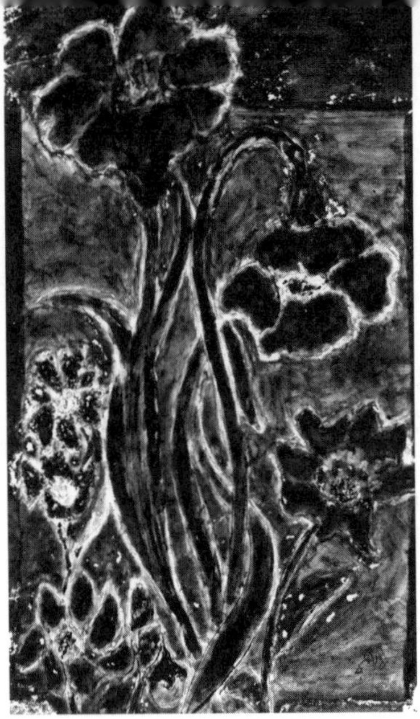

Rabindranath Tagore.
A Bunch of Flowers.
Coloured ink and poster colour on paper,
c. 1933-34

THE PARROT'S TRAINING

Once upon a time there was a bird.* It was ignorant. It sang all right, but never recited scriptures. It hopped pretty frequently, but lacked manners.

Said the Raja to himself: 'Ignorance is costly in the long run. For fools consume as much food as their betters, and yet give nothing in return.'

He called his nephews to his presence and told them that the bird must have a sound schooling.

The pundits were summoned, and at once went to the root of the matter. They decided that the ignorance of birds was due to their natural habit of living in poor nests. Therefore, according to the pundits, the first thing necessary for this bird's education was a suitable cage.

The pundits had their rewards and went home happy.

A golden cage was built with gorgeous decorations. Crowds came to see it from all parts of the world. 'Culture, captured and caged!' exclaimed some, in a rapture of ecstasy, and burst into tears. Others remarked: 'Even if culture be missed, the cage will remain, to the end, a substantial fact. How fortunate for the bird!'

The goldsmith filled his bag with money and lost no time in sailing homewards.

* Tagore's fable '*Tota Kahini*' (1917), a satire on the education system, was published in *Lipika* (1922). Tagore's English translation appeared in 1918. It was published in Kolkata and Simla by Thacker, Spink and Co., with a cover designed by Nandalal Bose, and eight drawings by Abanindranath Tagore.

The pundit sat down to educate the bird. With proper deliberation he took his pinch of snuff, as he said: 'Textbooks can never be too many for our purpose!'

The nephews brought together an enormous crowd of scribes. They copied from books, and copied from copies, till the manuscripts were piled up to an unreachable height. Men murmured in amazement. 'Oh, the tower of culture, egregiously high! The end of it lost in the clouds!'

The scribes, with light hearts, hurried home, their pockets heavily laden.

The nephews were furiously busy keeping the cage in proper trim. As their constant scrubbing and polishing went on, the people said with satisfaction: 'This is progress indeed!'

Men were employed in large numbers and supervisors were still more numerous. These, with their cousins of all different degrees of distance, built a palace for themselves and lived there happily ever after.

Whatever may be its other deficiencies, the world is never in want of fault-finders; and they went about saying that every creature remotely connected with the cage flourished beyond words, excepting only the bird.

When this remark reached the Raja's ears, he summoned his nephews before him and said: 'My dear nephews, what is this that we hear?'

The nephews said in answer: 'Sire, let the testimony of the goldsmiths and the pundits, the scribes and the supervisors be taken, if the truth is to be known. Food is scarce with the fault-finders, and that is why their tongues have gained in sharpness.'

The explanation was so luminously satisfactory that the Raja decorated each one of his nephews with his own rare jewels.

The Raja at length, being desirous of seeing with his own eyes how his Education Department busied itself with the little bird, made his appearance one day at the great Hall of Learning.

From the gate rose the sounds of conch-shells and gongs, horns, bugles and trumpets, cymbals, drums and kettledrums, tomtoms, tambourines, flutes, fifes, barrel-organs and bagpipes. The pundits began chanting mantras with their topmost voices, while the goldsmiths, scribes, supervisors, and their numberless cousins of all different degrees of distance, loudly raised a round of cheers.

The nephews smiled and said: 'Sire, what do you think of it all?'

The Raja said: 'It does seem so fearfully like a sound principle of Education!'

Mightily pleased, the Raja was about to remount his elephant, when the fault-finder, from behind some bush, cried out: 'Maharaja, have you seen the bird?'

'Indeed, I have not!' exclaimed the Raja. 'I completely forgot about the bird.'

Turning back, he asked the pundits about the method they followed in instructing the bird. It was shown to him. He was immensely impressed. The method was so stupendous that the bird looked ridiculously unimportant in comparison. The Raja was satisfied that there was no flaw in the arrangements. As for any complaint from the bird itself, that simply could not be expected. Its throat was so completely choked with the leaves from the books that it could neither whistle nor whisper. It sent a thrill through one's body to watch the process.

This time, while remounting his elephant the Raja ordered his State ear-puller to give a thorough good pull at both the ears of the fault-finder.

The bird thus crawled on, duly and properly, to the safest verge of inanity. In fact, its progress was satisfactory in the extreme. Nevertheless, Nature occasionally triumphed over training, and when the morning light peeped into the bird's cage it sometimes fluttered its wings in a reprehensible manner. And, though it is hard to believe, it pitifully pecked at its bars with its feeble beak.

'What impertinence!' growled the kotwal.

The blacksmith, with his forge and hammer, took his place in the Raja's Department of Education. Oh, what resounding blows! The iron chain was soon completed, and the bird's wings were clipped.

The Raja's brothers-in-law looked black, and shook their heads, saying: 'These birds not only lack good sense, but also gratitude!'

With text-book in one hand and baton in the other, the pundits gave the poor bird what may fitly be called lessons!

The kotwal was honoured with a title for his watchfulness, and the blacksmith for his skill in forging chains.

The bird died.

Nobody had the least notion how long ago this had happened. The fault-finder was the first man to spread the rumour.

The Raja called his nephews and asked them, 'My dear nephews, what is this that we hear?'

The nephews said: 'Sire, the bird's education has been completed.'

'Does it hop?' the Raja enquired.

'Never!' said the nephews.

'Does it fly?'

'No'.

'Bring me the bird', said the Raja.

The bird was brought to him, guarded by the kotwal and the sepoys and the sowars. The Raja poked its body with his finger. Only its inner stuffing of book-leaves rustled.

Outside the window, the murmur of the spring breeze amongst the newly budded *asoka* leaves made the April morning wistful.

(*Tota Kahini*, 1917)
Translated by Rabindranath Tagore

PLAYS

Rabindranath Tagore in
Valmiki Pratibha

CHITRA

PREFACE

This lyrical drama was written about twenty-five years ago.* It is based on the following story from the Mahabharata.

In the course of his wanderings, in fulfilment of a vow of penance, Arjuna came to Manipur. There he saw Chitrangada, the beautiful daughter of Chitravahana, the king of the country. Smitten with her charms, he asked the king for the hand of his daughter in marriage. Chitravahana asked him who he was, and learning that he was Arjuna the Pandava told him that Prabhanjana, one of his ancestors in the kingly line of Manipur, had long been childless. In order to obtain an heir, he performed severe penances. Pleased with these austerities, the God, Shiva gave him this boon, that he and his successors should each have one child. It so happened that the promised child had invariably been a son. He, Chitravahana, was the first to have only a daughter Chitrangada to perpetuate the race. He had, therefore, always treated her as a son and had made her his heir.

Continuing, the king said:

'The one son that will be born to her must be the perpetuator of my race. That son will be the price that I shall demand for this marriage. You can take her, if you like, on this condition.'

Arjuna promised and took Chitrangada to wife, and lived in her father's capital for three years. When a son was born to them, he embraced her with affection, and taking leave of her and her father, set out again on his travels.

* *Chitra* (1913) is Tagore's English transcreation of his Bengali play *Chitrangada* (1892), which was later recast as a dance drama.

THE CHARACTERS

GODS:
MADANA (Eros).
VASANTA (Lycoris).

MORTALS:
CHITRA, daughter of the King of Manipur.
ARJUNA, a prince of the house of the Kurus. He is of the Kshatriya or 'warrior caste,' and during the action is living as a Hermit retired in the forest.

VILLAGERS from an outlying district of Manipur.

NOTE.–The dramatic poem 'Chitra' has been performed in India without scenery–the actors being surrounded by the audience. Proposals for its production here having been made to Tagore, he went through this translation and provided stage directions, but wished these omitted if it were printed as a book.

SCENE I

Chitra
Art thou the god with the five darts, the Lord of Love?

Madana
I am he who was the first born in the heart of the Creator. I bind in bonds of pain and bliss the lives of men and women!

Chitra
I know, I know what that pain is and those bonds.–And who art thou, my lord?

Vasanta
I am his friend–Vasanta–the King of the Seasons. Death and decrepitude would wear the world to the bone but that I follow them and constantly attack them. I am Eternal Youth.

Chitra
I bow to thee, Lord Vasanta.

Madana

But what stern vow is thine, fair stranger? Why dost thou wither thy fresh youth with penance and mortification? Such a sacrifice is not fit for the worship of love. Who art thou and what is thy prayer?

Chitra

I am Chitra, the daughter of the kingly house of Manipur. With godlike grace Lord Shiva promised to my royal grandsire an unbroken line of male descent. Nevertheless, the divine word proved powerless to change the spark of life in my mother's womb—so invincible was my nature, woman though I be.

Madana

I know, that is why thy father brings thee up as his son. He has taught thee the use of the bow and all the duties of a king.

Chitra

Yes, that is why I am dressed in man's attire and have left the seclusion of a woman's chamber. I know no feminine wiles for winning hearts. My hands are strong to bend the bow, but I have never learnt Cupid's archery, the play of eyes.

Madana

That requires no schooling, fair one. The eye does its work untaught, and he knows how well, who is struck in the heart.

Chitra

One day in search of game I roved alone to the forest on the bank of the Purna river. Tying my horse to a tree trunk I entered a dense thicket on the track of a deer. I found a narrow sinuous path meandering through the dusk of the entangled boughs, the foliage vibrated with the chirping of crickets, when of a sudden I came upon a man lying on a bed of dried leaves, across my path. I asked him haughtily to move aside, but he heeded not. Then with the sharp end of my bow I pricked him in contempt. Instantly he leapt up with straight, tall limbs, like a sudden tongue of fire from a heap of ashes. An amused smile flickered round the corners of his mouth, perhaps at the sight of my boyish countenance. Then for the first time in my life I felt myself a woman, and knew that a man was before me.

Madana
At the auspicious hour I teach the man and the woman this supreme lesson to know themselves. What happened after that?

Chitra
With fear and wonder I asked him 'Who are you?' 'I am Arjuna,' he said, 'of the great Kuru clan.' I stood petrified like a statue, and forgot to do him obeisance. Was this indeed Arjuna, the one great idol of my dreams! Yes, I had long ago heard how he had vowed a twelve-years' celibacy. Many a day my young ambition had spurred me on to break my lance with him, to challenge him in disguise to single combat, and prove my skill in arms against him. Ah, foolish heart, whither fled thy presumption? Could I but exchange my youth with all its aspirations for the clod of earth under his feet, I should deem it a most precious grace. I know not in what whirlpool of thought I was lost, when suddenly I saw him vanish through the trees. O foolish woman, neither didst thou greet him, nor speak a word, nor beg forgiveness, but stoodest like a barbarian boor while he contemptuously walked away! . . . . Next morning I laid aside my man's clothing. I donned bracelets, anklets, waist-chain, and a gown of purple red silk. The unaccustomed dress clung about my shrinking shame; but I hastened on my quest, and found Arjuna in the forest temple of Shiva.

Madana
Tell me the story to the end. I am the heart-born god, and I understand the mystery of these impulses.

Chitra
Only vaguely can I remember what things I said, and what answer I got. Do not ask me to tell you all. Shame fell on me like a thunderbolt, yet could not break me to pieces, so utterly hard, so like a man am I. His last words as I walked home pricked my ears like red hot needles. 'I have taken the vow of celibacy. I am not fit to be thy husband!' Oh, the vow of a man! Surely thou knowest, thou god of love, that unnumbered saints and sages have surrendered the merits of their life-long penance at the feet of a woman. I broke my bow in two and burnt my arrows in the fire. I hated my strong,

lithe arm, scored by drawing the bowstring. O Love, god Love, thou hast laid low in the dust the vain pride of my manlike strength; and all my man's training lies crushed under thy feet. Now teach me thy lessons; give me the power of the weak and the weapon of the unarmed hand.

Madana
I will be thy friend. I will bring the world-conquering Arjuna a captive before thee, to accept his rebellion's sentence at thy hand.

Chitra
Had I but the time needed, I could win his heart by slow degrees, and ask no help of the gods. I would stand by his side as a comrade, drive the fierce horses of his war-chariot, attend him in the pleasures of the chase, keep guard at night at the entrance of his tent, and help him in all the great duties of a Kshatriya, rescuing the weak, and meting out justice where it is due. Surely at last the day would have come for him to look at me and wonder, 'What boy is this? Has one of my slaves in a former life followed me like my good deeds into this?' I am not the woman who nourishes her despair in lonely silence, feeding it with nightly tears and covering it with the daily patient smile, a widow from her birth. The flower of my desire shall never drop into the dust before it has ripened to fruit. But it is the labour of a life time to make one's true self known and honoured. Therefore I have come to thy door, thou world-vanquishing Love, and thou, Vasanta, youthful Lord of the Seasons, take from my young body this primal injustice, an unattractive plainness. For a single day make me superbly beautiful, even as beautiful as was the sudden blooming of love in my heart. Give me but one brief day of perfect beauty, and I will answer for the days that follow.

Madana
Lady, I grant thy prayer.

Vasanta
Not for the short span of a day, but for one whole year the charm of spring blossoms shall nestle round thy limbs.

SCENE II

Arjuna

Was I dreaming or was what I saw by the lake truly there? Sitting on the mossy turf, I mused over bygone years in the sloping shadows of the evening, when slowly there came out from the folding darkness of foliage an apparition of beauty in the perfect form of a woman, and stood on a white slab of stone at the water's brink. It seemed that the heart of the earth must heave in joy under her bare white feet. Methought the vague veilings of her body should melt in ecstasy into air as the golden mist of dawn melts from off the snowy peak of the eastern hill. She bowed herself above the shining mirror of the lake and saw the reflection of her face. She started up in awe and stood still; then smiled, and with a careless sweep of her left arm unloosed her hair and let it trail on the earth at her feet. She bared her bosom and looked at her arms, so flawlessly modelled, and instinct with an exquisite caress. Bending her head she saw the sweet blossoming of her youth and the tender bloom and blush of her skin. She beamed with a glad surprise. So, if the white lotus bud on opening her eyes in the morning were to arch her neck and see her shadow in the water, would she wonder at herself the livelong day. But a moment after the smile passed from her face and a shade of sadness crept into her eyes. She bound up her tresses, drew her veil over her arms, and sighing slowly, walked away like a beauteous evening fading into the night. To me the supreme fulfilment of desire seemed to have been revealed in a flash and then to have vanished. . . . But who is it that pushes the door?

Enter CHITRA, dressed as a woman.

Ah! it is she. Quiet, my heart! . . . . Fear me not, lady! I am a Kshatriya.

Chitra

Honoured sir, you are my guest. I live in this temple. I know not in what way I can show you hospitality.

Arjuna

Fair lady, the very sight of you is indeed the highest hospitality. If you will not take it amiss I would ask you a question.

Chitra
You have permission.

Arjuna
What stern vow keeps you immured in this solitary temple, depriving all mortals of a vision of so much loveliness?

Chitra
I harbour a secret desire in my heart, for the fulfilment of which I offer daily prayers to Lord Shiva.

Arjuna
Alas, what can you desire, you who are the desire of the whole world! From the easternmost hill on whose summit the morning sun first prints his fiery foot to the end of the sunset land have I travelled. I have seen whatever is most precious, beautiful and great on the earth. My knowledge shall be yours, only say for what or for whom you seek.

Chitra
He whom I seek is known to all.

Arjuna
Indeed! Who may this favourite of the gods be, whose fame has captured your heart?

Chitra
Sprung from the highest of all royal houses, the greatest of all heroes is he.

Arjuna
Lady, offer not such wealth of beauty as is yours on the altar of false reputation. Spurious fame spreads from tongue to tongue like the fog of the early dawn before the sun rises. Tell me who in the highest of kingly lines is the supreme hero?

Chitra
Hermit, you are jealous of other men's fame. Do you not know that all over the world the royal house of the Kurus is the most famous?

Arjuna
The house of the Kurus!

Chitra
And have you never heard of the greatest name of that far-famed house?

Arjuna
From your own lips let me hear it.

Chitra
Arjuna, the conqueror of the world. I have culled from the mouths of the multitude that imperishable name and hidden it with care in my maiden heart. Hermit, why do you look perturbed? Has that name only a deceitful glitter? Say so, and I will not hesitate to break this casket of my heart and throw the false gem to the dust.

Arjuna
Be his name and fame, his bravery and prowess false or true, for mercy's sake do not banish him from your heart—for he kneels at your feet even now.

Chitra
You, Arjuna!

Arjuna
Yes, I am he, the love-hungered guest at your door.

Chitra
Then it is not true that Arjuna has taken a vow of chastity for twelve long years?

Arjuna
But you have dissolved my vow even as the moon dissolves the night's vow of obscurity.

Chitra
Oh, shame upon you! What have you seen in me that makes you false to yourself? Whom do you seek in these dark eyes, in these milk-white arms, if you are ready to pay for her the price of your probity? Not my true self, I know. Surely this cannot be love, this is

not man's highest homage to woman! Alas, that this frail disguise, the body, should make one blind to the light of the deathless spirit! Yes, now indeed, I know, Arjuna, the fame of your heroic manhood is false.

Arjuna

Ah, I feel how vain is fame, the pride of prowess! Everything seems to me a dream. You alone are perfect; you are the wealth of the world, the end of all poverty, the goal of all efforts, the one woman! Others there are who can be but slowly known. While to see you for a moment is to see perfect completeness once and for ever.

Chitra

Alas, it is not I, not I, Arjuna! It is the deceit of a god. Go, go, my hero, go. Woo not falsehood, offer not your great heart to an illusion. Go.

SCENE III

Chitra

No, impossible. To face that fervent gaze that almost grasps you like clutching hands of the hungry spirit within; to feel his heart struggling to break its bounds urging its passionate cry through the entire body—and then to send him away like a beggar—no, impossible.

Enter MADANA and VASANTA.

Ah, god of love, what fearful flame is this with which thou hast enveloped me! I burn, and I burn whatever I touch.

Madana

I desire to know what happened last night.

Chitra

At evening I lay down on a grassy bed strewn with the petals of spring flowers, and recollected the wonderful praise of my beauty I had heard from Arjuna;—drinking drop by drop the honey that I had stored during the long day. The history of my past life like that of my former existences was forgotten. I felt like a flower, which has but a few fleeting hours to listen to all the humming flatteries and whispered murmurs of the woodlands and then must lower its eyes from the Sky, bend its head and at a breath give itself up to the dust without a cry, thus ending the short story of a perfect moment that has neither past nor future.

Vasanta
A limitless life of glory can bloom and spend itself in a morning.

Madana
Like an endless meaning in the narrow span of a song.

Chitra
The southern breeze caressed me to sleep. From the flowering Malati bower overhead silent kisses dropped over my body. On my hair, my breast, my feet, each flower chose a bed to die on. I slept. And, suddenly in the depth of my sleep, I felt as if some intense eager look, like tapering fingers of flame, touched my slumbering body. I started up and saw the Hermit standing before me. The moon had moved to the west, peering through the leaves to espy this wonder of divine art wrought in a fragile human frame. The air was heavy with perfume; the silence of the night was vocal with the chirping of crickets; the reflections of the trees hung motionless in the lake; and with his staff in his hand he stood, tall and straight and still, like a forest tree. It seemed to me that I had, on opening my eyes, died to all realities of life and undergone a dream birth into a shadow land. Shame slipped to my feet like loosened clothes. I heard his call—'Beloved, my most beloved!' And all my forgotten lives united as one and responded to it. I said, 'Take me, take all I am!' And I stretched out my arms to him. The moon set behind the trees. One curtain of darkness covered all. Heaven and earth, time and space, pleasure and pain, death and life merged together in an unbearable ecstasy. . . . With the first gleam of light, the first twitter of birds, I rose up and sat leaning on my left arm. He lay asleep with a vague smile about his lips like the crescent moon in the morning. The rosy red glow of the dawn fell upon his noble forehead. I sighed and stood up. I drew together the leafy lianas to screen the streaming sun from his face. I looked about me and saw

the same old earth. I remembered what I used to be, and ran and ran like a deer afraid of her own shadow, through the forest path strewn with shephali flowers. I found a lonely nook, and sitting down covered my face with both hands, and tried to weep and cry. But no tears came to my eyes.

Madana
Alas, thou daughter of mortals! I stole from the divine Storehouse the fragrant wine of heaven, filled with it one earthly night to the brim, and placed it in thy hand to drink—yet still I hear this cry of anguish!

Chitra [bitterly]
Who drank it? The rarest completion of life's desire, the first union of love was proffered to me, but was wrested from my grasp? This borrowed beauty, this falsehood that enwraps me, will slip from me taking with it the only monument of that sweet union, as the petals fall from an overblown flower; and the woman ashamed of her naked poverty will sit weeping day and night. Lord Love, this cursed appearance companions me like a demon robbing me of all the prizes of love—all the kisses for which my heart is athirst.

Madana
Alas, how vain thy single night had been! The barque of joy came in sight, but the waves would not let it touch the shore.

Chitra
Heaven came so close to my hand that I forgot for a moment that it had not reached me. But when I woke in the morning from my dream I found that my body had become my own rival. It is my hateful task to deck her every day, to send her to my beloved and see her caressed by him. O god, take back thy boon!

Madana
But if I take it from you how can you stand before your lover? To snatch away the cup from his lips when he has scarcely drained his first draught of pleasure, would not that be cruel? With what resentful anger he must regard thee then?

Chitra
That would be better far than this. I will reveal my true self to him, a nobler thing than this disguise. If he rejects it, if he spurns me and breaks my heart, I will bear even that in silence.

Vasanta
Listen to my advice. When with the advent of autumn the flowering season is over then comes the triumph of fruitage. A time will come of itself when the heat-cloyed bloom of the body will droop and Arjuna will gladly accept the abiding fruitful truth in thee. O child, go back to thy mad festival.

SCENE IV

Chitra
Why do you watch me like that, my warrior?

Arjuna
I watch how you weave that garland. Skill and grace, the twin brother and sister, are dancing playfully on your finger tips. I am watching and thinking.

Chitra
What are you thinking, sir?

Arjuna
I am thinking that you, with this same lightness of touch and sweetness, are weaving my days of exile into an immortal wreath, to crown me when I return home.

Chitra
Home! But this love is not for a home!

Arjuna
Not for a home?

Chitra
No. Never talk of that. Take to your home what is abiding and strong. Leave the little wild flower where it was born; leave it

beautifully to die at the day's end among all fading blossoms and decaying leaves. Do not take it to your palace hall to fling it on the stony floor which knows no pity for things that fade and are forgotten.

Arjuna
Is ours that kind of love?

Chitra
Yes, no other! Why regret it? That which was meant for idle days should never outlive them. Joy turns into pain when the door by which it should depart is shut against it. Take it and keep it as long as it lasts. Let not the satiety of your evening claim more than the desire of your morning could earn. . . . The day is done. Put this garland on. I am tired. Take me in your arms, my love. Let all vain bickerings of discontent die away at the sweet meeting of our lips.

Arjuna
Hush! Listen, my beloved, the sound of prayer bells from the distant village temple steals upon the evening air across the silent trees!

SCENE V

Vasanta
I cannot keep pace with thee, my friend! I am tired. It is a hard task to keep alive the fire thou hast kindled. Sleep overtakes me, the fan drops from my hand, and cold ashes cover the glow of the fire. I start up again from my slumber and with all my might rescue the weary flame. But this can go on no longer.

Madana
I know, thou art as fickle as a child. Ever restless is thy play in heaven and on earth. Things that thou for days buildest up with endless detail thou dost shatter in a moment without regret. But this work of ours is nearly finished. Pleasure-winged days fly fast, and the year, almost at its end, swoons in rapturous bliss.

SCENE VI

Arjuna

I woke in the morning and found that my dreams had distilled a gem. I have no casket to inclose it, no king's crown whereon to fix it, no chain from which to hang it, and yet have not the heart to throw it away. My Kshatriya's right arm, idly occupied in holding it, forgets its duties.

Enter CHITRA.

Chitra

Tell me your thoughts, sir!

Arjuna

My mind is busy with thoughts of hunting today. See, how the rain pours in torrents and fiercely beats upon the hillside. The dark shadow of the clouds hangs heavily over the forest, and the swollen stream, like reckless youth, overleaps all barriers with mocking laughter. On such rainy days we five brothers would go to the Chitraka forest to chase wild beasts. Those were glad times. Our hearts danced to the drumbeat of rumbling clouds. The woods resounded with the screams of peacocks. Timid deer could not hear our approaching steps for the patter of rain and the noise of waterfalls; the leopards would leave their tracks on the wet earth, betraying their lairs. Our sport over, we dared each other to swim across turbulent streams on our way back home. The restless spirit is on me. I long to go hunting.

Chitra

First run down the quarry you are now following. Are you quite certain that the enchanted deer you pursue must needs be caught? No, not yet. Like a dream the wild creature eludes you when it seems most nearly yours. Look how the wind is chased by the mad rain that discharges a thousand arrows after it. Yet it goes free and unconquered. Our sport is like that, my love! You give chase to the fleet-footed spirit of beauty, aiming at her every dart you have in your hands. Yet this magic deer runs ever free and untouched.

Arjuna
My love, have you no home where kind hearts are waiting for your return? A home which you once made sweet with your gentle service and whose light went out when you left it for this wilderness?

Chitra
Why these questions? Are the hours of unthinking pleasure over? Do you not know that I am no more than what you see before you? For me there is no vista beyond. The dew that hangs on the tip of a Kinsuka petal has neither name nor destination. It offers no answer to any question. She whom you love is like that perfect bead of dew.

Arjuna
Has she no tie with the world? Can she be merely like a fragment of heaven dropped on the earth through the carelessness of a wanton god?

Chitra
Yes.

Arjuna
Ah, that is why I always seem about to lose you. My heart is unsatisfied, my mind knows no peace. Come closer to me, unattainable one! Surrender yourself to the bonds of name and home and parentage. Let my heart feel you on all sides and live with you in the peaceful security of love.

Chitra
Why this vain effort to catch and keep the tints of the clouds, the dance of the waves, the smell of the flowers?

Arjuna
Mistress mine, do not hope to pacify love with airy nothings. Give me something to clasp, something that can last longer than pleasure, that can endure even through suffering.

Chitra
Hero mine, the year is not yet full, and you are tired already! Now I know that it is Heaven's blessing that has made the flower's term of life short. Could this body of mine have drooped and died with

the flowers of last spring it surely would have died with honour. Yet, its days are numbered, my love. Spare it not, press it dry of honey, for fear your beggar's heart come back to it again and again with unsated desire, like a thirsty bee when summer blossoms lie dead in the dust.

SCENE VII

Madana
Tonight is thy last night.

Vasanta
The loveliness of your body will return tomorrow to the inexhaustible stores of the spring. The ruddy tint of thy lips freed from the memory of Arjuna's kisses, will bud anew as a pair of fresh asoka leaves, and the soft, white glow of thy skin will be born again in a hundred fragrant jasmine flowers.

Chitra
O gods, grant me this my prayer! Tonight, in its last hour let my beauty flash its brightest, like the final flicker of a dying flame.

Madana
Thou shalt have thy wish.

SCENE VIII

Villagers
Who will protect us now?

Arjuna
Why, by what danger are you threatened?

Villagers
The robbers are pouring from the northern hills like a mountain flood to devastate our village.

Arjuna
Have you in this kingdom no warden?

Villagers
Princess Chitra was the terror of all evil doers. While she was in this happy land we feared natural deaths, but had no other fears. Now she has gone on a pilgrimage, and none knows where to find her.

Arjuna
Is the warden of this country a woman?

Villagers
Yes, she is our father and mother in one.

[Exeunt.

Enter CHITRA.

Chitra
Why are you sitting all alone?

Arjuna
I am trying to imagine what kind of woman Princess Chitra may be. I hear so many stories of her from all sorts of men.

Chitra
Ah, but she is not beautiful. She has no such lovely eyes as mine, dark as death. She can pierce any target she will, but not our hero's heart.

Arjuna
They say that in valour she is a man, and a woman in tenderness.

Chitra
That, indeed, is her greatest misfortune. When a woman is merely a woman; when she winds herself round and round men's hearts with her smiles and sobs and services and caressing endearments; then she is happy. Of what use to her are learning and great achievements? Could you have seen her only yesterday in the court of the Lord Shiva's temple by the forest path, you would have passed by without deigning to look at her. But have you grown so weary of woman's beauty that you seek in her for a man's strength?

With green leaves wet from the spray of the foaming waterfall, I have made our noonday bed in a cavern dark as night. There the cool of the soft green mosses thick on the black and dripping stone, kisses your eyes to sleep. Let me guide you thither.

Arjuna
Not today, beloved.

Chitra
Why not today?

Arjuna
I have heard that a horde of robbers has neared the plains. Needs must I go and prepare my weapons to protect the frightened villagers.

Chitra
You need have no fear for them. Before she started on her pilgrimage, Princess Chitra had set strong guards at all the frontier passes.

Arjuna
Yet permit me for a short while to set about a Kshatriya's work. With new glory will I ennoble this idle arm, and make of it a pillow more worthy of your head.

Chitra
What if I refuse to let you go, if I keep you entwined in my arms? Would you rudely snatch yourself free and leave me? Go then! But you must know that the liana, once broken in two, never joins again. Go, if your thirst is quenched. But, if not, then remember that the goddess of pleasure is fickle, and waits for no man. Sit for a while, my lord! Tell me what uneasy thoughts tease you. Who occupied your mind today? Is it Chitra?

Arjuna
Yes, it is Chitra. I wonder in fulfilment of what vow she has gone on her pilgrimage. Of what could she stand in need?

Chitra
Her needs? Why, what has she ever had, the unfortunate creature? Her very qualities are as prison walls, shutting her woman's heart in a bare cell. She is obscured, she is unfulfilled. Her womanly love must content itself dressed in rags; beauty is denied her. She is like the spirit of a cheerless morning, sitting upon the stony mountain peak, all her light blotted out by dark clouds. Do not ask me of her life. It will never sound sweet to man's ear.

Arjuna

I am eager to learn all about her. I am like a traveller come to a strange city at midnight. Domes and towers and garden-trees look vague and shadowy, and the dull moan of the sea comes fitfully through the silence of sleep. Wistfully he waits for the morning to reveal to him all the strange wonders. Oh, tell me her story.

Chitra

What more is there to tell?

Arjuna

I seem to see her, in my mind's eye, riding on a white horse, proudly holding the reins in her left hand, and in her right a bow, and like the Goddess of Victory dispensing glad hope all round her. Like a watchful lioness she protects the litter at her dugs with a fierce love. Woman's arms, though adorned with naught but unfettered strength, are beautiful! My heart is restless, fair one, like a serpent reviving from his long winter's sleep. Come, let us both race on swift horses side by side, like twin orbs of light sweeping through space. Out from this slumbrous prison of green gloom, this dank, dense cover of perfumed intoxication, choking breath.

Chitra

Arjuna, tell me true, if, now at once, by some magic I could shake myself free from this voluptuous softness, this timid bloom of beauty shrinking from the rude and healthy touch of the world, and fling it from my body like borrowed clothes, would you be able to bear it? If I stand up straight and strong with the strength of a daring heart spurning the wiles and arts of twining weakness, if I hold my head high like a tall young mountain fir, no longer trailing in the dust like a liana, shall I then appeal to man's eye? No, no, you could not endure it. It is better that I should keep spread about me all the dainty playthings of fugitive youth, and wait for you in patience. When it pleases you to return, I will smilingly pour out for you the wine of pleasure in the cup of this beauteous body. When you are tired and satiated with this wine, you can go to work or play; and when I grow old I will accept humbly and gratefully whatever corner is left for me. Would it please your heroic soul if the playmate of the night aspired to be the helpmeet of the day, if the left arm learnt to share the burden of the proud right arm?

Arjuna

I never seem to know you aright. You seem to me like a goddess hidden within a golden image. I cannot touch you, I cannot pay you my dues in return for your priceless gifts. Thus my love is incomplete. Sometimes in the enigmatic depth of your sad look, in your playful words mocking at their own meaning, I gain glimpses of a being trying to rend asunder the languorous grace of her body, to emerge in a chaste fire of pain through a vaporous veil of smiles. Illusion is the first appearance of Truth. She advances towards her lover in disguise. But a time comes when she throws off her ornaments and veils and stands clothed in naked dignity. I grope for that ultimate you, that bare simplicity of truth.

Why these tears, my love? Why cover your face with your hands? Have I pained you, my darling? Forget what I said. I will be content with the present. Let each separate moment of beauty come to me like a bird of mystery from its unseen nest in the dark bearing a message of music. Let me for ever sit with my hope on the brink of its realization, and thus end my days.

SCENE IX

CHITRA and ARJUNA

Chitra [cloaked]

My lord, has the cup been drained to the last drop? Is this, indeed, the end? No, when all is done something still remains, and that is my last sacrifice at your feet.

I brought from the garden of heaven flowers of incomparable beauty with which to worship you, god of my heart. If the rites are over, if the flowers have faded, let me throw them out of the temple [unveiling her original male attire]. Now, look at your worshipper with gracious eyes.

I am not beautifully perfect as the flowers with which I worshipped. I have many flaws and blemishes. I am a traveller in the great world-path, my garments are dirty, and my feet are bleeding with thorns. Where should I achieve flower-beauty, the unsullied loveliness of a moment's life? The gift that I proudly bring you is the heart of a woman. Here have all pains and joys gathered, the hopes and fears and shames of a daughter of the dust; here love springs up struggling toward immortal life. Herein lies an imperfection which yet is noble and grand. If the flower-service is finished, my master, accept this as your servant for the days to come!

I am Chitra, the king's daughter. Perhaps you will remember the day when a woman came to you in the temple of Shiva, her body loaded with ornaments and finery. That shameless woman came to court you as though she were a man. You rejected her; you did well. My lord, I am that woman. She was my disguise. Then by the boon of gods I obtained for a year the most radiant form that a mortal ever wore, and wearied my hero's heart with the burden of that deceit. Most surely I am not that woman. I am Chitra. No goddess to be worshipped, nor yet the object of common pity to be brushed aside like a moth with indifference. If you deign to keep me by your side in the path of danger and daring, if you allow me to share the great duties of your life, then you will know my true self. If your babe, whom I am nourishing in my womb be born a son, I shall myself teach him to be a second Arjuna, and send him to you when the time comes, and then at last you will truly know me. Today I can only offer you Chitra, the daughter of a king.

Arjuna
Beloved, my life is full.

(1913)
Rabindranath Tagore

Chandalika by Dancers' Guild, Kolkata

CHANDALIKA

SCENE 1

[*A group of flower girls going to sell flowers.*]*

GROUP We've brought trays of new spring's gifts to your doors,
Come, come,
Wear them as necklaces.
Madhavis die crying, having lost their creeper's bonds–
Bind them to the bonds of your braids,
Sway them on the swings of your hair,
Come, come.
Steal the forest's beauty
In your own new beauty–
It will wake raga Sohini
In veena strings of your body,
Come, come.

* Tagore wrote the play *Chandalika* originally in prose and published it in 1933. In 1938 he transformed it into a verse dance-drama set to music by him, the libretto of which he published. After performances in March directed and choreographed by him at Santiniketan and Calcutta, its revised and definitive text appeared in 1939. The present translation is based on this final version.

ଔ ଔ ଔ

In the flower petals of my garland is written
Spring's mantra script.
Youth's invitation is in its beauty.
Raga Sahana has been dyed
In its red hue,
Honeybees' hunger hums the strings
With unheard rhythms and scents.
Bring the trays and string the garlands,
Bring madhavi, malati and ashok clusters,
Come, all of you.
Bring karavi, rangan, kanchan and rajanigandha,
Full-blooming mallika,
Come, all of you.
Wear the garlands, O pretty ones,
Make haste, make haste.
The moon awakes on full-moon night,
The bakul bower
Sways and trembles in the south breeze
Quivering and softly rustling.
The dance-engrossed forest woman roams the forest clearing,
Her anklets hum encircling restless feet.
Do not let the vernal night pass in vain
Indifferent, alas.
Auspicious moment gone, it shall never get caught again,
The basket of nectar
Will fall empty in the dust,
The cane clusters dry up.
In moonlight-anointed night, cicada-clamorous forest shade,
Sleepless lovelorn-koel-calls-cacophonous south breeze,
My garden fills with flowers,
Kimshuk boughs grow restless with swaying.

[*When PRAKRITI wants flowers, they scorn her and go away.*
The Daiwala, or yogurt seller, enters.]

DAIWALA Do you want dai, anyone, dai?
Shyamali is my cow,
No one compares with her.

To the Kankana river's bank
I take her every dawn–
In the field thick with durba grass
The whole morning I let her graze.
Her body glossy black,
The more I see, the more I like.
Sitting near her I prattle,
She answers with her eyes,
On my back she puts her head–
I stroke her with my hand.

[*The Chandal daughter, PRAKRITI, wants to buy dai. A girl warns him.*]

GIRL Don't touch her, chhi,
She's a Chandal's daughter–
So the dai will get polluted
Don't you know that?

[*Daiwala exits.*

[*The Churiwala, or bangle seller, enters.*]

CHURIWALA O all you girls of the neighbourhood,
Come and take a look,
I've brought bracelet pairs
Ringed in golden wires.
Listen to my words
Wear them on your hands,
The one you want to capture
The bracelets will become chains
To bind up his mind–
I say this.

[*As soon as PRAKRITI takes bangles and stretches out her hands*]

GIRLS Don't touch her, chhi,
She's a Chandal's daughter.

[*Churiwala and others exit.*

PRAKRITI The one who sent me to
This darkness of insult
I won't worship that god, I won't.
Why should I give him flowers,
Why flowers to him–
Who for my entire life
Kept me in this humiliation?
Alas, I don't know for what impossible hope
I light puja lamps at the temple doors.
God steals their light
Deceitfully,
And keeps me in the dark.

[*Buddhist bhikkhus on the path.*]

BHIKKHUS To Him meditating seated
At the foot of the Bodhi tree,
Who vanquished Mara and his great cohorts,
Then attained His quest of boundless knowledge,
I pranam that supreme human, Buddha.

[*Exit.*

[*Prakriti's mother, Maya, enters.*]

MA What do you think, absent-minded
Without reason–
For the morning passes.
There rings the palace gong, dong dong,
Morning passes.
The sun has grown severe
The yard has not been mopped,
Water not drawn,
Fruit not been plucked,
When will you stoke the stove?
When graze the goats?
Make haste, make haste–
Draw water and go home.
There rings the palace gong
Dong dong, dong dong
O there, morning passes.

PRAKRITI It's no use, no use, Ma,
I've no use for household duties.
Let all get swept
Away in floods.
Why did you give me birth,
A life full of disgrace–
Being a mother you brought this curse!
Tell me what sin I committed on whom,
Without offence this is grave injustice.
MA Stay then, stay prone,
Crying false tears
Building false sorrows.

[*Exit.*

[*PRAKRITI draws water.*
Buddha's disciple, ANANDA, enters.]

ANANDA Water, give me water,
The sun is at its harshest, very long the path,
Give me water.
I am hot, parched,
Give me water.
I am fatigued,
Give me water.
PRAKRITI Forgive me, lord, forgive–
I'm a Chandal's daughter,
Water from my well is unclean.
I have no right to the virtue
Of giving you water,
I'm a Chandal's daughter.
ANANDA The human in me is the human in you, daughter.
That water is pilgrimage water
Which satisfies those athirst,
Which cools those hot and fatigued,
That is pure water.
Water, give me water.

[*She gives water.*]

Grace be with you, gracious one.

[*Exit.*

PRAKRITI Only one palmful of water,
Ah, taken in the lotus-bud of his cupped hands.
And my well became a shoreless ocean—
Here dance, here dance its waves,
Dance pervading my life—
Surging over my soul,
Dance pervading my life.
O what joy, what joy, what utter freedom!
One palmful of water—
Washed off the taints of my rebirths
Only one palmful of water.

[*Girls and boys enter.*
Welcome to the harvest.]

GIRLS AND BOYS The soil is calling for you, come along,
Come, come.
Her tray is full with ripe harvest today—
Ah, ah.
Intoxicated by the wind,
The spirits rise in harvest land,
The gold of sunlight streams upon the earth's anchal.
Ah, ah.
The sky is happy hearing the flute of the fields.
Who remains in their homes today, open the doors.
Laughter of light awakes,
Sparkling upon the leaves
The forest's happiness can't be caught, there it overflows—
Ah, ah.
PRAKRITI Oh don't call me, don't call.
My mind, forgetting work, is somewhere far—
Pursuing sadhana for a dream.
The elusive shadow will not be caught,
Enchanting magic composed in the mind—
Don't know if it's God's compassion,
Don't know if this is deception.
In the dark clearing I did not light lamps,
For I'm the gardener of a scorched grove,

I'm a beggar with empty hands
Spending time day and night.
If he comes then in the shade of his feet
I will spread out my agonies,
I will let him know my tear-drenched
Destitute life's desires.

SCENE 2

[*Buddhist women with offerings on their way to the temple.*]

With new golden-coloured champak petals brilliant
We sing the praises at the Muni's lotus feet.
The whole breeze is sweet-scented with the virtuous scent,
With floral garlands we sing praises at his feet.
[*Exit.*

PRAKRITI The flower says, I am blessed
Blessed on the soil.
O god, service to you
Is in my home.
I've taken birth in dust,
Have compassion, let me forget,
I have no dust within.
Cast down your glance,
The petals tremble fearfully.
Give the touch of your feet,
Make the dust's treasure heavenly,
The earth's pranam is mine for you.
MA You leave me speechless, girl.
One hears in the Puranas, Uma ascetically
Burnt in the sun,
Has that happened to you?
PRAKRITI Yes Ma, I sit on an ascetic's seat.
MA For whom is your sadhana?
PRAKRITI He who has called on me,
To me, the voiceless one, has given speech.
He who has known my name,
Oh let his name stay in my heart.

By his estrangement scorched
I practise asceticism in my inmost core.
Sorrow's inferno sanctifies
All that is dirty, shut within,
Uncoils the cobra of insult.

MA What call of yours, what call?
What underworld-dwelling antigod's beck
Will entice you away?
I will chant mantras to wreck his magic.

PRAKRITI He has played it inside my mind—
Give me water, give me water.

MA A curse upon my fate!
Who said to you "Give me water"!
Is he someone of your own caste?

PRAKRITI Oh yes Ma, that's exactly what he said,
He's a person of my own caste.
I'm a Chandali, that's a lie, a lie,
An unbearable lie.
The black clouds of Sravan,
If you name them "Chandal",
Will they lose their caste,
Will their water become unclean?
He said to me—
Don't blame yourself,
Yours is the human family,
Human blood in your veins.
Chhi Ma, don't circulate false blame about yourself,
That is a sin.
Countless maids are born in a raja's family,
I am not such a maid.
There are many Chandals in twice-born families,
I'm not a Chandali.

MA What words are you speaking,
I don't understand your language.
Who put these decrees in your mouth?
Has somebody possessed you in a dream,
The companion of your last birth?
I don't understand your language.

PRAKRITI This is a new birth,
A new birth for me.
The afternoon gong rang on that day,
The sun blazing down,
At the well I was bathing
The motherless calf.
In front of me came and stood
My Buddhist bhikkhu–
Said, give me water.
My body shivered,
Soul startled.
Tell me, Ma,
Is there no water anywhere in the whole city!
Why came he to the side of my well,
Suddenly gave me
The honour of quenching a man's thirst?

Saying: water, give me water.
I shall give, who has given such wealth?
Looking towards the black clouds
Came rushing
The agitated cuckoo–
Saying, give me water.
Lost under the ground
The stream of the source
In darkness
In prison.
Whose profound decree
Demolished
The black rocky floor–
Saying, give me water?
MA Child, whose mantras have cast a spell on you,
Who tugged your eagerly awaiting mind?
PRAKRITI He is my traveller,
My traveller of the heart's path.
Alas, he did not come again,
Not on this path,

He did not want water again.
So my heart became a desert,
Its liquid has dried up—
He did not want water.

Thirst in my eyes,
Thirst pervading my breast.
I'm a rain-deprived Baisakh day,
Overheated, my soul burns to ashes.
A storm has risen in the heated winds,
Rushing the mind to emptiness far-off—
The veil flies off.
The flower that used to light the grove,
Blackened and dried up.
Who blocked the waterfall—
Bound in cruel stone,
On the peak of sorrow's summit?

MA Child, speak to me plainly
Who is it your mind desires
Select a groom who suits your mind—
We have many of our own folk.
Don't stretch your hands
Out toward the moon in the sky.

PRAKRITI I want him
Who gave me a serving-girl's honour,
Who with his right hand
Picked the storm-blown datura flower from the dust.
O lord, lord,
String a garland with that flower,
Wear it on your neck,
Don't let it become futile.

[*An Attendant from the palace enters.*]

Attendant After searching in many lands
I've been saved by my good fortune,
Coming upon you finally in this place.

MA Why, what do you want?
Attendant The Rani's pet bird has flown off somewhere—
In that unbearable grief
She cannot close her eyes in sleep,
O minstrel's wife.
You must make it come back,
O minstrel's wife.
MA Do I know such spells
That a flown bird will come back?
Attendant I won't hear false pretexts,
Your Rani won't hear them.
You must bring it back by spells, by mantras,
Only then will you be freed,
O minstrel's wife.

[*Exit.*

PRAKRITI O MA, those words are right.
You know mantras,
Chant the mantras
To bring him here.
MA O ruinous girl, what words are you saying—
Playing with fire!
Hearing them my breast trembles,
Dying in fear.
PRAKRITI I don't fear, Ma,
Don't fear.
I fear, Ma, lest
My boldness wanes,
Lest my own value I forget.
I have such great audacity,
How marvellous!
He has caused this marvel—
Won't there be cause for something more,
Won't he come and sit,
By my side, affectionately?
MA If I'm able to bring him
Will you be able to pay the price?
Nothing in your life
Will remain.

PRAKRITI No, nothing will remain,
Nothing, nothing.
If my all is fulfilled
All is fulfilled,
Then I will stay alive
For evermore
When nothing will remain.
All together kept me
Forgetful of just this,
I have something to give—
Today I know, I am not an ill-fated girl;
I shall give, I shall give,
I shall exhaust myself giving.
I have no more fear left.
Chant your mantras,
Bring the bhikkhu beside the unhonoured,
Only she can give him honour—
Can anyone else give so much honour?
MA Child, you are the treasure torn from my breast.
Upon your words I take
The path to sin, sinful woman.
Mahapurush, pure man,
Your power of forgiveness
Is many degrees greater than
The power of my offence.
I shall dishonour you—
Pranam nonetheless, pranam nonetheless.
PRAKRITI Make me guilty.
The shrivelled blossom fallen in the dust
Hold underfoot.
The tray filled with offence
Unload with your own hands,
Afterward in that empty tray
Fill your pity—
Make me guilty.
You stand tall, I am small.
I will hold you ensnared
By my offence.
You will make my guilt your virtue

Emptied of stains—
String into forgiveness all faults
To wear around your neck.

MA What unlimited boldness, girl.

PRAKRITI My boldness!
No comparison to his boldness.
The words that no one could speak
He spoke so plainly—
Give me water.
That little decree—
It had such lustre;
Made my whole birth into light.
The black slab that was pressed on my breast,
It pushed asunder—
The liquid stream overflowed.

MA Who are they, passing by,
Sannyasis wearing yellow clothes?

[*Enter a group of Buddhist bhikkhus.*]

Bhikkhus We bow to the Buddha, the light of the day,
We bow to Gautama, glory of the moon,
We bow to the ocean of endless virtue,
We bow to the son of the Sakyas.

PRAKRITI Ma, there he goes
Before everyone else!
He didn't look back—
This new creation of his own hands
He doesn't see any more!
This soil, this soil alone
Then is your own!
Ill-fated one, who drew you into the light
Only for one instant?
You will have to stay in the soil
Beneath everyone's feet.

MA O child, I can't bear to see your sorrow—
I will bring him here, I will
Chanting mantras.

PRAKRITI Chant the most cruel among all mantras,
Let it hold his mind in an embrace

Constricted in coils.
Wherever he goes,
He will never, never be
Able to get rid of me.

[The mother calls her group of disciples to join in chanting the mantra of attraction.]

MA Come, all of you, come,
Come, all of you, come.

[They enter and dance.]

If he goes to the seacoast–
come, come back again.
I will keep his seat laid out
In my heart.
I'll soak the dust of the path
With my tears.
If he goes to mountain tops–
Come back again, back again.
I'll hide in the hilly caves,
Call him there–
My dreams will surround
His awakening.

[The mother's dance of magic.]

MA Do not worry–
See this magic mirror of mine,
When you dance with it in your hands
You'll be able to see his plight.
Now come, come, Rudra-Bhairav's sons,
Awaken the tandava dance.

[Exit.

SCENE 3

[The mother's dance of magic.]

PRAKRITI Look there, clouds thicken in the west,
The mantra works, Ma, works–
The sannyasi's dry sadhana flies off
Like withered leaves.
The lights go out, the paths grow dark,
Birds with nests broken in the storm
Will circle and fall at my door.
My breast palpitates, and
Lightning flashes within my mind.
It seems the ocean froths in the distance–
It has no floor, no shore.
The mantra works, Ma, works.

MA Let's see you dance before the glass,
Look, look what shadows fall on it.

[PRAKRITI dances.]

PRAKRITI Shame, chhi chhi, shame!
Both arms raised to the sky
He is cursing someone.
Striking himself with flaming whip,
Like a missile piercing his soul.

MA O child, if you are so uneasy now,
What will your condition be finally?

PRAKRITI I won't look, I won't look
I won't look into your mirror.
It's heartrending,
Oh, heartrending.
What a whirlwind of terrible sorrow–
Will the maha forest-lord roll in dust,
His air-cleaving pride break?
I won't, won't look in your mirror.
No, no.

MA Then let this magic be.
I'll call back the mantra at the cost of my soul–

Let my veins tear,
Let my breath cease.
PRAKRITI That's right, Ma, that's right.
Stop your mantra, stop—
It is no use any more, no use.
No no, chant your mantra, chant—
There is no other path left!
He will come, he will,
To the borders of my life and death.
The wayfarer will arrive in deepest night,
With the burning in my heart
I shall light the lamp—
He will come.

With sorrow I'll quench your sorrow.
Bathe it in the bottomless water
Of tremendous agony.
I shall burn up my existence,
The taint of this delusion rectify—
The pain of death present
As a gift at your feet.
MA Child, I have no more mantras left,
My soul reaches my throat.
PRAKRITI MA, it seems after so many days
He stirs in his seat.
There they come, they come.
From far away, lakhs of leagues away,
From beyond moon and sun,
There they come, they come—
My breast trembles in the earthquake.
MA Tell me, child, what do you see in the glass?
PRAKRITI Thick black clouds behind him,
Lightning sparkles on all sides.
Encircling his limbs
A fence of fire,

Like the lustre of Siva's blazing fury.
Your mantra manifest as a deadly cobra
Roars its venomous breath,
Defiling his virtuous crest.

[*ANANDA's shadow-acting.*]

MA O girl of stone,
What a cruel mind you have,
What a hard soul,
Yet you are still alive.
PRAKRITI Hungry love has no compassion,
It has no fear, no shame.
My vow is cruel,
I will not accept loss, not loss—
I shall bind him in magic bonds,
Embrace him in my laughs and tears.
Look there, he has crossed that river—
He walks alone on the thick forest path.
As if there's nothing in front of his eyes—
No truths, no lies;
No good, no bad.

[*Shaking her mother*]

Don't get weak, don't,
It is time to chant your Sesha cobra mantra—
The Nagpash noose mantra.
MA It has not awoken yet
The cobra staying in the lowest underworld.
Play the flute, play it
In raga Mahabhimpatali,
Wake up, black-magic cobra—
O listen to my mantra—
Pull, pull, pull.
Call him with venomous roar—
Coil, coil, coil.
Emerge from the cave,

Cross the seven seas.
Bind him and bring him—
Pull, pull, pull.
The cobra awakes, awakes—
Begins to coil, coil—
Pulls the magic pull.
Binds him and brings him.
It is time to welcome him in dance—
Start your song.
Come and join us, come
Band of yoginis.
Come, you all,
Come, all of you, come,
Come, you all.

ALL As dreams come from the thick core of sleep,
So rise, come, come.
As fire burns from the breast of shami boughs,
So come you, come.
As lightning comes suddenly at the northeast point
Splitting the black clouds' forbidding,
So shoot a spark into the bottom of the heart,
Come you, come, come.
When dark sends its call mutely beckoning,
As Kalpurush comes in the evening sky
So come you, so come, come.
When ascetic Baisakh transmits mantras
To the peaks of the distant Himalayas,
As hard thick ice melts in harsh heat
And flooded streams come down—
So come you, so come, come.

MA Don't delay any more, look, the mirror—
My power's getting destroyed.

PRAKRITI No, I won't look, won't look,
I'll hear—
Within my mind I'll hear,
Within dhyana I'll hear,
The sound of his footsteps.

Look there, a storm comes, comes,
That storm of his advent—
The world quakes violently,
My breast pulsates.

MA He comes with a curse on you,
Ill-fated one.

PRAKRITI Not a curse,
Not a curse—
He brings my rebirth,
He opens the gates of death.
The doors break,
The walls break,
Lies of this birth break.
O my ruin
O my everything,
You have come
Upon the summit of my insults.
Place your radiant feet
Above my darkness.

MA O cruel girl,
He can't bear it any more, he can't.

PRAKRITI O Ma, O Ma,
Your mantra, take it back
Right now, right now.
O demoness, what did you do,
What did you do—
Why didn't you die, sinful woman?
Where's my lustrous brilliant
Chaste and immaculate
Light from distant heaven?
Ah, how shrivelled, how tired—
How profound his defeat.
Let go, let go,
Let go of all—
Don't insult the hero,
Let him succeed,
Let him succeed,
Succeed.

[*ANANDA enters.*]

Lord, you have come to uplift me,
Paying such a price for it,
Receiving such sorrow for it.
Forgive me, forgive me—
I've pulled you down to the soil,
Brought you low,
Raise me up from the dust
To your virtuous abode.
Forgive me.
May you succeed, may you succeed.

ANANDA Grace be with you, gracious one.

[*Everyone pranams the Buddha.*]

ALL O Buddha the pure, great ocean of mercy,
Whose vision of knowledge is pure and perfect,
Slayer of human sins and their sufferings,
We sing your praises, Buddha, and adore you.

Translated by Ananda Lal

CHANDALIKA: NOTES

madhavi, malati, ashok, karavi, rangan, kanchan, rajanigandha, mallika, bakul.

madhavi—*Hiptage madablota*, a climbing shrub bearing fragrant white blossoms tinged with yellow

malati—*Aganosma caryophyllata*, a climber with very fragrant white flowers

ashok—*Saraca indica*, a tree bearing clusters of small delicately-scented reddish-orange blooms

karavi—*Nerium odorum*, the oleander, a large shrub with white, pink or red flowers

rangan—Ixora, shrubs of many species bearing diversely-coloured clusters of blooms

kanchan—Bauhinia, trees of many species with very showy flowers coloured from yellow to purple

rajanigandha—*Polianthes tuberosa*, the tuberose, a plant with stalks of sweetly-scented white flowers

mallika—*Jasminum sambac*, like all jasmines, produces very fragrant white flowers

bakul—*Mimusops elengi*, an evergreen tree with tiny white scented flowers

vina—or veena, ancient string instrument still extant and played in classical music

kimshuk—*Butea monosperma*, the flame of the forest, a tree whose leafless branches in early spring become covered with flamboyant orange or scarlet flowers, hence its English name

Bhikkhu—a Buddhist monk or devotee

Mara and his cohorts—Buddhist demon who sent his daughters to seduce the Buddha away from his objective under the Bo tree, and then an army of creatures to attack him, all in vain

anchal—the border or end of a sari draped usually over a woman's left shoulder

sadhana—disciplined practice or learning, especially in religion

champak—Bengalis use *champa* for various trees, but the original champak celebrated in Indian poetry is *Michelia champaca*, bearing very fragrant golden flowers

Muni—sage or ascetic; here, Sakya-muni, or the Buddha

pranam—the act of bending and touching another person's feet in reverence or respect

Sravan—the fourth month of the Bengali calendar, corresponding to July-August; heavy monsoon

Baisakh—the first month of the Bengali calendar, corresponding to April-May; hot summer
Mahapurush—"supreme man"
Sannyasis—Hindu religious mendicants [COD]
Rudra-Bhairav—is a compound of both names. Rudra was originally the Vedic god of storms, depicted as a terrible destroyer, but also had the epithet siva, 'benevolent', which in course of time became another name for him. In later mythology he turned into the awesome manifestation of Siva. Bhairav is Siva's name in his fearsome aspect as the Destroyer, in which his violent traits are said to be emphasized. Tagore had a particular fascination with Rudra-Bhairav, using the compound quite often, as for instance in the tragic drama Tapati.
Tandava—the god Siva's dance of destruction coinciding with the end of the world
Sesha cobra—the "ultimate" all-powerful snake; the god Vishnu, when he rests, sleeps under the protection of Sesha, whose seven hoods give him shade
Nagpash—legendary missile that released snakes to coil and bind enemies
shami—*Prosopis cineraria*, a sturdy tree
Kalpurush—the constellation Orion; in Indian mythology, envoy of Yama, the god of death
dhyana—profound meditation which is the penultimate stage of yoga [COD]

PROSE

Rabindranath Tagore.
Dancing Woman.
Crayon on paper,
c. 1932-33

THE MUSIC OF THE BAULS

Sameness and difference, both must be taken into account.* Without difference, the world cannot survive at all. All human beings are indeed equal, yet all human beings are different. To find two persons cast exactly in the same mould, with the same mindset, is impossible—no-one can deny that. Similarly, between two independent cultures, there is the common element of human nature, but there is also difference. That disparity, indeed, is the saving grace—that is how give-and-take, trade and exchange, can take place in literature. If the temperature everywhere became uniform, the wind would not blow, the river would not flow, our spirit would not survive. To merge completely into a uniform oneness means total dissolution. Hence, if our literature wants to live, it should strive to learn how to be Bengali.

The language of emotions cannot be translated. The dry language of scholarship can be cast into a mould, and its image reproduced. But the language of the heart grows and matures like a human child, nurtured on the milk of human emotion, rocked in the cradle of human joys and sorrows. Hence it has a life of its own. Pouring it into a mould, a lifeless replica of it can be produced, but that has no capacity to move. It remains static as a stone, a dead weight within the heart. . . .

High-sounding terms like 'Universal Love' sound very good when uttered by those from foreign climes, but when beggars come to our own doors singing of the same thing, why does their song fail to reach our ears?

* *Samalochana* was published on 26 March 1888. All the essays but one were earlier published in *Bharati*. 'Bauler Gaan' had appeared in the Baisakh 1290 (c. 1883) issue; a slightly longer version appeared in the volume *Sangeetchinta* (1966).

Come, O come, Jagai-Madhai, all and sundry, come!
Come join our dance if you will, chanting Hari's name.
O we've suffered, so what? We can suffer some more
But still we'll chant Hari's name. Come!

The Baul says:

To love like that you have to die

The one who dies no longer fears death. Loving the world, he becomes the world. He is not merely a small, insignificant 'I' that he should fear Yama the god of death—he is the whole universe. One who loves not will ask, of what use is such love? Why not ask the flower, what do you gain from spreading your fragrance? I cannot live without spreading my fragrance, the flower would reply; for that is my dharma. If I cannot share my fragrance, my life seems futile. Similarly, the lover would say: death is my dharma, without giving up my life, I cannot be happy. . . . The string of love's musical instrument vibrates with the electric charge of the boundless universe; in a single instant, tidings of the celestial world reach the heart's core. When you are close to the one you love, an electric current flows from one heart to the other, through an invisible wire. Likewise, if your heart is wired to the universe by the strings of love, you can tune in to the world's innermost secrets. Who else but the Baul has sung the glory of love in such a way!

Why don't we want to immerse ourselves in universal love? Because we want to preserve our own selves. We want to protect the independence of an entity called 'Myself', never to be relinquished. A web of love encircles the world. Day and night, the universe tries to draw you into itself. The universe does not want that any part of it, any single wave, should assume independence and reject the general flow to turn against the current. It wants that all waves should follow the same direction, sing the same song, for only then can the whole universe maintain a certain harmony—there is no discordant note in the supreme music of the universe. Hence any person who defies the universe to take a stand based on 'me, myself', cannot survive for long. His own insignificant self cannot compensate for what is lacking in himself. Ultimately, battered by sorrow, misery and remorse, he finds relief in seeking refuge in the world outside. How long can a fish survive in a tiny container of water? Within a few days, its source of nourishment is exhausted, the water becomes polluted, and its spirit longs desperately for the sea. At that point, if it cannot reach the sea, a large fish dies early, while a small fish remains alive for just a few days. Likewise, the large-hearted cannot remain self-absorbed for long; they long to pervade the universe. Chaitanyadev is proof of this. The small-minded manage to survive on their own for a long time, but not for ever; the 'me' does not have an eternal source of nourishment. Plagued by famine, they take to the streets, fleeing their homes. What I said here is expressed in the song, below:

O my soul-bird, how many clever tricks will you play on me?
Won't you fall into the Creator's web of love, just once?
Moving with care you stay out of things
You escape the web and fly away, eluding capture again and again!
Into the trap one day you'll fall; all your ploys will fail
When, sans food and water, you'll cry out in distress!

. . . . There is a reason why we want to pay special attention to the music composed by people from ancient times, and those untrained in English. The situation of contemporary educated people is more or less the same, across the board. We are educated together, all of us; our hearts are cast more or less in the same mould. Hence, we are not particularly wonderstruck if we find a resonance between other modern hearts and our own. But if we discover something in ancient literature that strikes a chord in our hearts, what wonder, what delight we experience! Why such delight? Because at once, for an instant, as in a flash of lightning, we catch a glimpse of the vast, eternal birthplace of our spirit. . . . Then we can see the connecting thread that binds our age with the endless succession of epochs. . . . When we see the oneness of our hearts with the poetry of ancient times, our spirit attains that state of delight. What an arid desert is the heart that allows the stream of ancient ages to dry up!

(From *Samalochana*, c. 1887)
Translated by Radha Chakravarty

Rabindranath Tagore, aged forty years.

WHAT IS A NATION?

The famous French thinker Renan has discussed the question: What is the entity called a nation? But to analyse his views on this subject, we need to first determine the meaning of a couple of terms.

We have to acknowledge that the Bengali language does not have an equivalent term for the word 'nation'. In colloquial usage, generally, *jati* is taken to mean 'caste', and it sometimes also implies what in English is called 'race'. We will use the word *jati* to connote only the English term 'race', and refer to the nation as *nation*. If the words 'nation' and 'national' are assimilated into the Bengali language, we can avoid a great deal of ambiguity in meaning and connotation. . . .

I feel no hesitation in accepting the word 'nation' without any distortions. We have received the idea from the English, hence we are also ready to acknowledge our debt by retaining the word in its English form. The words *Brahma* from the Upanishads, *Maya* from Shankara and *Nirvana* from the Buddha are generally left untranslated in English writings, and they should not be translated.

Renan says there was no 'nation' in ancient times. Egypt, China, and ancient Chaldea did not know what a 'nation' was. Assyria, Persia and Alexander's empire cannot be described as empires created by particular nations.

The Roman Empire had come close to the idea of the nation. But they had barely established their nationhood, before the assaults of barbarians broke it to fragments. All these fragments, over centuries, have passed through all sorts of conflicts to gradually coalesce into nations, and France, England, Germany and Russia have risen to supremacy above all other nations.

But in what respect are they nations? How did Switzerland, with its diverse communities and languages, become a nation? Why did Austria remain merely a state, not a nation?

Some political scientists say that the root of the nation is the monarch. At some moment in the distant past, a heroic warrior wages war and conquers a place; in time, the local people forget this episode. The dynasty established in those days now becomes the centre from which a nation develops. England, Scotland and Ireland were not united at first, nor was there any reason for them to be. But due to the power of the monarch, they have gradually come together. The reason why Italy is taking so long to emerge as a nation is that, from among its numerous minor rulers, no single figure has been able to act as a central force in uniting the entire country.

But this principle has not worked in all places. After all, the united states of Switzerland, and of America, which have gradually expanded through a process of amalgamation, have not received the support of a royal dynasty.

A nation that exists without a monarchy, or a nation that survives the downfall of the monarchy–such instances are not unknown to anyone. The idea no longer prevails that the authority of the king is the highest form of power; it has now been decided that national power is above the authority of the king. What is the basis of this national power? By what signs can it be identified?

Many people say that it is racial unity that is the sign of nationhood. The positions of the ruler, his viceroy and the royal assembly are artificially constituted and impermanent; but race is permanent, and its authority is sound.

Yet there is no country in Europe where there has been no mixing of races. England, France, Germany, Italy–nowhere is racial purity to be found. Everyone knows that. It is impossible now to determine who is Teutonic, and who is a Celt. In political science, there is no concern for racial purity. By the decree of political science, races that were one have been differentiated, and those who were different have become one.

The same is true of language. No doubt linguistic homogeneity aids the unification of the nation, but there is no force in the argument that it will inevitably act as a unifying factor. The United States and England share the same language; Spain and Hispanic America also share a language, but they are not the same nation. On the other hand, Switzerland has three or four languages, yet it is a single nation. Human desire is greater than language . Linguistic diversity notwithstanding, the collective desire of the whole of Switzerland has united the country.

Besides, it is also not true that language can indicate race. Today, Prussia speaks German, but a few centuries ago, it spoke Slavonic; Wales uses English, while Egypt converses in Arabic.

The nation is not subsumed by religious unity either. Whether individuals are Catholic, Protestant, Jewish or atheistic, whatever they might be, there is nothing to stop them from being English, French or German.

The bonds of material self-interest are very strong, no doubt. But in Renan's opinion, those ties are not sufficient to hold a nation together. Material self-interest might produce the Mahajan's panchayat group, but nationhood has a place for emotions–just as it has a body, it also does not lack a soul. Nobody quite thinks of a Mahajan group as a motherland.

It must be admitted that geographic, or in other words, natural borders, serve as a prime cause of the differentiation between nations. The current of the river may have borne a race along on its course, but the mountain blocks its path. But does that mean anyone can draw a map to demonstrate the exact limit upto which a nation's dominion may extend? In human history, natural borders are not the ultimate limit. Pieces of territory, races, languages–these do not bring nations into being. On a piece of territory, a battlefield or a place of work may be established, but that fragment of land cannot create the soul of a nation. It is the human being who constitutes the prime ingredient of the pure substance that the term 'human society' signifies. The profound, historic entity that is churned up–the nation–is a psychological entity. It is a psychological family, not bound by the contours of a piece of territory.

Clearly, race, language, material self-interest, religious unity and geographical location are not the fundamental ingredients for the creation of the psychological substance called the nation. What then is its basic ingredient?

The nation is a live entity, a psychological substance. Two elements constitute the inner nature of this substance, and those two elements are basically the same. One of them resides in the past, and the other in the present. One has become the ancient, treasured memory of the general public, while the other is the desire for mutual consent and collective co-existence—the desire to properly protect the unbroken legacy that has come into our possession. The human being does not create his identity on the spot, using what is presently at hand. Likewise, the nation, too, finds its source of self-expression in the effort, sacrifice and dedication that have come down from the remote, bygone ages. To a great extent, our selves have been already constituted by our ancestors. It is upon the heroism, greatness and achievements of the past that the national spirit is founded. In ancient times, a certain glory attained by the people in general, and in the present, a desire shared by the general public; formerly, the collective accomplishment of great feats, and again, at a later stage, the resolve to collectively perform similar feats—that is the ultimate basis for the creation of a general community. Our love will gain force proportionately, according to the extent to which we have accepted the idea of sacrifice, and the extent to which we have endured suffering. We love the home that we have built ourselves, the house that we will bequeath to our heirs. An ancient Spartan song says: 'What you were, the same are we; what you are, the same shall we become.' This very simple assertion can be taken as the national anthem of all countries.

Glorious memories of the past, and ideals of the future shaped by those memories—to suffer together, rejoice together, live together in hope—these are the real things. Despite diversity of races and languages, the greatness of these things can be apprehended; the value of these far exceeds that of collectively establishing a revenue office, or drawing territorial borders. The idea of suffering together is mentioned here because the bonds of suffering are stronger than those of joy.

The collective sharing of sacrifice and suffering in the past, and the collective readiness to undergo the same experience again gives the common people a unified, profound mode of expression. That is what a nation is. Indeed, there is a past behind it, but its visible sign is to be found in the present. That sign is nothing but collective consent, the clearly expressed desire to live together in collective unity.

Renan asks: what remains, now that we have banished royal power and religious dominance from the principles of statecraft? There remain humans, human desire, and all human needs. Many will argue that desire is something changeable, often uncontrolled and untutored. If it is given the task of protecting an ancient, great treasure such as the nationality of a nation, the whole thing will gradually disintegrate, and go to ruin.

Human desire is changeable—but is there anything in the world that is not? Nations are not immortal. They had an origin, and will also have an end. Perhaps, when these nations begin to change, a European union may be established. But we don't see signs of that yet. At present, it is the existence of differences between these nations that is beneficial; that is what is necessary. That is what now safeguards the freedom of all. To come under one law, one master, is dangerous for freedom.

Through diversity, and often through conflicting tendencies, the different nations are helping the process of spreading civilization. To the great music of humanity, each of them is adding a separate note. Combined together, all of this is creating in the real world an imaginative form of glory that is beyond the capacity of any individual effort.

Anyway, Renan says that humans are not slaves to race, language, religious belief or geography. The self-aware entity created by the great union of numerous disciplined and eager-spirited human beings—that is a nation. By means of the sacrifices made by particular individuals for the general good, as long as this image of a conscious entity demonstrates its own power, it can be recognized as authentic, and for that duration, it has complete right to exist.

I have finished recounting Renan's statements. Now let us prepare to discuss how Renan's profoundly significant statements may be applied to our own country.

(From *Nation Ki?*, c. 1901)
Translated by Radha Chakravarty

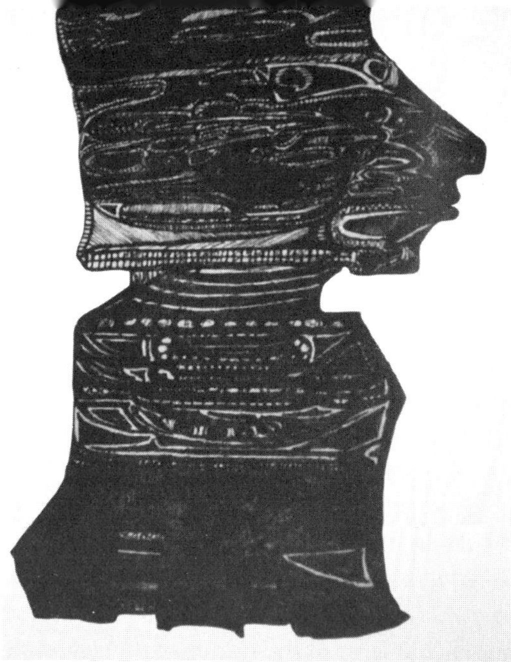

A page from the manuscript of Purabi

THE GREATER PART

A wealthy man's garden is larger than his home. Home is essential, but a garden is something redundant, superfluous; one can do without it. The largeness and liberality of wealth manifests itself through what is superfluous, non-essential. A goat has horns enough for its needs, but the antlers of a deer—the greater part of which is superfluous—fascinate us. A peacock's tail feathers are irresistible not only for their wealth of hues, but the amplitude of its plumage also decisively puts other birds to shame.

The man who has rendered his life completely indispensable is doubtless an ideal man, but fortunately there are not many who follow his ideal; had they done so, human society would have been like a fruit that is all stone, without any pulp whatever. There is no gainsaying the fact that the man who performs only beneficial acts is good and beneficent; but people are fond of the fellow who is redundant, superfluous.

The reason is that the redundant, superfluous man can give of himself in all kinds of ways. The benefactors of the world touch a part of our being only through the narrow aspect of the benefit done. They are hemmed in by the great wall of their beneficence on all sides except one where a door remains open—here we put out our hands and they give. And our superfluous man is a do-nothing, so he has no wall about him. He is of no help to us, he's only company. We go and acquire something from the benefactor and spend it in the company of the superfluous fellow. He who keeps us company while we spend is indeed a friend of ours.

Thanks to providence we are—most of us—superfluous like a stag's antlers and a peacock's plumage; the stories of our lives are not fit to be written up into biographies and fortunately, after most of us are dead and gone, nobody will raise a fund in a futile effort to build stone statues to us . . . .

Few people achieve posthumous immortality; that is why the world has become habitable. What would become of ordinary passengers if all train coaches were to be reserved? On the one hand great men take all; in other words, as long as they live, they grab all the space at least in the minds of their disciples and detractors alike. On the other hand they do not vacate the space even posthumously. And pressing home the advantage of being dead, many of them go on to annex more space, rather than vacating it. The fact that they are few in number acts as the only buffer in our favour. Otherwise legions of memorial columns would have left no space on earth for the hovels of the poor. The earth is such a poky place that the living have to fight one another for a foothold. There are heaps of people who are all too eager to court eternal damnation by committing sins like fraud and forgery only to gain a little more at the expense of others, be it an acre of land on earth or in the hearts of people. This struggle being waged by the living is a war of equals, but the tussle between the living and the dead is indeed a tremendous one. The dead are now beyond all weaknesses and limitations; they dally in never-never land—but we are mortal creatures subjected to and affected by a variety of forces of attraction and repulsion; how on earth can we match their strength? This is why Providence exiles most of the dead to the land of oblivion where there is room enough for everyone. If it was the intent of Providence to make us small people live utterly despondent, gloomy, constricted lives in the shadow of the great dead, then why did he make the earth so bright and beautiful in the first place? Why did the heart of man become so irresistibly coveted a thing?

The moralists reproach us. They say we are frittering our lives away. They are exhorting us—arise, awake, engage in action, work and do not waste your time.

No doubt many people sit back doing nothing and waste time. But those who only work end up wasting both work as well as time. The very earth is shaking under their feet and God has proclaimed

'Sambhabami yuge yuge' to save the helpless world precisely from their depredations.

Life is falling apart, it is an exercise in futility. Let it fall apart. Lives are there—for the most part—to fall apart and be wasted anyway. It is exactly these unnumbered, unnecessary, superfluous lives which demonstrate the superabundance of God's riches. We who are the failures are innumerable witnesses to the fact that there is no paucity in his fund of life and vitality. See our countless multitudes, our unaccountable superfluousness, and remember God's grace. We, the greater part of the world, proclaim God's grace through our failure the same way as a flute launches its notes through its own emptiness. It was for us that the Buddha renounced his family, Christ sacrificed his life, the rishis meditated and the sadhus are alert.

Life is falling apart, failing. Let it fail. Even being a failure is a fulfillment of some kind. The river is flowing—not all its water is exhausted though we bathe in it and drink it and irrigate the fields of autumn rice with it. The greater part of its water keeps the current going. Even if nothing else is done, keeping the current going has its own significant fulfillment. We dig canals to bring this water into our ponds, we bathe in it but do not drink it; that part of it which we carry in pots and store in big earthen barrels we drink, but it does not reflect the festive dalliance of light and shade like the water in the river. It is miserly to regard only benefit as success; it is jejune to consider the purpose as the only consequence.

We—who are the majority and multitude—should not look upon ourselves as slighted and despicable. We are the hope of the world. Here in the world our validation is in the heart of the people. We do not go and seize anything and hang on to it, we drift away. All the choral songs of the world are sung by us, all the interplay of light and shade centres on us. We laugh, we cry and fall in love, play with friends for no apparent reason, carry on small talk with near and dear ones for no specific reason, spend the best part of the day loafing about with folks around us, then marry off our sons in style, install them in office, die off in obscurity and get cremated and turn to ash—we are the ripples of the waves that keep rising and falling in the vast world in strange dalliance. It is our little antics and jests that jolly up the whole society and make it dazzle and it reverberates with our little conversations, cries and laments.

To be sure, the greater part of nature consists of what we call failure. Most sunlight is lost in space, very few of the buds in the trees last long enough to bear fruit. But all this is God's wealth and it is for him to take stock. Unless we go through Viswakarma's books of accounts, we cannot decide if it is a wasteful expenditure. Similarly most of us are of no use except as each other's companion, sidekick and minder. Therefore, instead of blaming others and beating up ourselves and fidgeting, we can very properly realize the goal of life in that very aimlessness if only we gain peace in a quiet obscure ending amidst hilarious laughter and happy songs.

I will count myself blessed if Providence has created me as nothing more than a failure. If, however, goaded on by advisors and counsellors, I begin to fancy that I must do good and make myself useful, the monstrous failure I end up begetting will be of my own making. And of course I will have to answer for it. It is not that everybody is called upon to do good to others, hence there's no shame in not doing any good. We have no call to play the missionary and save China. If one who stays back in the country and ruins himself through fox hunting and losing his bets on horse races is called a failure, it pales into insignificance beside the terrible catastrophic and hair-raising failure of the efforts to save China.

It is not that every blade of grass turns into rice. The earth grows infinitely more grass than rice. But there is no reason for grass to mourn its natural uselessness–it may well remember that it coats the earth's dusty crust with its green verdure and softens the harsh sun with its ever present emollient soothing properties. Perhaps the kush, of all varieties of grass, tried to muscle in on rice, perhaps it was only too anxious to stop being insignificant grass and fulfil its life by paying intense attention to others; yet it failed to become rice. But others know only too well what its concentrated effort to always pay keen attention to others is like. On the whole it can be said that such aggressive attention to others is not what God intends. Compared to this, the obscure and unsung, soothingly graceful, self-effacingly soft uselessness of ordinary grass is much better.

Briefly speaking, there are two kinds of people–ninety nine percent and the remaining one percent. The former are quiet and the latter are restive. Ninety nine percent are unnecessary and superfluous, while one percent is necessary and essential. The amount of dynamic and flammable oxygen in the air is much less than nitrogen which is static and inert. If it was the other way round, the world would blow up and be reduced to cinders. Similarly when some ninety nine percent in the world try hard to be as restive and necessary as the one percent, the world is in for trouble and those who are doomed to die must prepare to perish.

(*Ponero Anna*, 1903)
Translated by Subhransu Maitra

Rabindranath Tagore. Black silhouette female figure with raised hand. Black ink used with thin pen on paper. Signed 'Sri Rabindranath' vertically in Bengali script, c.1929-30

Monsoon day in Santiniketan

STATE vs. SOCIETY

The earth of Bengal, usually wet and green, is thirsting for water. But she is looking up at the authorities as the *chatak* bird looks up at the sky for clouds. She has no respite unless the authorities arrange for water.

The rumbling of the cloud has begun, the government has responded; some measure will be taken for quenching the thirst. But today we are not here to express our concern about this.

Our concern is that we had earlier a system in which society used to manage its own needs in a simple manner. Has even the last remnant of such a system vanished from this country?

Let the foreigners fulfil those needs which they have created and fostered among us. Lord Curzon is actively trying to create thirst for tea among the starving Indians; let the Andrew Yule group keep our cups of tea full to the brim. Thirst for the other more fiery liquid which has been progressively tempting us like the radiant hue of sunset at the time of deluge, is also a thing of the West and it is in the fitness of things that the Westerners will take charge of supplying it. But the thirst for water is an age-old indigenous thing. We had thirst for water before the British came and we had ways and means to quench it in a reasonably efficient manner. The spectre of the rulers was never unduly troubled for accomplishing this.

In our country, the king has fought wars to preserve the kingdom and delivered justice to the wronged. But all other works—from imparting education to providing water—have been accomplished by the society in such an easy manner that though the waves of alien rule washed over our country through the centuries over our country, they could not destroy the fabric of our society and make us wretches, nor could they displace us from the path of dharma and turn us into beasts. Kings have fought with each other endlessly, but in our murmuring bowers, under the shade of our mango and jackfruit trees, temples were being built, inns were being set up for wayfarers, ponds were being dug; the teacher taught in the pathsalas, the Acharya gave lessons on the shastras in the tols, the Ramayana was being recited in the Chandimandap, the annual prayer-pavillion and the sound of kirtans, devotional music, resounded in the village courtyards. The society did not care for outside help nor did it lose its grace because of the turmoil outside.

For ceaselessly maintaining all these propitious works and joyous celebrations for the people, rich and poor alike, it was never necessary for enthusiastic persons to go from door to door with subscription book in hand, nor was it necessary for the royal officers to make pompous declarations. Just as one need not appease anybody for the act of breathing, or call a meeting at the Town Hall for circulation of blood in one's body, similarly all the essential work conducive for society happens as a natural process.

That we are today lamenting the lack of water is not important. A much more grievous matter is at the root of this lamentation. Today the soul of society is missing. All our attention has been grabbed by the outside world.

If a river that has always flowed past a village suddenly decides to divert its course from that village, the water of the village is spoilt, its harvest is destroyed, its health is damaged, its commerce is jeopardised; the gardens of the village turn into jungles and over the ruins of its past glory grow huge banyan trees whose cracks and crevices become playgrounds for owls and bats.

The flow of the human mind is no less forceful than that of a river. That flow of mind always invested the shadowy villages of Bengal with mirth and comfort. Now the mind of the Bengali has been diverted from the lap of Bengal villages. Hence, his temples are dilapidated, there is no one to restore them; his ponds are contaminated, there is no one to clean them; once rich houses are abandoned, no sound of festive celebration is heard from them anymore. So, now the giver of water is the government, the giver of health is the government, even for education one has to beg at the door of the government. The tree that used to blossom on its own now spreads its thin branches towards the sky, appealing for the alms of flowers. Even if its appeal is granted, does it lead to any fulfilment?

What is called the State in English is called Sarkar in our modern language. This Sarkar was in existence as the king in ancient India. But there is a difference between the British State and our kingship. Britain has assigned all the welfare of the country to the hands of the State. India did it only partly.

It is not that the king did not look after and reward the preceptors who gave education and imparted knowledge of the shastras to the people without any fee, but it was only partly the king's duty; as a matter of fact, it was the duty of every household. If the king withdrew the support due to a sudden anarchy in the country, still the education and practice of shastra did not get altogether suspended. Not that the king would not dig a pond for the subjects, but he would do so like any other wealthy person. The king's indifference would therefore never cause emptiness of the country's water-bowl.

In Britain everyone is free to pursue his own comfort and pleasure selfishly. They are not burdened by heavy work; most of their heavy duties are assigned to the state machinery. In our country, state power is comparatively free, the common man is bound by social duty. The king may go to war or go a-hunting, he may do his royal duty or spend time in pursuit of pleasure; he will be answerable for his deeds in the final day of reckoning. But people never depend on him totally for their own well-being. In a marvel of achievement the duties of society were meticulously distributed among each member.

Due to such a long-standing system, what we understand as dharma is an all-enveloping aspect of society. Each of us has to learn to eschew self-interest and practise self-denial. All of us are bound to observe dharma.

From the above analysis, it should be clear that the life-forces of different civilizations are founded in different areas. The soul of the country is where the greatest benefit of the common people converges. The whole country is seriously wounded if that spot is attacked. In Britain, if the State power is in turmoil, the whole country will be devastated. This is why politics occupies the pride of place in Europe. In our country, if society is paralysed, real danger looms close. This is why, we have never gone all out for the freedom of the State, but have always guarded the freedom of society in all respects.

There is scope for misunderstanding me here. I am not saying that everyone should cling to his own village, that there is no necessity for going out to earn knowledge, respect and wealth. We must be grateful to the magnetic force which is drawing the Bengali people out of the house, for it is energising the mind of the Bengali and enlarging his heart by widening the scope of his work.

But this is the time when the Bengali needs to be repeatedly reminded that the natural balance between the home and the world should not be topsy-turvy. One has to earn in the world to save at home. Your heart must be in your home if you want to employ your energy in the world. We will learn in the world, but apply the knowledge at home. But today we have:

> *made our home alien and the alien home,*
> *made the other our own and the own other.*

Consequently, we are aimlessly afloat like the 'water-moss', as the poet says. But happy signs are visible from many corners that the Bengali has turned his mind towards the home again. Not only that our ancient knowledge is commanding our respect or that our indigenous literature is being enriched in our mother tongue, the art and handicrafts of our country are also being loved and promoted, the ancient history of our country is arousing the interest of our researchers. Gradually, the passage money that we gathered to reach the royal court with begging bowl is slowly but steadily helping us to return to our own doorstep.

Against this background, we may safely assert that the work for the country has begun in right earnest. Now, we shall point out a few strange incongruities which need to be rectified. One glaring example is the Provincial Conference. The Conference has been convened to counsel our country, and yet its language is foreign. We feel close only to the Western-educated people. We fail to realise that we will reach nowhere unless we can associate the common people whole-heartedly in our endeavour. We are creating an unbridgeable gap with the common man. We have kept them standing outside, away from all our deliberations. We have been trying all the ways and means to win over the heart of Britain, but have not even understood that the heart of our country is much more precious and winning it also demands a lot of piety and penance.

The ultimate goal of political penance is only to unite the hearts of the people. But unfortunately, what goes by political education in this wretched country today is to organise different activities only to attract the heart of the foreigner at the cost of our own language and our own customs.

If we agree that gaining the confidence of the people is the ultimate goal, we have to shun those habits which we have got accustomed to and bring those ways into focus which are forever open to reach out to the people of our country. Suppose we were to employ the Provincial Conference for really counselling the country, what should we have done? Instead of an organisation in the British mould, we should have organised a huge fair, native-style. People from far and wide would come there to enjoy a get-together with jatra, theatre, music and merriment. There would be exhibitions of indigenous handicrafts and agricultural products. The best story-teller, kirtan-singer and jatra party would have been given awards. People would have been advised on different aspects of health, hygiene and sanitation through the magic lantern and other devices. Whatever we wanted to say, to advise, we would have done it there together, heart to heart, in simple Bengali.

Our country is based in rural society. When this rural society feels in its pulse the blood circulation of the wider world, it organises a fair. It is these fairs through which we invite the world to our home. During these festive days the village forgets all its narrowness. These are the occasions when it gives and receives gifts open-heartedly. Just as the advent of the rainy season fills the ponds with water from the sky, these fairs are the fitting occasions to fill the village with intimations of the world.

These fairs are very spontaneous in our country. If you call people for a meeting, they will come with a lot of trepidations. It would take time for them to open up. But those who assemble on the occasion of a fair do so naturally and open-heartedly. Hence, this is the right occasion to win the mind of the people. It is when the villagers have taken a holiday from their ploughs and burrows that the time to go and sit with them has come.

There is no district in Bengal where some fairs or other are not held at various places at various times of the year. We should first collect data on them and prepare a descriptive catalogue. Then we ought to take advantage of this information to make real contact with the people in some way or other.

If the genteel educated community in each district takes the initiative to reconstruct the fairs in a new manner and to instill a fresh lease of life in them, it will be a great service. They have to put their heart in this work and utilise the fairs to establish harmony between the Hindus and the Muslims, to advise people on their different needs with regard to schools, roads, water-tanks, pasture-land etc. in the district. If they accomplish this work without any connection with the barren politics, then they would be really able to activate their motherland in a short span of time.

India laid greatest emphasis on establishing a relationship between man and man. One has to maintain contact with distant relatives also; the bond with children will not loosen even after they grow up; different persons of the village are to be addressed as relatives, irrespective of their caste and social station. Relationships have all been well-defined with the priest, the guest, the beggar, the zamindar and the subject. These are not just ordained by social ethics; these are relationships of the heart. Some of them are like fathers, some like sons, some like brothers, and some jesters. If we come in real contact with any person, we eventually establish such a relationship with him. This is why we can never think of a person only as a means to achieving our selfish goal. This attitude may have both good and bad sides, but this is the trait of our country, and more importantly, of the East. . . . We adopt the relationship of utility only after purifying it with the relationship of the heart. Hence, occasionally we are required to take unnecessary responsibilities too. The utility-based relationship is narrow; it ends at the door of the office. If the relationship between a master and a servant ends there, the responsibility remains confined to extracting work and paying wages. But the moment you allow the heart to play a role in this relationship, the responsibility continues to the marriage of the sons and daughters of the servant and even up to the performance of his funeral rites.

Hinduism has suggested the path for each individual perceiving himself in conjunction with the world beyond the small interests of the home, and the village. Hinduism has induced every individual to remember his harmonious relationship with gods, rishis, forefathers, all men and birds and beasts every day. If this teaching is properly followed, it would be propitious for every individual in particular and for the whole world in general.

From this lofty standpoint, is it not possible for us to define a daily relationship for every member of our society with the country? Can't we sacrifice a paisa or a fistful of rice in the name of our motherland every day? Will Hinduism fail to bind us with our motherland in a thread of devotion–the land where our gods played, our rishis built their ashrams and did penance and our ancestors lived? Won't the harmonious relationship with the country be a personal matter for all of us? Are we going to totally alienate our country from our thoughts and endeavours by shrugging off all our concern for water, education and other beneficial works to the foreign rulers ? Today, the government has granted fifty thousand rupees for alleviating the water-scarcity of Bengal. Even if they had granted fifty lakh rupees under the pressure of our demands and the problem of our water-scarcity were totally solved, still what we would have actually gained? The net result will be that the heart of the country which has so long remained in tune with the society through co-operation and propitious work will now be bestowed upon the foreigners. The country will naturally give her unconditional loyalty to whomsoever gives her all the benefits. We often lament that the wealth of our country is being siphoned off to the foreign land through various ways. But it will be a matter of greater regret if the heart of the country goes to the foreigner, which is bound to happen if the foreigner gradually takes over all the propitious works connected with the core of our society. Do we hold meetings and draw up resolutions to this end? Is this endeavour to hand over the heart and soul of the motherland to the other called patriotism? It cannot be. It will never take root in India permanently, because it is against the grain of the Indian psyche. Our pride, our dharma is in the feeling that every one of us will bear all the burdens of our country everyday. The time has come when our society will evolve into a huge Swadeshi Samaj, or indigenous society. Time has come when each individual will feel in his heart: I am not alone, no one can forsake me even if I am small; similarly, I can also never forsake anyone, even if he is the smallest. . . .

It is the perception of harmony among the many, establishing unity in the midst of diversity that is the internal dharma of India. India never considered difference as opposition, never imagined the other as enemy. This is why she strives to accommodate everyone in a particular system rather than denouncing or destroying anyone. This is why she recognises all the paths and finds greatness in the core of everyone.

Because of this distinctive virtue, we are not afraid of any other society as our detractor. At the end of every new clash we shall expect more expansion of our mind. The Hindu, the Buddhist, the Muslim, the Christian will not die mutually fighting each other on Indian soil. They would discover a harmony here. That harmony would be characterised by the essence of the Hindu way of life. Its limbs may be from different parts of the world, but its soul is of India, Indian.

If we constantly keep in mind the role of India as ordained by God, we will discover that never-say-die spirit which distinguishes India. At this discovery, our shame will be erased and our aim will be fixed. We must remember that we should not receive the scientific knowledge of Europe like students forever. Our Mother Goddess Saraswati will reconcile all schools and thoughts of knowledge, round off their incompleteness and make them blossom into a hundred-petal lotus. Our scientist Dr Jagadish Chandra Bose worked towards bringing materialism, botany and zoology within one parameter. One cannot say for sure if one day he will not bring even psychology within the same bracket. Search for this harmony is the main task for an Indian talent. India is not in favour of forsaking anyone or keeping anyone at a distance. One day in this warring, faction-ridden world, India will show the path of acknowledging and accepting everyone, merging and yet perceiving with pride his individual identity in a great unitary entity.

(From *Swadeshi Samaj* (*Atmashakti*), c.1904)
Translated by Nirmalkanti Bhattacharjee

Rabindranath Tagore. Landscape with trees on a mound. Ink and watercolour on paper. 14 May 1936

THE WELFARE OF THE PEOPLE

Of late we have been surmising that after all there is such a thing as common people in our country and we have suddenly taken it into our head that 'something should be done for the common people.' *Yadrisi bhabana yasya sidhhirbhabati tadrisi.* That is why even such thoughts worry us and make us think.

Even if we decide to do good to others, we cannot start doing good right away. One needs to have the right to do good. He who is powerful can easily harm the weak, but in order to do good to the weak, one has to be not only powerful, but weak as well, and the equal of the weak. Men will never accept what is truly good as a dole measured out for beggars or as a debt; they will be able to accept it only as their due.

But when we go overboard with the welfare of the people, oftener than not a kind of intoxicating egotism lies at the bottom of this state of inebriation. Our attempts to do good are but a handle for us to luxuriate in the belief that we are superior to the common people in all kind of ways. Thus we end up doing them harm and we don't do ourselves any good, either.

There is only one god-given right to do good to the people and that is love, compassion. There is nothing humiliating about anything given with love and affection. But charity tainted with a do-good attitude tends to offend and humiliate people. It is a way to make a man look smaller than the rest—do him good and benefit him without any love for him.

It is often said that men are naturally ungrateful—it is their nature to shun their benefactor to whom they are indebted. *Mahajana yena gata sa pantha.* Nobody usually follows this advice. They altogether give up the path trodden by great souls.

The reason behind this is not that the human mind is naturally perverse. The reason is that the money lender has to be paid interest, and the interest exceeds the principal. The interest extracted by a person who wishes to do good is man's self-respect; extracting this as well as claiming gratitude is out-Shylocking Shylock.

That is why we must not forget that doing good is fraught with risk. If we try to do good while keeping our distance from the people, the latter will really do themselves a world of good if they refuse to put up with this nuisance.

It is only recently that we learnt a lesson in this regard. When we suddenly grew intensely fond of things swadeshi, indigenous things—whatever the reasons might have been—we started fraternizing with the Muslims of the country and took to addressing them as our own, our brothers, all too stridently!

When they did not ecstatically burst into grateful sobs in reply, we were very cross with them. We thought it was a satanic ploy on their part. But it never occurred to us that though there was an urge in our call, there was no truth in it. People engage in social intercourse which is very common and it draws us together, we call on one another, prompted by simple affection, eat together and even if there are differences between us, we smooth them over. When we are unable to accept the Muslims as brothers even in the sphere of very common social intercourse, our very carefully calibrated theatrical effort—dictated by compulsion—to clasp them to our breast like brothers in the political sphere can never be successful.

Differences assuredly exist between men and between communities, but common social intercourse smoothes over them and conceals their rude visibility. There are differences galore between the rich and the poor. However, if a rich man, instead of concealing these differences, thrusts the same blatantly to the fore when his poor neighbour calls on him, it will be neither sincere nor proper for the former to look to the latter for a shoulder to cry on in difficult times.

We have been displaying the Hindu-Muslim divide in our society so flagrantly in all its nakedness that in the recent past when the Swadeshi movement was very much on, a Hindu swadeshi agitator did not at all hesitate to ask a Muslim colleague of his to step off his veranda because he wanted to drink a glass of water. In the field of action where there is competition, people jostle, shove, even insult one another; it does not do anyone much harm. In wrestling bouts often a wrestler's feet land on his opponent's body and nobody takes any notice of it. But if it happens at every step in the social arena, it cannot be easily forgotten. In the fields of education and employment we have vigorously shoved the Muslims away and I admit it is not entirely pleasant or amiable. Yet this scramble does not hurt mentally, though it may hurt physically. But humiliation inflicted by society does not hurt physically, it leaves your mind scarred because it is the very purpose of society to smoothly and decorously paper over mutual differences.

The partition of Bengal did not affect our livelihoods, but hurt our mind. The pain was felt continuously, seamlessly as far as that mind was indivisible. The Muslims of Bengal were not at one with us in sharing this pain because we never ever allowed our mind to connect and merge with theirs.

There is a saying in Sanskrit: it is useless to try digging a well when your home is burning. During the partition of Bengal when the need suddenly arose for us to rope in the Muslims, we didn't even try to dig a well—we thought that water would spurt out of the earth if only we tapped the earth with water pots. When no water spurted up and dust rose and flew about, our amazement knew no bounds. Till today we have forgotten all about digging the well. We will end up hammering the earth repeatedly and finally our foreheads, too, with empty water pots.

We of the genteel society are exactly in the same position as far as the common people, are concerned. It is our eternal habit to humiliate them in every possible way. If we look within ourselves and introspect, we cannot but admit that the India we know is genteel India. The only reason why the number of Muslims has increased among the lower classes in Bengal is that the genteel upper class Hindus did not accept these classes from the heart.

There has been no change in our attitude and yet we are discussing with great zest the question of the welfare of these classes. That is why it is time we reminded ourselves that no purpose is served by exerting ourselves ostentatiously for their welfare and thereby intensifying the humiliation to which we always subject them by keeping them at a distance.

In the past when we sallied forth and went about waving the flag of the welfare of the country, the country was for the most part missing from our show; what loomed large was our ego trip. In those days when we tried our hands at doing good, we were aping Europe and not following any heart-felt urge. Even today there is a lot that we have copied in our concern for public good. Of late the masses of common people have occupied centre stage as the main protagonists in European politics. As spectators we are so far away that though we can somehow espy their body language, gestures and movements, we cannot exactly hear what they are saying. So, when we imitate, gesture and body language is the only thing we can fall back on. . . .

Inequality and disparity form the very nature of wealth. When shared by many, knowledge, religion and aesthetic beauty increase instead of decreasing; if it is extracted through exploitation of others and kept away from them, wealth fails to exist and tends to disappear. Therefore, seekers of wealth breed poverty and disparity in their own interest.

Thus when differences crop up in society due to disparity of wealth, the rich do not want to entirely remove these gaps and yet when they grow dangerously wide, they only want to somehow fend off the crisis with half measures.

That is why when the labouring classes out in those countries are smouldering, lullabies are being sung to make them go to sleep instead of giving them much-needed food; efforts are on to divert their attention by offering them lollies. Some are saying, 'put their houses in better repair', some others suggest, 'make arrangements to give them soup to eat before they go to work'; while others still go and call on them and enquire after them or send them their redundant winter clothing in winter.

Trapped in the vast net of wealth, people are thrashing about in desperation. If the impact of wealth had not struck them so powerfully, they would not have succeeded—nor would it have occurred to anybody that they were a force to reckon with. People are not only the subject of census reports today in those countries, they are a force in their own right. They no longer go begging, but demand instead. That is why those countries can no more afford to be oblivious of them. They have caused consternation in all circles.

Every day we get to read in their newspapers the debates and discussions currently raging in the west over these issues. And the result is that our dharmabuddhi—our conscience—is sometimes shocked into awareness. It tells us, why we too should initiate and get under way the same kind of debate.

We tend to forget that in the west they are debating and discussing, not merely for the sake of debate and discussion, but in deadly earnest. There is a wide range of calculations and groping for solutions going on behind these debates, because out there it is a tussle between opposite forces which is far removed from the extravagant ego trip of those who want to spend their leisure and divert themselves by showing favours to the weak.

Even now the common masses in this country are not aware of themselves, and hence cannot make their presence felt. We will get to know them from reading English books and do this as a favour to them. This awareness on our part neither gives them strength nor helps them in any way. The wants, the misery from which they suffer, they regard as personal and isolated events. Had they been aware that their individual miseries are but parts of a much vaster misery, such misery then would have posed a problem for the entire society. Then society would have set about resolving this problem not as a favour shown, but in its own interest. We start seriously thinking about others when others give us cause for serious concern. When we do the thinking as a favour shown to others, we fail to pay attention at almost every step and the thinking tends to veer round to ourselves.

The same thing can be said about literature as well. If we are thrilled by our alleged superiority and fancy in a fit of conceit that we will create folk literature for those common people, then we will end up producing such trash that the country will have a hard time getting rid of it. It is beyond us to do it. As we cannot eat on behalf of others, we cannot live on behalf of others, either. Literature is a natural articulation of life; surely it is not an expression driven by any necessity. In all ages people have created their own folk literature by themselves. It is not that they have placed orders with us kind-hearted gentlemen and are waiting anxiously for us to emerge with the goods from our college halls. Folk literature is no different from other kinds of literature in that it, too, has its share of good, mediocre and bad things. The good things in it are really incomparable—they can easily hold their own in any literary circle in the world. Therefore it does not behoove our educated degree holders to plead their case as so called patrons of folk literature. Even god himself cannot create the world as a mere favour bestowed, he has created everything from a motiveless joy. Whenever motive intrudes as a patron, creativity and creation are ruined alike. And wherever doing a favour takes the pride of place, welfare takes leave and departs.

So far it has been smooth sailing for our genteel society because our common masses have not yet come into their own. That is why the zamindars beat them up, the money lenders and loan sharks trap them, the master and employer abuse them, the police fleece them, the ancestral guru lives by sponging off them, petty lawyers—the moktars—drain them of their money, and they only bemoan and blame that fate which can by no means be summoned to appear in a court. At most we appeal to their conscience and tell the zamindar, 'do your duty', we tell the loan shark, 'slash your rate of interest' or exhort the police, 'do not commit any injustice'—but how long can we go on so feebly fending off attacks from all sides! It is just like making someone carry water in a sieve and asking them 'save as much water as you can by stopping up the holes with your hands.' It may work for a moment or two but not for ever. In society, compulsion is more powerful than kindness.

Therefore, the first priority is linkage or connectivity among the people—a connectivity which is visible to all. In other words, they should have a way to communicate among themselves. It may not be a highway, but it has to be a country lane at any rate.

It is the spread of the ability to read and write which paves the way. If I use the term *gynansiksha*—the cultivation of wisdom—they will argue that our farmers lead the rest in this field, thanks to the Jatra troupes and Kathakthakurs. If I use the phrase 'higher education', it will provoke guffaws of laughter in genteel society—I could have put up with that, too, if this proposal had possessed some immediate usefulness. . .

The common people in our country today depend on the kindness of zamindars, loan sharks, government officers—in short, the entire genteel society. Consequently they have dragged down the latter. We can beat up our servants with impunity and easily dupe the illiterate.

We need to learn how to deal justly and fairly with subordinates, to behave politely with the lowly who are not normally treated with respect. The latter depend on our whims rather than their own power. It is precisely with a view to saving ourselves from this ceaseless predicament that we need to empower the lower classes. However, as soon as we proceed to empower them, we will have to give them a means to gradually come together and unite and it boils down to teaching them reading and writing skills.

(From *Lokahita*, c. 1914)
Translated by Subhransu Maitra

At the Loom: Boys at Shilpa Sadan in Santiniketan

Sriniketan: Rural Reconstruction Training Camp

CONSTRUCTION vs. CREATION

We all know that when at first a people became clearly aware of its oneness, it expressed it in some symbolism of divinity.* This means that it felt some indefinable touch of the supreme personality in the heart of its social existence, which could claim for its sake the loyalty of love even when this love was fraught with danger. This personality was held to be divine, because through it we felt an emancipation from the too narrow bonds of self, and urged by its call we could rise above the fear of death and resist the downward pull of personal gain. Through it we reached a plane of existence totally different from that to which we had been accustomed. It was our translation to the moral plane of OUGHT from the physical plane of IS. This great feeling of the person in the centre of our social unity brought its members together, into a profound intimacy of relationship, and this sense of personality broke out in an amazing outburst of creative energy.

But science is producing a habit of mind which is ever weakening in us this spiritual standpoint of truth that has its foundation in our sense of a person at the ultimate and innermost reality of existence. Science has its true sphere in analysing this world as a construction just as a grammarian has his legitimate mission in

* This extract is from text of a lecture given by Rabindranath Tagore on April 2, 1920 at the Gujarati Sahitya Parishad, as a reply to their felicitation of Tagore. It was published three years later as 'Dr. Tagore's Reply' in *Chhaththi Gujarati Sahitya Parishadano Report–1920* ('Report of the Sixth Gujarati Sahitya Parishad—1920'; published 1923; pp. 112–132). A revised version of the lecture was later published as 'Construction vs. Creation.'

analysing the syntax of a poem. But the world as a creation is not a construction: it is also more than its syntax. It is a poem, which we are apt to forget when, by exclusive attention, grammar takes complete possession of our mind.

Upon the loss of the sense of a universal personality, which is religion, the reign of the machine and of method has been firmly established. It is the simplification of man by jettisoning a great part of his treasure, spiritually speaking he has been made a homeless tramp, getting a freedom which is negative because superficial. Its concentrated hurt had been felt by all the world in the late war. Freed from the bond of spiritual relationship as the medium of the brotherhood of man, the different sections of society are continually being resolved into their elemental character of forces. Labour is a force and also capital, so are the Government and the people; the man and the woman. It is said that when the forces lying latent even in a handful of dust are liberated from their bond of unity, which is their bond of creation, they can lift St. Paul's Cathedral to the height of a mountain. Such disfranchised forces roving as irresponsible freebooters may be useful to us for certain purposes, but St. Paul's Cathedral is, generally speaking, better for us standing secure on its foundation than shattered into pieces and scattered in the void. To own the secret of mastering these forces is a proud fact for us but the power of self-control and self-sacrifice within is a truer subject of exultation for mankind. The genii of the Arabian Nights may have their lure and fascination for us, but God is infinitely more precious for imparting to our society its spiritual power of creation. But these genii are abroad everywhere, and even after their death-dance in the late war, incantations addressed to them are secretly being muttered, and their red-robed devotees are still getting ready to play tricks upon humanity by suddenly spiriting it away to some hill top of desolation. The thunder-clouds of revolution which are ominously gathering, flashing their angry teeth and growling out their throat are the outcome of a long process of separation of human personality from human power reducing men into a ghost of abstraction.

Modern science has outwardly brought all mankind close together. The situation requires the spiritual realization of some great truth of relationship to save human societies from constant conflict of interest and friction of pride. The people who are mere forces when not organically united must prove their humanity by some creative transfusion. This is not a mere problem of construction and therefore does not chiefly fall within the province of science which deals merely with discovery and invention and not with creation. The outer bonds of telegraph wires and railway lines have helped men all the more efficiently to tear one another to pieces and to rob their weaker fellow beings of food, of freedom, and of self-respect. Must the sword continue to rule for ever and not the sceptre, and must science after her great achievement of mastering the geography of the earth remain at the head of the administration? Can she establish peace and unity in this world of diverse races? Has it not been sufficiently proved that her material law of ruthless skillfulness can only commandeer the genii of power for her agents but cannot conjure up that spirit of creation which is the love of God and man? And yet science does not show any sign of vacating her seat in favour of humanity or submit to any curtailment of her jurisdiction after her own proper work has been finished. The powerful races who have the scientific mind and method and machinery have taken upon themselves the immense responsibility of the present age. They have lustily set revolving the innumerable wheels of their engines for moulding alien races like ourselves which can not be wholly for our own benefit. And yet they are surprised with a vehemence of anger when we are hurt. We complain not of their law and Government, which are scientifically efficient, but of the desolating deadliness of their machine domination. These people in their dealings with subject races all over the world forget that science and law are not a perfect medium for human communication. They refuse to acknowledge what an ordeal it can be for human beings meekly to have to receive gifts from animated pigeon-holes or condescension from a steam-engine of the latest type. We feel the withering fierceness of the spirit of modern civilization all the more because it beats directly against our human sensibility not affording to us for its medium even a rarefied atmosphere of kinship to temper it with sympathy. And it is we of the Eastern hemisphere who have the right of suffering to say that those who represent this great age of great opportunities are furiously building their doom by their renouncement of the divine ideal of personality, for the ultimate truth in man is not in his intellect or in his material wealth, it is in his imagination of sympathy, in his illumination of heart, in his activities of self-sacrifice, in his capacity for extending love far and wide across all barriers of caste and colour, in his realizing this world not as a storehouse of mechanical power but as a habitation of man's soul with its eternal music of beauty and its inner light of a divine presence.

Before I finish my lecture I must, to be fair, express with all humility and sorrow our shame for our own failure in India to justify the trust placed upon us by Providence. Men of various races came to this country and the only thing we could think of in order to accommodate them was to make elaborately permanent the walls of our social compartments. We are tenaciously proud of their exclusiveness. We make it a matter for boast that in this world only our own society has come to a dead finality in the classification of its living members. Yet in our political agitations we conveniently try to forget that any unnaturalness in the relationship of the governors and the governed which humiliates us is also a wrong classification when it is sought to be artificially fixed for ever under a threat of persecution. In the time of its fullest vigour of vitality when India produced its harvest of immortal thoughts its men had the fearless spirit of the seekers of truth. The great epic of our national soul—the Mahabharata gives us a wonderful vision of a seething life, full of the freedom of enquiries and experiments, of shifting points of view, of the boldly claimed prerogative of men in using errors as stepping stones to truth. Then came the age of Buddha, who stirred up, in our country, humanity to its uttermost depth, and the freedom of mind which it produced expressed itself in a wealth of creation in all departments of life, ever flowing in its richness the continent of Asia. With the ebb of life in India the age of creation died away. It hardened into an age of inert construction when the organic unit of variedness gave way to that conventional division of classification, which proves its artificiality by its inexorable exclusiveness. Life has its inequalities, I admit, but they are natural and are in harmony with our vitality. The head keeps its difference from the feet not through some external arrangement or conspiracy of coercion. If the body is compelled to turn, the head never changes its position into that of feet. But have our social classifications the inevitableness of an organic truth? If we have the hardihood to say so then how can we blame an alien people for subjecting us to a political classification, which they are tempted to believe as eternal? By squeezing human beings in the grip of an inelastic rigidity and forcibly holding them fixed we have ignored the law of change, the law of growth, the law of life, which is God's law of creation. We have reduced living soul into a permanence of passivity, making incapable of moulding circumstances into the shape of their own design and mastering their own destiny. Borrowing our own ideal of life from a dark period of our degeneracy, smothering our sensitiveness of soul under the immovable weight of a remote past we have set up an elaborate ceremonial of cage worship and plucked all the feathers from the wings of the living spirit of our people till it has become dependent for the welfare upon the charity of those fortunate nations who are on their pilgrimage to the future, in all the pride of their freedom of initiative. And, for us, the punishment has been terrible with the centuries of degradation and insult, with the amorphousness of our national unity, the incoherence of our power and purpose, with our ever-growing helplessness to stem the tide of disaster from outside and unreasoning self-obstruction from internal sources. Our stupefaction has become so absolute that we do not even realise that this age-long persistency of misfortune cannot be for us a mere accident of history, removable only by another accident from outside. Unless we have a true faith in freedom, knowing it to be creative, manfully taking all the risks, we not only shall not have the right to claim freedom in politics as a favour from others but shall also lack the power to maintain it with all our strength. For that would be like assigning the service of God to a confirmed atheist in belief and practice. And men who contemptuously treat their own brothers as eternal babies never to be trusted in the most insignificant details of their personal life, coercing them at every step by the cruel threat of persistent persecution into following a blind lane leading to nowhere, driving a number of them into the ditch of hypocrisy or the strength of moral perversion will fail ever again to rise to the height of the severe responsibility to hold a just freedom in politics and fight for its cause.

This great world where it is a creation, an expression of the infinite, where its morning sings of joy to the newly awakened life and its ensuing stars sing of peace to the life weary and worn, sinking to its rest, has its call for us. It is ever claiming from us co-operation with God, reminding us of our divine nature which can only find itself in freedom of spirit, freedom of higher opportunities, freedom from fear, from greed, freedom from self in a creative overflow of renunciation. Let us respond to this claim and make our creation worthy of eternity and be worthy of it, let us wipe off from our hearts the accumulating traditions of hatred, of contempt for men whom we have done our best to make and keep contemptible, and of that hardness of pride which makes us liable wrongly to judge others, and carelessly to inflict injury upon them. Let us join our voice to that of our forefathers who realised and said, 'Nothing is greater than the Person, he is supreme, he is our ultimate object,' and make that prayer our own, the prayer for that unity which can only come from love and goodness.

He, who is one, and without caste and colour,
Who with his manifold power provides people of all colours
with what are their intrinsic needs;
Who is in the beginning and in the end of all, the shining one,
Let him unite us with the wisdom, which is good.

(*c.*1920)
Rabindranath Tagore

Rabindranath Tagore and Mahatma Gandhi

CHARKHA, THE SPINNING WHEEL

Due to my lack of enthusiasm for using the Charkha, Acharya Prafullachandra has condemned me in black and white.* But since he cannot be totally ruthless in indicting me, the Acharya has bracketed Brajendranath Sil also with me in this serious sin of omission.

This has alleviated my pain; moreover, it provided a new proof to an old adage that some people are of the same opinion, while some are not. In other words, it was not the creator's intention that all people will build the same kind of hives as the bees do. But the creators of society at times intend to do that. They do not hesitate to treat man as a lump of earth in their desire to make their work easy. They put human-trees through moulding machines to produce thousands of match-sticks of the same size and shape. The sylvan goddesses may remain silent when the forest-good is thus converted to consumer goods, but reducing human intelligence to the level of bees in the name of work may lead to a heavy penalty on the day of final judgement. During my boyhood, when I would go for a boat-ride at the Jagannath Ghat of Ganga, all ferry-men would jostle with each other to entice me as a prospective passenger. But when I finally settled for a particular boat of my choice, there was no fear of reprimand for any bias or favour. For there were many boats, there were many passengers and their destinations were also many. But if

* Published in *The Modern Review* in 1925, this is one of Tagore's responses to Gandhian politics.

Lord Tarakeswar had commanded in a dream that only a particular boat could lead to salvation, then who could have prevented the tyranny of the custodians of that boat? The poor human race could only cry from the bank: O mighty fellow, even if the shore is one, the ghats are many—some in the north, some in the south.

Our shastra says, God manifests himself in many ways. That is why the five elements combine together to maintain life. It is in death that the elements flee; and in a deluge, all become the same. God has granted man that multi-dimensional power, and hence human civilization is so rich. God intends that the many would be woven together to create one; but the rulers of a particular dispensation want to crush and grind the many in the mould of sameness. This is why there are so many labourers in the same mill, so many soldiers in the same uniform, so many puppets on the same string. The revolt against this pulverising sameness also continues wherever man's human qualities have not been frozen yet. If I do not find the symptom of that anywhere, if I find that mankind can calmly and timidly accept being consigned to a bed of dust, be it by the whipping of the ruler or the command of the guru, I would know that the day of mourning for that sightless, pulseless, frozen country has arrived.

In our country, the evil practices arising out of social equation have been in force for many days. This religion of death has assigned a particular variety of work for every man belonging to each caste. At the same time, the secret that was whispered in their ears was that their ancestor, right at the beginning of creation, had accepted advance wages for a particular work for eternity. Hence, it will be going against dharma if one wants to shift from that work. Such imitation of the society of ants may be useful for some practical work, but is a great obstacle to the process of becoming human. This kills the creative energy of mankind; it only enhances the physical skill of a slave or labourer. This is why in India there is a perpetual repetition of the old order. And today's aversion to the existential aspects of life is because of the constant grind of this mortar and pestle of repetition. Alarmed at the imagination of the cycle of life and rebirth, man is trying to suppress all his natural tendencies so that he can strike at the root of all work. He has seen the terror of this repetitiveness in his own day-to-day habitual drudgery. The loss is even greater: those who turned into machines lost their libido;

they did not have the strength to resist any onslaught. As a result, the clever cheated them through the ages, gurus duped them, the powerful oppressed them. They cannot even think of any redressal of this situation, because they are convinced that all this was ordained by God; the four-headed Brahma has wound up their motor at the beginning of creation and it will not exhaust till the end of creation. The raft of their life and death, made of monotonous work, has been placed in the flow of eternity. But whatever the ancient shastras say, what Brahma actually did with man at the beginning of creation was totally different. Instead of inserting the motor of monotonous cyclic movement, he slipped into the shell of man an extremely restless element called the mind. It is impossible to make a machine out of man unless that damned thing is banished. The rulers manage to nearly kill that mind partly by coercion, partly through temptations, and partly with the help of the infatuation of religion. By doing so, they are extracting handloom cloth from one group, mill-produced oil from another; if one group is supplying the urn as per their order, another is supplying the ploughshare for them. After all this, if you call them for a higher human cause where the mind is involved, they will ask, 'Mind? What's that rubbish? Give us orders, issue instructions!'

If you want to fence your house with a hedge, all the plants are required to be pruned to the same size. Similarly, in this land of pruned minds, the natural human instincts have been suppressed through the ages. And yet, if today a few branches here and there show mischievous signs of revolt by growing haphazardly beyond the prim and proper, if today all the minds do not sing in the same tune like the crickets at night, then let not anyone be anxious or irritated; because it is then that we can really hope for swaraj, or self-rule.

This is why I am not ashamed to confess (though with much apprehension of a public outcry) that my mind did not resonate with the Charkha movement. Many will misconstrue it as my audacity and get furious with me. For, when many fish are caught in the net, the one that escapes becomes the target of all our abuses. Still I hope there are people who are of a kindred spirit with me. It may be difficult to target all of them; because their hands may not be active with the Charkha, but their mouths are active, fast and furious.

Wherever a society has given more priority to work over knowledge, all human endeavours have been doomed to failure.

It we look at the great men who came with a profound message for the world, right from the Buddha to the saints of the mediaeval Bhakti movement, we find that all of them were against mindless external rituals. They appealed to the inner soul of man for overcoming all obstacles. Unlike a spendthrift, unlike a calculative wise man, they never said that externals come first, then internal matters; or material necessities first, then the holistic development of inner power. They accorded man great honour by making great demands on him. And it is because of this demand that the latent wealth of the human mind blossomed to enrich society with literature, music and other fine arts. They gave man light, the wakening call; in other words, they gifted him with the realisation of his own soul,—a gift complete in itself.

Today, if our whole country is ridden with poverty, both mental and physical, we have to understand that its root lies in our inner self. If we select only one external symptom of this disastrous condition and the whole country descends upon it with one external practice, it would have no impact on the evil. If mankind were an inanimate mass, his appearance could have been reshaped by hammering. But if poverty is manifested on the external appearance of man, his internal energy should be addressed. The indiscriminate hammering will only hurt that inner mind. . . .

We have to remember that the day on which man invented the wheel was a great day for him. The moment the immovable object was made dynamic on a wheel, much of the burden from his shoulder was shifted to the inanimate matter. That was the correct move, for it is the mass which is sudra; along with its external existence, there is no internal existence. Man has an inner life, hence everyman is a brahmin, twice-born. He has to preserve his external life as well as internal life. So, whatever burden of work he cannot put upon the inanimate mass, he has to depend on man. Thus man has to be turned into mass and hence become sudra to that extent, otherwise society cannot sustain itself. No one can bestow dignity upon these people by talking about the dignity of labour. The wheel has liberated numerous sudras from their sudra-ness. It is this wheel which has reduced man's burden through the Charkha, the potter's wheel, the automobile and many other crude and subtle forms. Eons ago, the day on which the wheel moved, man realised that no other component of wealth compared with this reduction of burden. At the beginning of history, when the movement of the wheel started generating wealth, it did not stop at the Charkha only. Can't we build a theory on this information? The power of Lord Vishnu lies in two items—the lotus and the wheel. The moment man reached that power of Lord Vishnu, he was liberated from the moment of inertia. It is this inertia which is the main poverty. All divine power is limitless. This is why we have not yet reached the end of the moving wheel. If we accept that the primitive Charkha is the last word for weaving, we shall never be blessed by Lord Vishnu's propitiousness, and hence Goddess Lakshmi will turn her face away. If we forget that science is increasing the capacity of this wheel of Lord Vishnu, we shall be exterminated by the conspiracy of those who have maintained their respect for Vishnu.

Through the lens of science, the huge power of the great wheel is understood. When we forget this and accept unthinkingly a particular form of Charkha of a particular time as the ultimate machine for spinning threads, the Charkha becomes inwardly dumb and no longer speaks of progress as it once did, leading to power and wealth. Not that it does not speak in sounds that reach our ear, but it does not address our mind. . . .

I have to repeat the age-old wisdom that the basis of swaraj is not sameness but the harmony of mind. This harmony of mind has a great role to play in the sphere of livelihood. In fact, if the unity has to be great, the space also must be large. But if a particular fraction of man's entire business of living is isolated and given special emphasis, then one will get thread, cloth and all, but the harmony of life with life will go out of focus.

In India it is not possible to achieve total unity in the field of religion. And there was never a concept of everyone being united under one nation. It has just started, but it will still take a lot of time for the idea to truly occupy the mind of ordinary people. So, we have to concentrate on basing a broad unity on the foundation of livelihood. The area of livelihood is the most wide; everyone—small and big, wise and ignorant—is welcome in this area. Its call is universal, like that of death. If this field does not become a battlefield, if we can prove that even here cooperation and not competition is the ultimate source of human power, we can wrestle a huge kingdom from the clutches of primitive instinct, of turmoil. Moreover, we should remember that we have practised this harmony in the rural society of India. Even if the thread of that harmony has been broken, it can easily be joined again, for our basic nature has not altogether changed.

Just as it is the livelihood in case of an individual, similarly it is the state policy in the case of a people. The nature of a people or its leaders expresses itself in its state policy. Diplomacy is the art of creating divisions. So far this is the policy that is practised. Individual nations are busy in achieving their own interests. The burden of their forged documents and stock of weapons are becoming heavier by the day. There is heavy competition to increase this burden. It has no end, hence there is no peace in the world. The day on which mankind will distinctly realise that the real goal of the welfare of every nation can be achieved only through the co-operation of all the nations (because mutual dependence is the basic human nature), national policies will also become the wider sphere of man's quest for truth on that day. It is only on that day that the state will also respect the same principles of life which the society recognises as truth. That means the state will understand that acts such as cheating someone, stealing someone else's property, indulging in vain self-glorification—these are not only against one's ultimate salvation but also against the interest of united humanity. Perhaps the founding of the League of Nations is the first step towards establishment of an ego-less humanity in the matter of state policies.

Just as state policies are invariably bound by the freedom of the state, livelihood also is bound by the freedom of the individual. This is why there is so much competition, jealousy, fraud and indignity. But man being man, even his livelihood should have been a field for cultivating humane nature, rather than power. It should have been achievable that even in the field of livelihood man will not only earn material prosperity but also realise his own truth. A few years back when I heard about the co-operative method of work, a complicated knot in my mind was undone to a great extent. I felt that the truth of humanity which was neglected in the field of livelihood due to the differences of self-interest was today asserted by the convergence of self-interest. It is striving to convince us that poverty lies in the practice of difference whereas wealth lies in the practice of harmony. From all angles, this is the basic truth of human civilization. I refuse to believe that this truth can ever be limited by time and space. . . .

Any difference of opinion with Mahatmaji on any matter is extremely unsavoury for me. Looked from a bigger perspective there is nothing wrong in this, but my mind refuses to think so. For, can there be any greater pleasure than assisting in the work of someone whom I love and respect? His noble character is a matter of great wonder to me. The maker of India's destiny has sent us a bright, invincible, divine power. Let this power not overwhelm the Indians, but strengthen them; let it teach them to think, to determine and to relinquish. This is what I pray for. There is an internal reason which prompted Mahatmaji to call a great intellectual like Rammohun Roy a pigmy—and yet I consider Rammohun as the greatest man of the modern age. It is due to the same internal nature that Mahatmaji's programmes of work have of late taken turns that I cannot accept as my own dharma. I regret this difference of conviction. But I believe God intends different paths of sadhana, the sacred pursuit, otherwise why should there be difference of nature in the world? On many occasions, because of my personal devotion to him, I was tempted to accept the mantra of Charkha from Mahatmaji. But I desisted from it lest I accord more importance to the Charkha than its due. I am sure Mahatmaji will appreciate my position; he has shown such patience towards me earlier also. Acharya Roy also respects individual opinion, irrespective of the popular trend of thought. I hope he would not be unkind to me in his heart, although he may attack me in public meetings at times. And I hope my countrymen, who have already forgotten both the good and bad deeds that I have done so far, would also forgive me. If they don't, at least they would forget. If they don't even forget, if their persecution of me continues, then let me hope I would get a companion like Acharya Brajendranath in my persecution, someone unloved in his country but before whose brilliance all public censure pales into insignificance.

(From *Charkha*, 1925)
Translated by Nirmalkanti Bhattacharjee

Rabindranath Tagore in Upaasana Griha, the Prayer Hall at Santiniketan

AN EASTERN UNIVERSITY

In the midst of much that is discouraging in the present state of the world, there is one symptom of vital promise. Asia is awakening. This great event, if it be but directed along the right lines, is full of hope, not only for Asia herself, but for the whole world.

On the other hand, it has to be admitted that the relationship of the West with the East, growing more and more complex and widespread for over two centuries, far from attaining its true fulfilment, has given rise to a universal spirit of conflict. The consequent strain and unrest have profoundly disturbed Asia, and antipathetic forces have been accumulating for years in the depth of the Eastern mind.

The meeting of the East and the West has remained incomplete, because the occasions of it have not been disinterested. The political and commercial adventures carried on by Western races—very often by force and against the interest and wishes of the countries they have dealt with—have created a moral alienation, which is deeply injurious to both parties. . . .

The demoralising influence of the constant estrangement between the two hemispheres, which affects the baser passions of man,—pride, greed and hypocrisy on the one hand; fear, suspiciousness and flattery on the other,—has been developing, and threatens us with a world-wide spiritual disaster.

The time has come when we must use all our wisdom to understand the situation, and to control it, with a stronger trust in moral guidance than in any array of physical forces.

In the beginning of man's history his first social object was to form a community, to grow into a people. At that early period, individuals were gathered together within geographical enclosures. But in the present age, with its facility of communication, geographical barriers have almost lost their reality, and the great federation of men, which is waiting either to find its true scope or to break asunder in a final catastrophe, is not a meeting of individuals, but of various human races. Now the problem before us is of one single country, which is this earth, where the races as individuals must find both their freedom of self-expression and their bond of federation. Mankind must realise a unity, wider in range, deeper in sentiment, stronger in power than ever before. Now that the problem is large, we have to solve it on a bigger scale, to realise the God in man by a larger faith and to build the temple of our faith on a sure and world-wide basis.

The first step towards realisation is to create opportunities for revealing the different peoples to one another. This can never be done in those fields where the exploiting utilitarian spirit is supreme. We must find some meeting-ground, where there can be no question of conflicting interests. One of such places is the University, where we can work together in a common pursuit of truth, share together our common heritage, and realise that artists in all parts of the world have created forms of beauty, scientists discovered secrets of the universe, philosophers solved the problems of existence, saints made the truth of the spiritual world organic in their own lives, not merely for some particular race to which they belonged, but for all mankind. When the science of meteorology knows the earth's atmosphere as continuously one, affecting the different parts of the world differently, but in a harmony of adjustments, it knows and attains truth. And so, too, we must know that the great mind of man is one, working through the many differences which are needed to ensure the full result of its fundamental unity. When we understand this truth in a disinterested spirit, it teaches us to respect all the differences in man that are real, yet remain conscious of our oneness; and to know that perfection of unity is not in uniformity, but in harmony.

This is the problem of the present age. The East, for its own sake and for the sake of the world, must not remain unrevealed.

The deepest source of all calamities in history is misunderstanding. For where we do not understand, we can never be just.

Being strongly impressed with the need and the responsibility, which every individual to-day must realise according to his power, I have formed the nucleus of an International University in India, as one of the best means of promoting mutual understanding between the East and the West. This Institution, according to the plan I have in mind, will invite students from the West to study the different systems of Indian philosophy, literature, art and music in their proper environment, encouraging them to carry on research work in collaboration with the scholars already engaged in this task. . . .

The Western Universities give their students an opportunity to learn what all the European peoples have contributed to their Western culture. Thus the intellectual mind of the West has been luminously revealed to the world. What is needed to complete this illumination is for the East to collect its own scattered lamps and offer them to the enlightenment of the world.

There was a time when the great countries of Asia had, each of them, to nurture its own civilization apart in comparative seclusion. Now has come the age of co-ordination and co-operation. The seedlings that were reared within narrow plots must now be transplanted into the open fields. They must pass the test of the world-market, if their maximum value is to be obtained.

But before Asia is in a position to co-operate with the culture of Europe, she must base her own structure on a synthesis of all the different cultures which she has. When, taking her stand on such a culture, she turns toward the West, she will take, with a confident sense of mental freedom, her own view of truth, from her own vantage-ground, and open a new vista of thought to the world. . . .

In this belief, it is my desire to extend by degrees the scope of this University on simple lines, until it comprehends the whole range of Eastern cultures—the Aryan, Semitic, Mongolian and others. Its object will be to reveal the Eastern mind to the world. . . .

In India our goddess of learning is 'Saraswati'. My audience in the West, I am sure, will be glad to know that her complexion is white. But the signal fact is that she is living and she is a woman, and her seat is on a lotus-flower. The symbolic meaning of this is, that she dwells in the centre of life and the heart of all existence, which opens itself in beauty to the light of heaven.

The Western education which we have chanced to know is impersonal. Its complexion is also white, but it is the whiteness of the white-washed class-room walls. It dwells in the cold-storage compartments of lessons and the ice-packed minds of the schoolmasters. . . .

Universities should never be made into mechanical organisations for collecting and distributing knowledge. Through them the people should offer their intellectual hospitality, their wealth of mind to others, and earn their proud right in return to receive gifts from the rest of the world. . . .

Where society is comparatively simple and obstructions are not too numerous, we can clearly see how the life-process guides education in its vital purpose. The system of folk-education, which is indigenous to India, but is dying out, was one with the people's life. It flowed naturally through the social channels and made its way everywhere. It is a system of widespread irrigation of culture. Its teachers, specially trained men, are in constant requisition, and find crowded meetings in our villages, where they repeat the best thoughts and express the ideals of the land in the most effective form. . . . Evidently, according to this system, the best function of education is to enable us to realise that to live as a man is great, requiring profound philosophy for its ideal, poetry for its expression, and heroism in its conduct. Owing to this vital method of culture the common people of India, though technically illiterate, have been made conscious of the sanctity of social relationships, entailing constant sacrifice and self-control, urged and supported by ideals collectively expressed in one word, 'Dharma'.

Such a system of education may sound too simple for the complexities of modern life. But the fundamental principle of social life in its different stages of development remains the same; and in no circumstance can the truth be ignored that all human complexities must harmonise in organic unity with life, failing which there will be endless conflict. . . .

The main source of all forms of voluntary slavery is the desire of gain. It is difficult to fight against this when modern civilization is tainted with such a universal contamination of avarice. I have realised it myself in the little boys of my own school. For the first few years there is no trouble. But as soon as the upper class is reached, their worldly wisdom—the malady of the aged—begins to assert itself. They rebelliously insist that they must no longer learn, but rather pass examinations. Professions in the modern age are more numerous and lucrative than ever before. They need specialisation of training and knowledge, tempting education to yield its spiritual freedom to the claims of utilitarian ambitions. But man's deeper nature is hurt; his smothered life seeks to be liberated from the suffocating folds and sensual ties of prosperity. And this is why we find almost everywhere in the world a growing dissatisfaction with the prevalent system of teaching, which betrays the encroachment of senility and worldly prudence over pure intellect. . . .

A most important truth, which we are apt to forget, is that a teacher can never truly teach unless he is still learning himself. A lamp can never light another lamp unless it continues to burn its own flame. The teacher who has come to the end of his subject, who has no living traffic with his knowledge, but merely repeats his lessons to his students, can only load their minds; he cannot quicken them. Truth not only must inform but inspire. If the inspiration dies out, and the information only accumulates, then truth loses its infinity. The greater part of our learning in the schools has been wasted because, for most of our teachers, their subjects are like dead specimens of once living things, with which they have a learned acquaintance, but no communication of life and love.

The educational institution, therefore, which I have in mind has primarily for its object the constant pursuit of truth, from which the imparting of truth naturally follows. It must not be a dead cage in which living minds are fed with food artificially prepared. It should be an open house, in which students and teachers are at one. They must live their complete life together, dominated by a common aspiration for truth and a need of sharing all the delights of culture. In former days the great master-craftsmen had students in their workshops where they co-operated in shaping things to perfection. That was the place where knowledge could become living—that knowledge which not only has its substance and law, but its atmosphere subtly informed by a creative personality. For intellectual knowledge also has its aspect of creative art, in which the man who explores truth expresses something which is human in him—his enthusiasm, his courage, his sacrifice, his honesty, and his skill. In merely academical teaching we find subjects, but not the man who pursues the subjects; therefore the vital part of education remains incomplete.

For our Universities we must claim, not labelled packages of truth and authorised agents to distribute them, but truth in its living association with her lovers and seekers and discoverers. Also we must know that the concentration of the mind-forces scattered throughout the country is the most important mission of a University, which, like the nucleus of a living cell, should be the centre of the intellectual life of the people.

The bringing about of an intellectual unity in India is, I am told, difficult to the verge of impossibility owing to the fact that India has so many different languages. Such a statement is as unreasonable as to say that man, because he has a diversity of limbs, should find it impossible to realise life's unity in himself, and that only an earthworm composed of a tail and nothing else could truly know that it had a body.

Let us admit that India is not like any one of the great countries of Europe, which has its own separate language; but is rather like Europe herself, branching out into different peoples with many different languages. And yet Europe has a common civilization, with an intellectual unity which is not based upon uniformity of language. It is true that in the earlier stages of her culture the whole of Europe had Latin for her learned tongue. That was in her intellectual budding time, when all her petals of self-expression were closed in one point. But the perfection of her mental unfolding was not represented by the singularity of her literary vehicle. When the great European countries found their individual languages, then only the true federation of cultures became possible in the West, and the very differences of the channels made the commerce of ideas in Europe so richly copious and so variedly active. We can well imagine what the loss to European civilization would be if France, Italy and Germany, and England herself, had not through their separate agencies contributed to the common coffer their individual earnings.

There was a time with us when India had her common language of culture in Sanskrit. But, for the complete commerce of her thought, she required that all her vernaculars should attain their perfect powers, through which her different peoples might manifest their idiosyncrasies; and this could never be done through a foreign tongue. . . .

All great countries have their vital centres for intellectual life, where a high standard of learning is maintained, where the minds of the people are naturally attracted, where they find their genial atmosphere, in which to prove their worth and to contribute their share to the country's culture. Thus they kindle, on the common altar of the land, that great sacrificial fire which can radiate the sacred light of wisdom abroad.

Athens was such a centre in Greece, Rome in Italy; and Paris is such today in France. Benares has been and still continues to be the centre of our Sanskrit culture. But Sanskrit learning does not exhaust all the elements of culture that exist in modern India. . . .

Let me say clearly that I have no distrust of any culture because of its foreign character. On the contrary, I believe that the shock of such extraneous forces is necessary for the vitality of our intellectual nature. It is admitted that much of the spirit of Christianity runs counter, not only to the classical culture of Europe, but to the European temperament altogether. And yet this alien movement of ideas, constantly running against the natural mental current of Europe, has been a most important factor in strengthening and enriching her civilization, on account of the sharp antagonism of its intellectual direction. In fact, the European vernaculars first woke up to life and fruitful vigour when they felt the impact of this foreign thought-power with all its oriental forms and affinities. The same thing is happening in India. The European culture has come to us, not only with its knowledge, but with its velocity.

Then, again, let us admit that modern Science is Europe's great gift to humanity for all time to come. We, in India, must claim it from her hands, and gratefully accept it in order to be saved from the curse of futility by lagging behind. We shall fail to reap the harvest of the present age if we delay.

What I object to is the artificial arrangement by which foreign education tends to occupy all the space of our national mind, and thus kills, or hampers, the great opportunity for the creation of a new thought-power by a new combination of truths. It is this which makes me urge that all the elements in our own culture have to be strengthened, not to resist the Western culture, but truly to accept and assimilate it; to use it for our sustenance, not as our burden; to get mastery over this culture, and not to live on its outskirts as the hewers of texts and drawers of book-learning. . . .

So, in our centre of Indian learning, we must provide for the co-ordinate study of all these different cultures,—the Vedic, the Puranic, the Buddhist, the Jain, the Islamic, the Sikh and the Zoroastrian. The Chinese, Japanese, and Tibetan will also have to be added; for, in the past, India did not remain isolated within her own boundaries. Therefore, in order to learn what she was, in her relation to the whole continent of Asia, these cultures too must be studied. Side by side with them must finally be placed the Western culture. For only then shall we be able to assimilate this last contribution to our common stock. A river flowing within banks is truly our own, and it can contain its due tributaries; but our relations with a flood can only prove disastrous.

There are some who are exclusively modern, who believe that the past is the bankrupt time, leaving no assets for us, but only a legacy of debts. They refuse to believe that the army which is marching forward can be fed from the rear. It is well to remind such persons that the great ages of renaissance in history were those when man suddenly discovered the seeds of thought in the granary of the past. . . .

The time has come for us to break open the treasure-trove of our ancestors, and use it for our commerce of life. Let us, with its help, make our future our own, and not continue our existence as the eternal rag-pickers in other people's dustbins. . . .

The great use of Education is not merely to collect facts, but to know man and to make oneself known to man. It is the duty of every human being to master, at least to some extent, not only the language of intellect, but also that personality which is the language of Art. It is a great world of reality for man,—vast and profound,—this growing world of his own creative nature. This is the world of Art. . . . From the educational point of view we know Europe where it is scientific, or at best literary. So our notion of its modern culture is limited within the boundary lines of grammar and the laboratory. We almost completely ignore the æsthetic life of man, leaving it uncultivated, allowing weeds to grow there. Our newspapers are prolific, our meeting-places are vociferous; and in them we wear to shreds the things we have borrowed from our English teachers. We make the air dismal and damp with the tears of our grievances. But where are our arts, which, like the outbreak of spring flowers, are the spontaneous overflow of our deeper nature and spiritual magnificence ? . . .

Ours is the education of a prison-house, with hard labour and with a drab dress cut to the limits of minimum decency and necessity. We are made to forget that the perfection of colour and form and expression belongs to the perfection of vitality,—that the joy of life is only the other side of the strength of life. The timber merchant may think that the flowers and foliage are mere frivolous decorations of a tree; but if these are suppressed, he will know to his cost that the timber too will fail. . . .

I have already hinted that Education should not be dragged out of its native element, the life-current of the people. Economic life covers the whole width of the fundamental basis of society, because its necessities are the simplest and the most universal. Educational institutions, in order to obtain their fullness of truth, must have close association with this economic life. The highest mission of education is to help us to realise the inner principle of the unity of all knowledge and all the activities of our social and spiritual being. Society in its early stage was held together by its economic co-operation, when all its members felt in unison a natural interest in their right to live. Civilization could never have been started at all if such was not the case. And civilization will fall to pieces if it never again realises the spirit of mutual help and the common sharing of benefits in the elemental necessaries of life. The idea of such economic co-operation should be made the basis of our University. It must not only instruct, but live; not only think, but produce.

Our ancient tapovanas, or forest schools, which were our natural universities, were not shut off from the daily life of the people. Masters and students gathered fruit and fuel, and took their cattle out to graze, supporting themselves by the work of their own hands. Spiritual education was a part of the spiritual life itself, which comprehended all life. Our centre of culture should not only be the centre of the intellectual life of India, but the centre of her economic life also. It must co-operate with the villages round it, cultivate land, breed cattle, spin cloths, press oil from oil-seeds; it must produce all the necessaries, devising the best means, using the best materials, and calling science to its aid. Its very existence should depend upon the success of its industrial activities carried out on the co-operative principle, which will unite the teachers and students and villagers of the neighbourhood in a living and active bond of necessity. This will give us also a practical industrial training, whose motive force is not the greed of profit.

Before I conclude my paper, a delicate question remains to be considered. What must be the religious ideal that is to rule our centre of Indian culture? The one abiding ideal in the religious life of India has been Mukti, the deliverance of man's soul from the grip of self, its communion with the Infinite Soul through its union in ânanda with the universe. This religion of spiritual harmony is not a theological doctrine to be taught, as a subject in the class, for half an hour each day. It is the spiritual truth and beauty of our attitude towards our surroundings, our conscious relationship with the Infinite, and the lasting power of the Eternal in the passing moments of our life. Such a religious ideal can only be made possible by making provision for students to live in intimate touch with nature, daily to grow in an atmosphere of service offered to all creatures, tending trees, feeding birds and animals, learning to feel the immense mystery of the soil and water and air.

Along with this, there should be some common sharing of life with the tillers of the soil and the humble workers in the neighbouring villages; studying their crafts, inviting them to the feasts, joining them in works of co-operation for communal welfare; and in our intercourse we should be guided, not by moral maxims or the condescension of social superiority, but by natural sympathy of life for life, and by the sheer necessity of love's sacrifice for its own sake. In such an atmosphere students would learn to understand that humanity is a divine harp of many strings, waiting for its one grand music. Those who realise this unity are made ready for the pilgrimage through the night of suffering, and along the path of sacrifice, to the great meeting of Man in the future, for which the call comes to us across the darkness. . . .

In other words, this institution should be a perpetual creation by the co-operative enthusiasm of teachers and students, growing with the growth of their soul; a world in itself, self-sustaining, independent, rich with ever-renewing life, radiating life across space and time, attracting and maintaining round it a planetary system of dependent bodies. Its aim should lie in imparting life-breath to the complete man, who is intellectual as well as economic, bound by social bonds, but aspiring towards spiritual freedom and final perfection.

(From *Creative Unity*, c.1927)
Rabindranath Tagore

Rabindranath Tagore.
1892

THE CO-OPERATIVE PRINCIPLE

At a critical juncture of civilization cities inevitably became more important than villages. It is not that the soul of a country finds its best expression in a city; the reason for its enhanced status is that the centre of power of a nation is consolidated in it.

At the heart of human habitation is man's instinct for socializing. But socializing is not something that takes root in a city. One reason for this is that as cities grow over time the ties that bind their denizens automatically loosen. Another reason for the lack of interaction between people in a city is that as it becomes a centre of trade and commerce and as facilities of all kinds develop in it, its population tends to swell in size. In a city, a man's priority is meeting his basic needs and not meeting other people. That is why even where the people of a neighbourhood do not know each other they find no cause for shame in such lack of knowledge. As life becomes more and more complex the distance between people in cities has increased. In my youth I saw people of our neighbourhood mingling freely with us in our house. It is as if they were our kinsmen. People who lived nearby would come to our tank to bathe; neighbours would stroll in our garden; and no one would be prevented from plucking the flowers needed for prayer-offerings. Someone or the other would sit on the bedstead in our veranda and ask for tobacco so that he could have a smoke there. Everyone in the neighbourhood had a right to be part of all the activities going on in our house; they would take part in our feasts and the events we would organize. The buildings that were constructed in those days had large courtyards, not merely because they allowed light to stream in and the shade to spread easily but also because they provided areas of open access to all. Then one had to make allowance for the needs of the community while meeting one's own needs; one's property was meant to be used strictly in proportion to one's requirements. The wealthy man would have one door for his use but another would open to admit the people of the community. The good fortune of the rich would extend to the people around him. Observance of social or religious ceremonies was a way of acknowledging that even the uninvited and otherwise unwelcome could come in at those times.

From such a way of life I can conclude that once upon a time the sociability that characterizes village life had its place in the city too. Even though our cities did not resemble our villages in their external features, they were similar in their dispositions. Without a doubt the big cities of our country were of this kind. Though puffed up with pride at having developed as cities they would acknowledge their kinship with villages. It was like the relationship between the public and private quarters of a mansion. For sure the hall would display more marks of wealth and grandeur than the other parts, but true ease and rest would be provided in the innermost parts of the house. But of course the passage was open for a meeting of hearts between the two.

It is obvious to us that no such bond exists in our time. Before our very eyes cities have become completely urbanised in the last fifty years; even their back doors no longer provide access to villages. This is the import of the saying: 'From the home the yard outside seems foreign'. Villages still surround cities but these days they appear hundreds of miles away from them in spirit.

Such an imbalance in the relationship can never be a good thing. It has to be emphasized that this situation is not something that is unique to our part of the world in modern times; it is a phenomenon characteristic of the era everywhere. In fact, a wind from the west is now blowing all over the world and spreading the seeds of self-division everywhere. This trend is not only destroying mankind's peace and happiness, it is destroying life from within. Consequently, people everywhere must pay attention to solving this problem.

What in European languages is called civilization is something that drains the ordinary spirit to nurture, something all too potent, something that can be likened to the bamboo flower, which blooms by sucking the sap of the plant. In trying to become distinctive it starts bending in one direction; its asymmetrical distribution of weight ultimately leads to cracks in the entire structure. Inevitably, it self-destructs. I see evidence of Europe cracking up through many such forms of self-rupturing. The Klu Klux Klan, the creation of the Soviet, Fascism, and workers' uprisings, feminist revolts and many other forms of self-destruction make it evident that the moorings of society are fraying. What in English is called 'exploitation' seems to be the dominant tendency of present-day civilization. The part wants to grow by suppressing the whole; that leads to the expansion of a small segment of society but does not nurture an entire people. What it ultimately results in is anti-social individualism.

I have indicated already that cities are where power is concentrated while villages harbour the soul of the country. It is essential to have special mechanisms in place for the exercise of financial, political and administrative power. But these mechanisms do not operate according to principles that are humane. This is because in cities the mechanical usurps humanitarian considerations. Whoever commandeers these mechanisms ends up becoming all powerful. This is the major reason why the city is mainly a site of fierce competition; it is not a place where cooperation is encouraged.

Qualities needed to generate power are pride and competitiveness. But when these exceed limits their consequences can be grave. In modern civilization the pursuit of such traits has had far-reaching effects. This is because contemporary civilization is not sparsely populated but densely so. For its manifestation and protection a lot must be done; to bear its costs much energy must be expended. In such a civilization to have limited possessions is a crime, since it must be propped up by innumerable components. Wherever it encounters scarcity of resources it tends to become confrontational. Whether it is a question of setting up centres providing knowledge, healthcare, or leisure, or offering infrastructure like roads and markets, law courts and chanceries, or developing eateries and residential quarters, or creating establishments to conduct wars or maintain law and order, the costs involved are enormous. Such a civilization treats poverty with constant contempt since the poor citizens become stumbling blocks in its way.

No wonder wealth is considered to be the primary source of all influence in modern times and why it is appreciated more than anything else. In effect, the basis of state policy is not the desire for kingly power but the craving for wealth to be amassed through expansion of trade. When civilization was not as materialistic as it is now [,] pundits, gifted people, heroes or philanthropists enjoyed more esteem than the wealthy. Paying homage to those men was a way of honouring the humane elements in mankind. At that time the merely wealthy would be treated disdainfully by ordinary people. Now civilization itself appears to be sponging on wealth. This is why there is a tendency to not merely accumulate wealth but worship it too. Worship of the wrong kind of god is ruining the good in mankind. The consequence of such damage to our human qualities is evident everywhere in the world today. Men were never such bitter foes of each other before; there is nothing so cruel and so conducive to injustice as the blind pursuit of riches. Modern civilization's endless thrust for power is manifest everywhere in schemes undertaken to acquire wealth; the desire to be rich has overtaken all other impulses.

But we must all understand that greed leads to sin, and sin to death. This is because greed is an anti-social tendency. The more man enervates his social instincts the more he moves towards self-division. He is then unable to extinguish the flames of discontent. Ultimately, man undermines the stability of society and then fragments it.

I can see in the west that the conflict between those who have amassed wealth and those who laboured to make the rich richer is not getting resolved by any means. And there appears to be no way of reconciling the two sides. This is because those who become rich are greedy, but, those who help them accumulate these riches are no less covetous. Both sides need a great deal of money for sufficient access to the many material benefits offered by civilization. Given such a situation, one cannot expect the conflict between the two sides to cease at any point

In a situation where the excitement created by desire for material benefits and the worship of power results in crack-ups in society a man will be unable to devote himself to cultivating the humane elements in him. This is because he wants to be powerful and not fulfilled as a human being. In such a situation cities tend to get disproportionate power and villages tend to get neglected. Then all creature comforts, all that are required for feasts and celebrations, tend to be concentrated in cities. Villages take the role of slaves who must work to supply their overlord with food. What they get in return is just enough to sustain them. Such a situation splits society in a manner that leads to the brightening of the one and the darkening of the other. City-based civilizations that developed in Europe resulted in splitting people in this manner. In ancient Greece, for example, all civilizational activities were based in the city. But that led to a condition where cities had short life spans; they would eventually disappear from sight. There was a clearly marked division between the master and the slave then. Ancient Italian civilization too was overwhelmingly urban. For a while its urban civilization augmented its power intensely. But power is intrinsically anti-social—whoever is powerful tends to isolate himself from whatever laboured to make him powerful. The consequence is that a few masters become parasites living off innumerable slaves. Such parasitism erodes the foundations of humanity.

Western civilization is urban; the people of the west have been spreading its dark side as well as its light among people throughout the world. They have such limitless ambition that they cannot satisfy it with their own resources. The wealth that the people of England consider to be essential to civilized life can only be acquired and then maintained by making India its possession. If it is to relinquish its hold on India it can only do so by curbing its spirit of conspicuous consumption. It needs slave-states since they are prime resources for its ultimate goal—the exercise of power. This is why the entire British race feeds off the whole of India like a parasite. This is also why the leading nations of Europe have become so eager to divide Asia and Africa amongst themselves. The alternative would mean that the civilization they have founded on limitless consumption will go hungry. This is the reason too that even in their own countries Europeans are witnessing the tendency of the minority to scrounge off the majority. The fruits of such a tendency towards excessive consumption cannot be shared equally among everyone in society for if the few are to dominate with the wealth they have accumulated the majority must be deprived. This is the problem that has now reared its head in the western world.

The conflict between the workers and the wealthy in the west has at its root the amassing of the kind of wealth needed by the few so that they can indulge in unlimited consumption. That has led to division between the rich and those who labour to make them rich just as divisiveness is obvious in the relationship between master-states and slave-states. These lines of division have deepened over time. But such extreme signs of divisiveness go against whatever is human. Where the unity of mankind is threatened by such abrasive tendencies, the seeds of destruction sprout invisibly or even openly. That is why in civilization the master quite visibly abuses his slaves and also why the slave surreptitiously assaults his master in an even more aggressive way by eroding the religious impulse in him. The consequence for humanity is that the humane element in us is then imperilled. After all, if want of food kills the animal in us, want of religion destroys our human impulses.

A fable of Aesop's tells us of a one-eyed deer which though alert, died of an arrow that struck the very eye that was blind. The blind side of present-day civilization is its materialism. What we can see in Europe now is that its nations collaborate in the acquisition of knowledge but compete with each other fiercely in the case of material interests. The result of the former tendency is that the modern age has been illuminated brilliantly by the lighting up of one flame that then kindled a hundred more flames. Europe has left all other continents behind because of its pursuit of knowledge. In the festival of knowledge European nations have been the priests and presiding authorities at the ceremonies. The sacrificial fires have come together from different directions and have resulted in something that will seemingly never die out, for such is the effort that has gone behind it. The history of mankind has not witnessed so much collaboration as far as knowledge is concerned. Previously each country would evolve its knowledge systems independently of each other. Greece's knowledge flourished in Greece and Rome's in the Roman world; this was also the case with India and China. It was fortunate that the European nations are closely bunched together and natural barriers do not pose insuperable obstacles in the continent—they have not been isolated by extensive desert areas or immense mountain peaks. Then came a period when the same religion conquered the entire continent; moreover, the centre of that religion was Rome.

For centuries, the Latin language alone was the basis of learned discourse throughout European countries. Religious unity led to unity in the pursuit of knowledge in the continent. The distinctive nature of the Christian religion was also homogeneous, for its soul was love of Christ and its dictum was love of all mankind. Ultimately, each country managed to come out of the nursery that was Latin and began to cultivate knowledge in the vernacular. But a policy of collaboration was adopted so that the knowledge that was evolving in different countries could be uniformly channelised and stored. And this is how western civilization developed, becoming a civilization based on knowledge amassed through cooperation. It is a civilization that brings together different branches of learning until it becomes a part of one central storehouse of knowledge. We tend to talk of an eastern civilization, but it is not the consequence of coming together of the minds of different eastern cultures. It can be known only as a binary; in other words all that can be said about this civilization is that it is not western! After all, is it not true that not only did Arab learning fail to integrate with Chinese forms of knowledge but also that in many ways they are quite contrary? If a comparison is carried out of the external features of civilization as well as its inner nature it will be obvious that there are major discrepancies between the Indian Hindu world and the Semitic civilization of west Asia. The intellectual riches of these two civilizations are kept in different storehouses. It is because knowledge has not been stockpiled in Asia that the history of ancient civilization in the continent is split into different phases. Conflicts that took place in ancient times meant that in a few cases some exchanges took place, but Asia's mind was never cast in one mould. That is why when we talk of 'ancient civilization' in the continent we tend to see only a part and not a whole!

These different civilizations of Asia have failed to have any kind of impact on the contemporary world, but Europe has succeeded. This is because cooperation is the foundation of all that is human; we have become humane by collaborating with each other. The meaning of civilization is the coming together of peoples.

But where in European civilization is the seed of destruction being sown? It is where it is opposed to the religion of man, that is to say, where it has not been able to make people come together. And this has happened in the case of material things. This is where Europe's different nations have gone their own ways and are in conflict with each other. This conflict over material things has acquired massive proportions. This is because, with the help of science, the organization and accumulation of wealth has reached gigantic proportions. The consequence is that the European world is witnessing a remarkable rise in conflicts. On the one hand I can see the rapid and everyday advance of knowledge dedicated to preserving life. Mankind has never seen such increases in soil fertility, cures for the body and control over whatever tends towards inertia in life. It is almost as if Europeans have acquired from the heavens what is needed to acquire immortality. But what we see on the other hand is quite contrary. No previous age has seen such a great obsession with the pursuit of death. All the countries of the west seem to be fervently cultivating this desire for whatever can invite death and destruction. Mankind has never before witnessed such determination displayed in the pursuit of self-annihilation. The tremendous strength that Europe had gathered in its hands because of cooperation in the field of knowledge is something that it now seems bent on using for its own destruction. History has never seen such incredible instances of the fruits of a policy of cooperation existing alongside a policy of confrontation. In the cultivation of knowledge contemporary man has embarked on a course of cooperation but in the pursuit of material things he has chosen the path of self-annihilation. It is difficult to predict which side will win.

Some are of the opinion that it is only when these machines of destruction are banished from human use will the danger disappear. This notion is utterly negligible. Four-footed creatures have legs and no hands; they somehow manage to perform the activities necessary for survival. It is in this bare survival that they show their wretchedness and futility. Man has by some stroke of good fortune found himself with a pair of hands, designed only for work. His hands have greatly increased his capacity for work. Because of this advantage man has been able to triumph over all other creatures; the whole world has become his domain. Subsequently, whenever he has augmented his working capacity with mechanical contrivances, he has progressed triumphantly along the path of life. The lack of this ability characterizes other animals and its full presence is reserved for mankind. No one can say that man's ability to use such contrivances must be curbed and even if anyone says so, he will never listen. A nation that has not been able to master the machines that are the vehicles of the human capacity for work is bound to be defeated, just as other animals were destined to be defeated by mankind.

How to not hurt others while utilizing the power generated by mankind's inventions, how to strike a balance here, is the point to ponder over.

When any one person or group takes over the agencies of power or controls their constituent parts, others find themselves in difficulties. At one time in every country of the world state power rested in the hands of one individual and his followers. In such a situation the wishes of one person or a select few individuals could overwhelm the wishes of all others. This was the time when religion was used as an excuse to protect people from the powerful and their unjust, unfair and perverse rule. But as they say, 'the thief never stays back to hear a sermon'. In most cases, the ears of the powerful are not attuned to sermons. That is why in some countries, subjects have forcibly taken away the king's powers. They have declared: 'the king's might stems from us. We were deprived of our strength when we bestowed power on one person. If we could find a way of using that might ourselves, our combined strength would create a kingdom ruled collectively by all of us.' This opportunity for collective rule arose in England. Many other countries did not witness such a change because their citizens lacked the education and attitude required for sharing power and combining it with work.

One can say the same thing about financial power. In our age such power has become confined to the moneyed class. This has resulted in power for a few and misery for the multitude. But the wealthy became empowered only because they were able to benefit from the labour of the multitude. The capital the rich man has accumulated represents the labour of many. In reality it is the industry of his workers that is the true capital, for it is this capacity for work that is manifest in each of his workers. If they are able to say with conviction, 'we shall pool our individual strength in one place', that will be the true capital. But those who, owing to flaws and weaknesses in their nature, are unable to unite with others or draw others together, will have to suffer. They will not gain any lasting benefits from abusing others or taking recourse to robbery!

Because of material interests people have been ignoring their own humanity for ages. They have assumed that their prowess was the means of satisfaction for their own greed alone. That explains the extent and range of the pervasive wretchedness and humiliation all around us. Countless workers have been harnessed and whipped so that the chariots of the rich could move on. The afflicted and their dear ones have been told by way of consolation, 'keep saving your wages and hold on to your religious beliefs (as well)'. But the attempt of the powerful to protect the weak by using the ploy of religion has not been successful till this day. The weak will one day have to tell each other, 'our scattered strength has been bestowed on the powerful all this time and has been the source of their might. We can assault them from the outside and shatter them, but we cannot mend the broken bits; and we cannot achieve any results if we are unable to do so. Consequently, we will have to strive to combine the fruits of our labour and utilise them for the general good.'

This is the basic principle of cooperation. This principle has made mankind's knowledge its greatest asset; this principle is also what allowed man's instinct for religion to spread far and wide. And it is the lack of such a principle that is creating such sorrow, envy, enmity, malice, cruelty and unhappiness throughout the world.

All over the world the powerful have been battling each other and spreading the flames of violence. Individual greed has been inclined to sacrifice humanity worldwide. If we cannot counter this trend, a catastrophic conclusion to human history is inevitable. The empowered will never get together to oppose this trend; it will only be taken care of when the disempowered come together. This is because in the case of material interests the difference between the empowered and disempowered is now critical. There is also a discrepancy between the knowledgeable and the ignorant, but men do not build walls of separation over the right to knowledge. Intelligence and aptitude do not team up to welcome collective power. But in every country and every home, the endless desire to amass wealth has created walls of difference that, if accepted, will cause men to encounter obstacles and humiliation at every step. Such forms of difference existed earlier, but their walls were not sky-high, as they are today. Generally, the profits and the preparations they required were relatively modest. As a result the desire for profit had not cast a shadow on human relations, as they have been doing lately. The lust for profit did not pervade and tarnish literature, the arts, politics and domestic life as they do now. The fields in which men could mingle with each other extended far beyond their financial spheres.

Hence the poor have been striving for change in our time, and not the rich. It is the poor who bear the responsibility of freeing a society that has been trampled upon by the wealthy. It is for them to restore peace and harmony in society. The task of building a passageway for the human element through a field fenced off by financial considerations. The weakness of the poor had left civilization weak and incomplete till now. Now the poor must strive to empower themselves so that they can come up with the remedy.

At present the principle of cooperation is being applied in the realm of business in Europe. One advantage they have there is that people are much smarter and more practised at working with each other, compared to people in our country. We, or at least those of us who are a part of Hindu society, are very weak in this respect. But we can hope that the path of any union based on the desire for food and clothing, will gradually become easier because of the intolerable poverty and sorrow here. If this is not the case, we will not be able to protect ourselves from poverty at all. And in such a case we cannot blame anyone.

One hears from time to time that if we revert to the kind of lifestyle where we were able to make do with very little, then the roots of poverty would be eliminated. In other words, if we were content with the bare minimum, we would not want anything more! But that cannot be described as deliverance.

The history of the human race does not suggest that people will continue to survive in the same way forever. Mankind would have been doomed to extinction if it had not possessed the ability to come up with new inventions from one era to the next. A new age demands that men bring new offerings; those who fail to innovate fall by the wayside. It is the ingeniousness innate in mankind that has allowed it to create new opportunities for itself again and again. That enables it to develop more ingredients for life than it had in a previous age. When they did not have the plough and the spade men would make do with fruits and berries that people plucked from the forests. No one imagined mankind was deficient in any way then. As soon as the plough and the spade appeared, the concept of dividing land into portions, appliances for farming, granaries, and laws about land ownership automatically came into existence. Of course, many problems cropped up at the same time—friction leading to violence, robbery, fraudulent schemes, and malicious accusations. The same race of men who created the plough and the spade must devise ways of tackling such problems. But just because one encounters friction there is no reason for one to recommend that the plough and the spade should be abandoned for good, for that would be like having our head screwed on backwards. History reveals that instead of walking along the road to progress, some races of men have reverted to all that they had preserved in the past, turning their head backwards and becoming moribund, as it were. They are worse off than the dead; they are afflicted by death-in-life. It is true that death does not cost anything. But who would therefore conclude that death is the best solution to the problem of poverty? It is not for a man to survive somehow with the little that he has stored from the past. A man's wants are many and the preparations they require are innumerable, but the capacity he has to meet them is great too. What is that we would consider as luxury? To use a kerosene-lighted lamp instead of one that uses castor-oil? To use electric lights instead of kerosene lamps? Never! If you consider any kind of artificial lighting unnecessary once daylight is gone you can of course dispense with electric lights. But the necessity that led to the use of castor oil in lighting up lamps in the evening once upon a time is still there and electric lights are far superior for that purpose. If we use electric lights now it will not be indulging in luxury; indeed, not using it would be a sign of indigence. When men so used to walking from one place to another began using bullock carts, it was a sign of their increasing affluence. But in those bullock carts lay the seed of our current devotion to the motor car. If the man who drove a bullock cart does not ride a motor car now, it would signal his indigence. That is why what is considered wealth in one era is considered to be a sign of impoverishment in another. To return to such poverty in order to get rid of poverty is a sign of cowardice and impotence.

It is true that most of the opportunities that have been created for mankind in modern times have benefitted the rich. In other words, the few have been able to enjoy those benefits while most people have been deprived of them. This misfortune is what characterizes society as a whole. This state of things has given rise to widespread disease, heated conflict, and crime. The whole of society has to pay for this situation all the time. The solution does not lie in reducing wealth, or seizing their riches from the wealthy by force, or donating wealth in a show of munificence. The way out of this situation is to spread as far as possible amongst everyone the ability to generate wealth, that is, to adopt a policy that promotes the cooperative principle among the general public.

I do not believe that discrepancies in income can ever be completely removed by force or guile. This is because inequitable distribution of power is inbuilt in the human condition. The discrepancies in the distribution are bound to show in all sorts of ways. Besides, people differ in their natures–some like to save money while others like to spend it. This is how wealth becomes distributed unevenly. In no sphere of human existence is it possible to have absolute equality and homogeneity enforced forever; nor is such enforced equality desirable. It will not do any good either. This is because, in the case of mankind as in nature, complete equality will lead to the death of enterprise and slacken the mind. On the other hand, excessive unevenness is wrong too. The reason is that the distance created between human beings then leads to obstacles in the path of socialization. Wherever there are no checks and balances, an abyss is formed where harmful forces congregate in many shapes. As I have said previously, boundless inequality characterizes our age. That is why the forces that can destroy societal harmony are amassing everywhere.

There must be ways of ensuring that the opportunities created in our time for the people of our time, in education, health and the workplace, are not beyond the reach of most people. They must have in their hands the means of accessing these things. It cannot be desirable for most people to merely survive and make do with the bare minimum. Such a limited option for living can only be humiliating. Every person needs more than that by way of income and leisure, so that the human element in them can flourish

At present, the burden of upholding the glories of civilization rests on very few people. But the burden of supporting these few people rests on the unwilling labour of innumerable people. Owing to this, a large number of people spend their days deprived of knowledge, good health and adequate nutrition, in a state of ignorance and stress. The burden of such limitless ignorance, misery, poor health and self-abuse oppresses human habitations. Because we have got habituated to them and deemed them to be inevitable, we have not given any thought to the possibility that they can do immense harm to us all. But there is no way we can remain indifferent anymore. All over the world, we can see signs of trepidations in the social sphere. Such inauspicious signs have become visible only because of the excessive pressure of the collective force that has been narrowly confined. It is imperative to free this force at this time.

In our predominantly rural and agricultural country the cooperative principle was, to a great extent, in place for a long while. But that was a time when people were more spread out than they are now. Because their needs were limited, mutual contact between them remained easy. Naturally, there were relatively few wealthy people around. But while the rich have now created barriers through excessive self-absorption, the rich had at that time established a connection with the poor through self-sacrifice. Rich people of our country find it difficult to give up anything nowadays due to increased expenditure and restricted income. But in a way this trend is welcome; now the populace as a whole must act to empower themselves. Doing so alone will benefit them permanently. If this path is pursued in India and livelihoods are built on the cooperative principle, then villages—the cradle of Indian civilization—will be rejuvenated, and will save the whole country. In India poverty is widespread in our time; accumulated capital—soaring though it is—has not in its triumphant march obstructed the path of small savers. That is why we have no alternative except to go for the cooperative principle; in our country, there are few impediments in its path. And so with all my heart I wish that wealth will be freed completely in our country and through the collective efforts undertaken by us all in a pure spirit, may Annapurna, the goddess of plenty, find her supreme place amongst us, firmly and surely.

(*Samabayniti*, c.1928)
Translated by Fakrul Alam

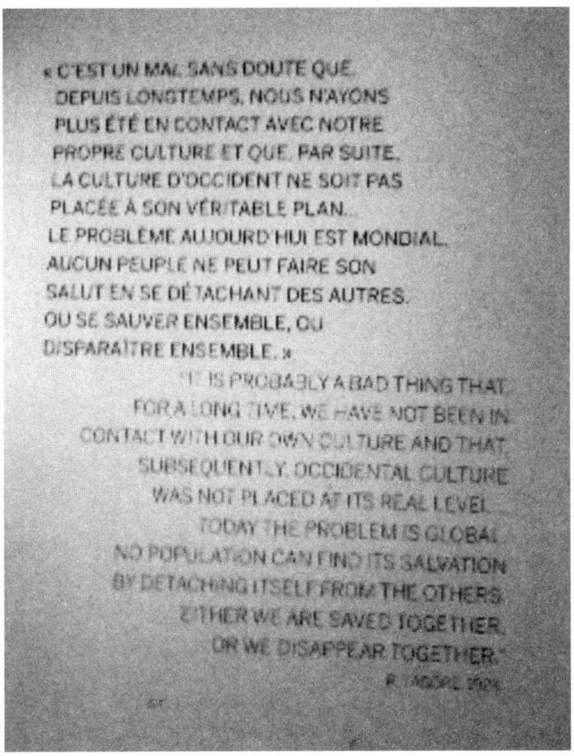

Tagore Wall.
Pompidou Centre.
Paris

Rabindranath Tagore. Seated figure design. Ink on paper, c.1928-29

RHYTHM

1

Our spirit is mobile, but words are static. . . . To impart mobility to words, to make them the very stuff of our soul, rhythm is essential. Rhythm is not just a vehicle that allows words to reach our hearts swiftly; it also adds its own vibrancy to the resonance of the word.

It is impossible to quantify the exquisiteness that the meaning of words acquires when this vibrancy is added to it. That is why the creation of verse is a wonderful affair. Its subject is framed in the poet's mind, but the aim of poetry is to exceed its subject matter; that very excess is the part that cannot be described in words. The movement of rhythm awakens that indescribable element within the word. . . .

Rhythm winds itself around the word, as leaves encircle the stem and twine their way upwards, in rhythm. A tree's substance remains embedded in its trunk and branches, but its grace, its restlessness, its dialogue with the breeze, its exchange of glances with the sky—all these things happen largely through the rhythmic movement of its leaves. . . .

The ground of colloquial Bengali is not even. If not according to the laws of Sanskritized formal Bengali, then by its own laws, it has its own play of undulations, like the waves of the ocean. . . .

This Prakrit, or colloquial Bengali, has found its natural expression in women's nursery rhymes, Baul songs, and in the verses of Ramaprasad. But because it has not gained respect in classical Bengali, it has not been able to tell the world all about itself, and the full extent of its power remains unknown. Even in today's democratic era, it proceeds timidly and with hesitation; regarding its status, where the line is drawn is still undecided. Its sense of identity is being eroded by this diffidence. One thing we forget: in the treasure-chest of colloquial Bengali, blessed by Lakshmi the goddess of wealth, there is an accumulation of words from Sanskrit, Persian, English, and various other languages; hence one should not assume that a sparse vocabulary is natural to colloquial Bengali. As required, we can obtain Sanskrit terms for the storehouse of Prakrit or colloquial language. Hence where the needs of meaning or sound dictate the necessity of Sanskrit words, colloquial Bengali will pose no obstacles. And we can arrange Persian words alongside, as well. In Sadhu Bangla or classical Bengali, that would create problems, for there, protecting one's ethnicity amounts to the preservation of purity. This broad-mindedness of colloquial language is a supreme value in our literature, in prose or verse—that is something to be borne in mind.

(From *Chhanda*, 1917)

2

The lively, natural resonance of colloquial Bengali verse, when it encountered Sanskritized Bengali—what we call formal Bengali—found itself confined within four walls like a woman in purdah, kept within the zenana, the secluded quarters reserved for women. The reason being, that classical Bengali is an artificial language; there, external rules reign supreme, while the laws of its own nature are often circumscribed. In a public meeting, there is a place, an asana, assigned to each member. Some people are lean; when they occupy their asanas, there is room to spare. Others are heavily built, and must stuff their bodies into their seats. However, the square seats are of measured dimensions, with fixed parameters. . . . But with an eye to prestige, one must freeze the laws of human nature to fit the fixed laws of civilization. Even if that causes some discomfort, it has a certain value where matters of gravity are concerned. That is why there are inevitably some differences between the ways of public meetings and the ways of the home. Seeing Shakuntala clad in tree-bark, Dushyanta said: *kimiba hi maduranam mandanam nakritam*—what can fail to enhance the loveliness of a form that is naturally beautiful? But when he took her to the inner quarters of the royal palace, surely he did not dress her in tree-bark. Then, he had added adornments to Shakunṭala's natural beauty, not to enhance her charm, but to preserve his prestige. The beauty of the royal consort varies according to the individual, but the prestige of her position is designated by the society to which kings belong. Hence, though Dushyanta had admitted that the wild vine had surpassed the garden creeper, he surely did not have the courage to beautify his garden according to the ideals of the forest. Hence, though I am personally fond of akanda blossoms, my civilized gardener uproots the tiniest seedling of that plant as soon as he catches sight of it. Had he been a poet, he would not have composed verse save in the classical style. . . .

Once upon a time, when I began to play around with verse, it was the formal language that enjoyed a monopoly in Bengali literature. . . . Afraid of stumbling, I was completely flattening out the rhythms of my lines of verse. I didn't always succeed, but on the whole, that was my endeavour. . . . My heart was full of doubt, it did not please my ear . . . .

In classical language, there is a profusion of resonant vowels, and in colloquial Bengali, these are scarce—that indeed is the fundamental difference between the two languages, as far as sound is concerned. . . . Both are of special value. Bengali poets want to reap the advantages of both styles, at appropriate points in their poetic compositions. Because they revel in the intricacies of sound, they do not wish to exclude either form. . . .

Hence, in Bengali, we follow the divergent rules of both Sanskrit and Prakrit, formal and colloquial styles. It is impossible to do otherwise. Hence, in Bengali verse, in the flowing stream of these two languages, if the rhythmic forms have taken divergent courses, then I am not at all in favour of objecting to this and blending everything into a uniform oneness by smearing purifying cow-dung over it. *Dwau kartavyau*, I say: we have a double duty. For, in matters of rhythm, my tongue is tempted by this very duality of taste.

(From *Chhanda*, 1931)
Translated by Radha Chakravarty

HINDUS AND MUSLIMS (2)

The leaders of the country have vowed to awaken a great nation based on the unity of all the provinces and all the societies in India and craft a unique asana—a constitution—for it.

Now this asana which is called constitution is an external thing; we will flesh out its bones as we go on to ascertain and determine each other's rights. We have seen a variety of examples in the history of different countries; a plan is being evolved by picking and choosing from among these. So long we were under the impression that the obstacles to giving it a final shape and putting it in place lay outside, that is, in the inclinations or disposition of the authorities; but of late we have thrown ourselves into negotiating and arguing with them.

When it seemed that progress was being made, a sudden jolt shook us and we saw that a formidable hurdle lay right in our midst. Contesting its supremacy and finally getting rid of the hostile power with which we have an external relationship is an awesome but not an insurmountable challenge. It is winning or losing. But when the row is between insiders—people fighting each other and when one side wins, such a victory is on the whole no different from a defeat or loss and loss does not usher in peace either. It is not possible to leave out or exclude anybody and to hold anybody down is to perpetuate and precipitate trouble. . . .

It is needless to say that in our country the need to create a great nation is much greater than the need to create a super constitution. There is no end to our social, religious, linguistic and ritual-centric differences. This divisiveness militates against our political unity; but what is more harmful is the fact that such divisiveness has vitiated our pursuit of humanism. There are people who live close to one another, yet never see eye to eye, there is no meeting of their minds, nor do they work together and they come to blows and fight at every turn—all this is a sign of barbarity. And yet the self-rule we are demanding is not something to be bestowed on barbarians. With what contrivance can a fragmented people—who are apt to smash everything to pieces at the drop of a hat because their religion, society, rituals and mental faculties are infected with such a virus of divisiveness—invent the identity of a united state?

A country where only religion can unite people is doomed. And the divisiveness such a country manufactures using religion is the most monstrous divisiveness of all. Real piety—dharmabuddhi—consists in lovingly accepting the value of humanity because we are human. How can political pragmatism save the country where dharma itself vitiates dharmabuddhi?

It has often been witnessed in history that when a great nation launched a political revolution inspired by a new vision of life, it simultaneously displayed a fierce abhorrence of religion. One hundred and fifty years ago the French Revolution exemplified it. The Soviet Union is implacably opposed to traditional religious systems. Of late this religion destroying fire is raging in Spain. In Mexico the Roman Catholic church has been again and again assailed by revolts.

Though the new Turks did not supplant traditional religion, they have forcibly reduced its power. In all these instances the basic fact remains that the ancient exponents and prophets of certain religions delivered sermons to unite humanity in the name of the Lord and liberate them from greed, envy and pride. Later on religious communities and sects ganged up and distorted the sermons and gospels and narrowed their meaning and used this mockery of religion as a more deadly weapon than acquisitiveness to wipe out others. They wiped out lives, wiped out dignity, human intelligence and power, they destroyed the greatest wealth of man. The unspeakable atrocities perpetrated by the Spanish Christians in ancient Mexico in the name of religion are without any parallel in history. Monarchies are increasingly being abolished now and they are disappearing from history because kings enjoying unchallenged power have often indulged in evil despotism and visited ruin and destruction on the people while posing as their saviour. Similarly, with regard to religion, history has of late witnessed numerous attempts to save man from the ravages of religion and crush the tremendous irreligiousness of religious systems. And people have achieved real freedom precisely in those countries where religious mania has not overcome the minds of people and fomented in various ways mutual indifference or hostility among them.

In Hindu society rituals have appropriated the name of religion. This is why ritualistic differences incurably drive people apart. Vegetarian neighbours in the other provinces cannot easily persuade themselves to accept the fish-eating Bengalis as their own. Usually, when Bengalis visit places in the other provinces, they harbour only indifference to local departures from familiar rituals. The kind of mindset which sets much store by external rituals has very little room for kindness and pity in it. This is what one encounters on every hand even at political conferences and it is seen that the invisible differences that we carry wherever we go are based on faith, very subtle and almost insurmountable. Even when we verbally deny that there are any differences, these lurk, unknown to us, in the depths of our mind. Religion has not been able to unite us; on the contrary it has erected myriad barriers and sanctified them by claiming that they transcend history and are eternal. The British call themselves British. If they had called themselves Christian instead, they would have surely come to blows with those among them who call themselves Buddhist, Muslim or atheist-while constituting the state. Our chief identity is that we are either Hindu or Muslim. . . .

A few years ago my British friend Andrews and I were touring the Malabar region. The moment we set foot in a Brahmin locality, an educated gentleman of the Tia community left our company and ran away. Andrews who was amazed at this followed and caught up with him, enquired and found out that people of the Tia community were debarred from entering that locality. Needless to say, according to the Hindu social code Andrews' conduct and behaviour was many times more unscriptural and improper than that of the Tia gentleman. Since Andrews belonged to the ruling class, he was powerful; but on the other hand a Hindu cannot expect any consideration on grounds of kinship from other Hindus. As far as he is concerned, even the gods save their caste by keeping him at arm's length. . . . Even a stepson has the right to sit on his mother's lap, then why so many restrictions, so many deprivations when her children come to sit on world mother India's lap? A refusal to acknowledge kindred relations and affinities is ingrained in us, it is part and parcel of our conduct and behaviour. Yet we are shocked if we do not receive their kinship and support to shore up our political needs. It is said that during the recent anti-Hindu disturbances in east Bengal the Namasudras mercilessly went over to the Muslims. Should not one ponder why they displayed no fondness, what prevented them from performing their duties of kinship?. . . . When we stridently declare that we are united and one, Providence whispers in our heart, 'you do not have the broad-mindedness and large heartedness to unite and be one in dharma-karma—belief and action, conduct and behaviour.' We are reaping the harvest of it and we are angry with the harvest, but not with the seeds sown.

When the Bengalis were sore about the deadly decision to partition Bengal, they tried to implement a policy of boycott in the last resort. Taking advantage of those troubled days in Bengal, the mill-wallas of Bombay mercilessly extracted maximum profit and did not hesitate to frustrate our utmost efforts. Alongside it was also seen that the Muslims of Bengal turned against us. It was in those days too, that the first disgraceful, sinister incidents involving Hindus and Muslims took place. There is no need to argue about who were chiefly responsible and whence suddenly incitement and instigation came aiding and abetting those disturbances. Unfriendly non-cooperation with Bengali Hindus was possible in those days because we lack the affinity and kinship to sympathetically realise that if Bengal had really been partitioned, the Bengali race would have been paralysed and that such paralysis would have proved to be the nemesis of all the Bengali communities and indeed India in its entirety. This is what we need to reflect on. And it is imperative to keep this in mind while assembling the basic framework of the state. . . .

Many people were furious about it at that time. But if the water pot is leaking, it is no use pouring water in it and what's the good of blaming the pot or water?. . . . It is our shame and it will show in good time; there will be no miracle to prevent it.

It has been agreed that a federal not unitary administrative structure should be introduced in the country. In other words, it has been conceded that we do not possess seamless unity. Let us accept this as a practical resolution of our political problems. Yet a formidable problem remains; the problem of Hindu-Muslim division and strife. This division or rift has now really grown serious for a variety of reasons. It cannot be mended by patching it up politically. The crack will resurface whenever the temperature rises for any reason. . . .

A group of Muslims are against the joint electorate, they are demanding a separate electorate and many special facilities, besides, to further strengthen their position. It seems that Mahatmaji is ready to accept even such demands in order to achieve a rapproachment if the entire Muslim community or the majority of them unanimously demand a separate electorate and want to improve their bargaining position. Because it is he who has conceived in his mind a clear image of the political rights we must win for India and the means of achieving them. It is only he who has so far made headway against very heavy odds in carrying the whole movement forward with superb skill. Judged from the viewpoint of the ultimate success of this enterprise, it is only proper that he should lead and guide us. Yet, while relying on the personal tolerance of an individual or a group, we must not forget that ordinary human nature will not tolerate the injustice if in conferring rights undue fondness is bestowed on one group, a festering hostility resulting from this will refuse to go away. In fact it is not the way to resolve a quarrel. There will be no reason for alarm if all concerned come together and amicably agree to arrive at a compromise. But the human mind! If a chord in it is stretched too tautly, it goes awry, produces discordant noise and music becomes a casualty. I do not exactly know what Mahatmaji thinks of this. Perhaps he thinks that the imperative need of the hour is to relentlessly maintain the pressure of our joint demands at the Round Table Conference. It is true that no progress can be made if both sides stubbornly stick to their inflexible positions. The situation can be saved for the time being if one side climbs down and compromises. This is what is called diplomacy. In politics you may well end up a loser if you insist on hogging everything. . . . The British are wise, to stop the boat sinking they do not mind throwing much of the cargo overboard. . . . They are celebrated for their famous pragmatism in politics, they can give up a lot keeping in mind what is really at stake. Only a headstrong fool will contend that we have no need for wise pragmatism of this kind and the headstrong fool loses at the end of the day. The surest way to gladden the enemy is to let Hindus and Muslims go on bargaining aggressively, stubbornly and let the consequent stand-of go too far.

My opinion is that if it is possible to reach a compromise by toning down our demands at the moment in order to save the situation at present, let us do it although the nub of the problem will remain. The external patch-up possible in the political sphere will not serve our long-term needs. And there is not much hope that even this patch-up in the political sphere will remain intact for ever. The half-baked patchwork will be subjected to pressure and strain again and again. . . . We will have to begin at the beginning and unite, otherwise no good will come of it.

As long as our sense of religion was easy and simple, we did not come to blows though fanaticism was not lacking. But later when the pride of religion sharply grew, the communities began to fend off and repel one another as if barbed wire fences had been erected to keep them apart. For our part, we used to beat our drums more violently when our processions carrying the idols for immersion after Puja passed a mosque on the way and they, for their part, performed korbani (sacrificial animal slaughter according to Islamic scripture on religious occasions) more ardently than before. All this was done not to satisfy the demands of religion, but to hurt each other's religious pride. These troubles started in the first place in the cities where people are not fond of one another because they hardly ever mix in the real sense of the term.

It must be admitted that there are not only differences, but even opposition between Hindus and Muslims as far as religious doctrines and social customs are concerned. Therefore, we should strive for effective harmony and unity in spite of all this. We must succeed in this. . . . Mahatmaji once thought that he would be able to build bridges between the two by standing up for the Khilafat Movement. . . . But this is not the primary point. I do not consider it wrong to have different opinions about this Khilafat. It has been proved that such differences can exist even among Muslims themselves.

We (of both the communities) need to visit and accompany each other and talk to each other certainly when an occasion comes along and also when no occasion presents itself. If we walk side by side and come closer, we will at once discover that accepting others as one's own becomes easier when they are considered as human beings. . . . Whenever people come closer, get to know each other better, doctrine lags behind and the human in each of us comes to the fore. Occasionally Muslim students and teachers came to Santiniketan, we never felt they were any different from us and there was absolutely no difficulty in establishing ties of friendship and affection. There are also Muslim villages among the neighbouring villages with which Santiniketan is associated. When the riots which broke out in Kolkata were being exported outside through agents provocateurs, a canard was whipped up in the Bolpur region to the effect that the Hindus were hell-bent on destroying the mosque. Hoodlums were also brought over from Kolkata. But we had no difficulty in maintaining peace among the local Muslims because they knew for a certainty that we were their real friends.

Most of my tenants are Muslims. When the country was terribly exercised about korbani, my Hindu tenants urged me to ban it altogether in the area under my jurisdiction. I did not think that it was a just request. Nevertheless when I called my Muslim tenants and asked them to perform korbani in such a way as not to hurt Hindu sentiments unnecessarily, they at once agreed to it. Till now no disturbance has occurred in my jurisdiction out there. I believe that the chief reason for this is that my relations with my Muslim tenants are easy and unhindered.

It can never be expected that the religious differences of doctrine, faith and rituals among the different communities in our country will cease altogether. Yet it must be hoped for the sake of humanity that there will be unity among us. If only we do not keep each other apart and at arm's length, this unity will come into its own by itself. Instead of giving each other company, Hindus and Muslims have gone apart and fomented communal disharmony and suppressed the harmony of humanity. Speaking on behalf of the Hindus I suggest that we stop finding fault with the Muslims for the time being and if we have not succeeded in bringing the

Muslims closer to ourselves, let us admit the failure and shame of it. When I had first gone on a tour of inspecting my zamindari estate and its offices as a young man, I noticed that the mattress which was spread over the cot and on which the Brahmin manager sat in the office was tucked up at one end to make room for the Muslim tenants to sit while the Hindu tenants sat on the mattress itself. I was revolted to see this. Yet this manager is one of the modern patriots. He revels in using vituperative language to criticise the British for humiliating Indians at official forums and yet he was so reluctant to show proper courtesy to his own countrymen. This reluctance has penetrated our society and sphere of work to such a great extent now that where Hindus call the tune Muslims take the back seat and vice versa. . . . The origin of the current dispute over joint electorate lies exactly here. Why don't we think of its natural cause when we get impatient about this dispute?

Meanwhile we have had to repeatedly endure unspeakable atrocities in Bengal. Outrages of this kind often took place in Czarist Russia. Demonic incidents of this kind were unheard of in our country before the current revolution-prone political age. The wonderfully glorious Law and Order thing in British ruled India has been scornfully violated and humiliated repeatedly right under the nose of the vigilant police in major cities particularly at this time. . . . And this has happened exactly at the moment when fortune would have smiled on us if we Hindus and Muslims could have spoken in one voice, and then we would not have disgraced ourselves before the whole world as we did. . . . Be that as it may, we cannot abdicate our responsibilities. It is stupid to fumble angrily trying to untie a knot which has become all too tangled up and making it still more tangled. . . . Owing to a variety of immediate and remote reasons and accumulated sins of the past, the problem of Hindu-Muslim disharmony has grown really formidable; that is why we must set about resolving the issue at once and determinedly. . . .

Prodded by the current political initiative the movement progressed most spectacularly in the province of Bombay because there was not enough provocation to set off a Hindu-Muslim row. Nor was it easy to play off the Parsis and the Hindus against each other because the Parsis are usually an educated community, they can think intelligently about the welfare of the country and besides, they are free from fanaticism. On the other hand Bengal is a powder keg and does not take long to blow up. Whenever we try to come to terms with each other here in Bengal, it becomes impossible to put our own house in order. The cause of this malady, it must be admitted, has struck deep roots here. If we in these circumstances fail to arrange a ceasefire between ourselves in an intelligent and calm manner, if we, driven by our typical Bengali impulsiveness, only foment obstinacy and violent pride, there will be no end to our misery and it will be almost impossible to embark on the path of welfare of our race.

There are some men among us who go about with their eyes and ears closed and say all problems will be sorted out when we ourselves start running the country. In other words it is an excuse for sitting idle and passing the buck by blaming everything on the changed circumstances. Let us take a closer look at this kind of argument.

Let us assume that we get the power to run the country ourselves after the Round Table Conference. Even then there is bound to be a long interlude before the actual transfer of power takes place. The tenure of the Civil Service is bound to last for a period of time. But the Civil Service of this period will be like a wounded wolf, fierce and growling. It will be necessary for the Civil Service to engrave it upon the minds of the people both at home and abroad, 'Look, we are unable to assume the responsibility of running the administration of the country because with the withdrawal of the British Raj the evil serpents of anarchy have at once slithered out of the holes and are poised to strike.' And the Civil Service will also be naturally inclined to persuade our own people to admit that it was a better state of affairs under the previous regime. In this period of transition salt will be liberally rubbed into the wounds inflicted by us on each other. This will be a fierce ordeal for us. And we will have to pass through this ordeal before the whole world. From now on we will have to be prepared and on our guard in all possible ways to ensure that no stupidity, no barbarity disfigures our new history right under the gaze of the whole world.

(From *Hindu Musalman 2*, 1931)
Translated by Subhransu Maitra

ON GANDHI AND THE BIHAR EARTHQUAKE

It has caused me painful surprise to find Mahatma Gandhi accusing those who blindly follow their own social custom of untouchability of having brought down God's vengeance upon certain parts of Bihar, evidently specially selected for His desolating displeasure.* It is all the more unfortunate, because this kind of unscientific view of things is too readily accepted by a large section of our countrymen. I keenly feel the iniquity of it when I am compelled to utter a truism in asserting that physical catastrophes have their inevitable and exclusive origin in certain combinations of physical facts. Unless we believe in the exorability of the universal law in the working of which God himself never interferes, we find it impossible to justify His ways on occasions like the one which has sorely stricken us in an overwhelming manner and scale.

* Tagore and Gandhi differed in their views on the Bihar earthquake of January 1934. In response to Tagore's reaction, Gandhi declared: 'Visitations like droughts, floods, earthquakes and the like, though they seem to have only physical origins are, for me, somehow connected with man's morals. Therefore, I instinctively felt that this earthquake was the visitation for the sin of untouchability'. Both Tagore's comments and Gandhi's answer were published in the same issue of Gandhi's newspaper, *Harijan*.

If we associate ethical principles with cosmic phenomena, we shall have to admit that human nature preaches its lessons in good behaviour in orgies of the worst behaviour possible. For, we can never imagine any civilized ruler of men making indiscriminate examples of casual victims, including children and members of the Untouchable community, in order to impress others dwelling at a safe distance who possibly deserve severer condemnation. Though we cannot point out any period of human history that is free from iniquities of the darkest kind, we still find citadels of malevolence yet unshaken, that the factories that cruelly thrive upon abject poverty and the ignorance of the famished cultivators, or prison-houses in all parts of the world where a penal system is pursued, which most often is a special form of licensed criminality, still stand firm. It only shows that the law of gravitation does not in the least respond to the stupendous load of callousness that accumulates till the moral foundation of our society begins to show dangerous cracks and civilizations are undermined. What is truly tragic about it is the fact that the kind of argument that Mahatmaji uses by exploiting an event of cosmic disturbance far better suits the psychology of his opponents than his own, and it would not have surprised me at all if they had taken this opportunity of holding him and his followers responsible for the visitation of Divine anger. As for us, we feel perfectly secure in the faith that our own sins and errors, however enormous, have not enough force to drag down the structure of creation to ruins. We can depend upon it, sinners and saints, bigots and breakers of convention. We, who are immensely grateful to Mahatamaji for inducing, by his wonder working inspiration, freedom from fear and feebleness in the minds of his countrymen, feel profoundly hurt when any words from his mouth may emphasize the elements of unreason in those very minds—unreason, which is a fundamental source of all the blind powers that drive us against freedom and self-respect.

(1934)
Rabindranath Tagore

Rabindranath Tagore.
Face of a woman.
Pen and coloured ink on paper.
26 October 1934. Adyar

WOMAN

Woman is eternal in the human paradigm. In human society feminine power can be called adyasakti. This is the power which conveys life in the living world and sustains it. Aeons passed before the earth could be hammered into shape as a place fit for the living to inhabit. But the process of shaping was only half done when nature commenced creating living beings and pain came to the world. Nature imparted this primal pain of rearing life to her blood and heart and inextricably intertwined the web of life-nurturing instinct with all the fibres of her being. Naturally all this instinct has lodged more in her heart than in her mind. And this is the instinct which creates a network of love, affection and solicitous patience inside her to hold together itself and others. This is the ancient bonding for building up and holding in place the human family which in turn provides the basis for all societies and civilizations. Without this primary bonding humans everywhere would have scattered and evaporated and could not have come together to create a meeting point for all to come and merge. This primary task of social bonding is a woman's responsibility. . . .

All the creative processes of nature are profound and secret, their self-motivation decisive, located in female nature. That is why men call female nature mysterious, enigmatic. That is why the sudden exuberance of emotion which is often seen in a woman's life is beyond logic. . . .

The enigma of love, the enigma of affection is very ancient and inscrutable. It brooks no argument on the way to its fulfilment and demands swift solutions to its problems. Thus, the moment a woman enters the house, she becomes housewife or mother; no sooner does the baby arrive than the mother appears. Mature intelligence developed much later in the animate world. It takes time to overcome hesitation and move ahead, but both strength and success are gained from this hard tussle with hesitation. As these ups and downs take place, centuries pass; hideous mistakes occur and disrupt human history. Man's civilization with all its feats sinks, he has to start all over again . . . such ups and downs have always been taking place in civilization created by males, from ancient times. Meanwhile woman the beloved and woman the mother have been steadily enacting these roles decided by nature and sometimes setting off conflagrations in the world as well, as a result of the conflict of strong emotions. . . . Such disastrous emotional upheavals are just like natural cataclysms, annihilating gale or forest fire—sudden, suicidal. Man again and again returns to his own world like a stranger. How often he re-makes his own laws and customs. His path has never been straight, such is his fate; he has had to hammer it out in different lands in different ages. What was the right path once became the wrong path later, his history was overturned, and he disappeared.

On the other hand, the fundamental stream of woman's life has been flowing along a broad course through the ups and downs of civilization. The wealth of the qualities of the heart with which she has been endowed by nature has not been subjected to ever new tests of perseverance by inquisitive, probing intelligence. Woman is ancient. Oftener than not a man finds himself scouring the vast office circuit looking for a job. In order to make a living most men are compelled to do jobs which do not at all agree with their bent of mind or ability. They have to learn a number of trades and acquire expertise in difficult things, which involves very hard work–and again most of them do not attain the level of success they desire. But what a woman does as a housewife and as a mother are her own tasks which are congruous with her nature.

Braving a lot of hurdles and getting the better of hostile circumstances through prowess and valour, man achieves greatness. But men who have succeeded so spectacularly are few and far between. Yet a woman who has made a home as wonderful as rich fertile soil, pouring out all her affection and love, can be found almost in every home. From nature women have received untutored skills; abundance of grace is their natural wealth. Unfortunately a woman who temperamentally lacks this grace cannot succeed in her world. Artificial means or education would not help in such a predicament. What can be gotten easily has its peculiar dangers. One of the reasons behind this is that it is coveted by many. Powerful countries want to annex other countries rich with natural resources, to satisfy their own needs. It is easier for a relatively poor, less endowed country to remain free. If a man can capture and cage a bird of wonderful plumage and voice, he feels proud; these greedy men forget that the glory of the bird belongs to the entire forest. For a long time men have jealously guarded women's gracefulness and willingness to serve as their personal rights. Women are naturally prone to bondage; that is why it has been so easy everywhere. . . .

Woman's intelligence, her beliefs, her conduct have for centuries been influenced by definite restrictions. Her education, her beliefs have not had adequate opportunity to mature in the thick of external, wide-ranging experiences. That is why she has been worshipping and offering gifts to all kinds of aggressors unquestioningly. If we look at the entire country, we will see how ruinous is the mischief caused by this beguiling faith, how difficult it is to advance up the tough path of development while struggling under such a burden. Not that there is any shortage of harebrained men in the country; they have been brought up by women and it is precisely these men who bully and push around women more than others. Yet they chiefly depend on the blind, unquestioning loyalty and judgement of women. Thus the mind is being fettered everywhere in the country and the fetters are getting stronger everyday. On the other hand, in almost all the countries of the world, women are moving beyond the boundaries of their own families. And the signs of this trend can be seen in modern Asia, too, because an age has arrived when all kinds of frontiers and boundaries are crumbling. The countries which were once absolutely confined within their geographical and political barriers are now being increasingly exposed to one another because the old barriers cannot box them up as they used to in the past. The spheres of experience are constantly widening. . . .

In our childhood days women used to ride in palanquins when they went out. Palanquins belonging to wealthy households had coverings with side screens. My elder sister was a notable member of the very first batch of students who went to Bethune School. She used to go to school in a palanquin with its doors open which surely militated against what an aristocratic family considered ideal conduct. In those days wearing a chemise was considered an act of shamelessness. Travelling by train without disturbing the prevailing standards of decency was no easy matter. Today the age of covered palanquins has receded far into the past, not slowly but post-haste. Alongside the changes taking place on the outside, this change came about on its own—nobody organized meetings or protests to bring it about. The marriageable age of women has also gone up over the years and this, too, has come about rather easily. If the volume of water flowing down a river increases, the shores naturally start receding, too. What is happening today in women's lives is that the shores are receding on all sides and the river of life has become a great river. Now the external changes in behaviour do not remain confined to the outside but make their presence felt in the inner nature as well. The female mentality which perfectly adjusted to life in a confined family cannot just remain static in an emancipated, free family. As it finds itself on the threshold of a major role in life, the female mind begins to think and judge on a big scale of its own accord. It naturally commences assessing its former beliefs and practices. At this stage it is likely to make mistakes, but it will have to rectify the mistakes as it negotiates a variety of obstacles. If it clings to its old habits of judging things narrowly as it formerly used to, it will find itself out of tune at every step with its surroundings. This process of changing habits is a painful one and not without its misery and hazards, but the current of the modern age cannot be reversed for fear of these. . . . Owing to the changing times, the field of women's life is constantly expanding and women now increasingly find themselves in a world free of the old restraints and inhibitions. That is why it has become essential for them to cultivate intelligence and learning for self-defence and self-esteem. And the obstacles on this path have all but disappeared. The shame attached to being illiterate is today the biggest shame for women of decent society and it surely exceeds the shame once attached to women's use of umbrellas and shoes. In other words, even in the marriage mart, the old argument that a girl's worth is best measured by domestic standards does not hold complete sway today. . . . In this way the mind of modern women in our country is every day progressing beyond the domestic sphere and graduating to the society of the world. . . . Today everywhere in the world women are stepping out of home into the wide open arena of the world. Now they must accept the responsibility for this large world family; doing otherwise will bring them shame and failure. I think a new age has arrived in the world. For a very long time men were in charge of human civilization. It was men who built up the politics, economics, social codes and administrative system of this civilization. Seamlessly concealed behind this façade, women performed only domestic roles at home. Thus this civilization was lopsided. It was substantially deficient in the wealth of the human mind which was locked in the hearts of women, as if hoarded by a miser. The hoard has now been unlocked. . . . Women, so long confined to home, are now emerging as women of the world. Thus, this new addition of the female mind to the creative human mind has surely infused a new spirit into human civilization and this is at work both directly and indirectly. It is now hoped that the civilization created by men, which often tends to plunge into catastrophe due to lack of balance and symmetry, will gradually move towards a state of equilibrium. The old civilization is now suffering massive and frequent jolts and quakes because the causes of disruption and catastrophe have been accumulating inside it for a long time; hence nobody will be able to stop its disintegration. The only big reason for optimism and hope is that women have stepped forward to build a new civilization at the end of the millennium—they are getting ready everywhere. It is not only that the veil which so long hid their faces is coming off now; the veil which so long hid them from the greater part of the world is coming off, too. The human society into which they have been born is now becoming more and more visible in every aspect. . . . Now their natural life-nurturing instincts will be devoted to the preservation, not only of their near and dear ones, but all humanity. From very ancient times men have subjected fellow men to repeated blood-baths to erect the castle of civilization. Individuals have been mercilessly slaughtered to establish a general principle or law; the labouring classes have been exploited and squeezed to create the wealth of the rich; the powerful, the mighty have flourished by slaughtering the unnumbered weak;

the subjects have often been harnessed as beasts of burden to the chariot of state power in order to pull it. This civilization is driven by power, there is but little room in it for clemency and mercy. . . . Let us hope that a new millennium in which a new civilization will be built is arriving. If this hope takes shape, there is no doubt that women will find themselves fully engaged this time in this creative endeavour. If the call of the new age is knocking at their doors, I urge women not to allow their conservative minds to cling passionately to the age-old unhealthy rubbish–let them liberate their hearts, brighten their intellect and devote themselves to the cultivation of wisdom. They must remember that indiscriminate and blind conservatism is completely at odds with creativity. The new age of creativity lies ahead.

(From *Nari*, 1936)
Translated by Subhransu Maitra

Rabindranath Tagore. Six seated women. Coloured ink on paper, c. 1929-30

Rabindranath Tagore.
Landscape with Trees.
Ink on paper, c. 1937-38

THE DIVINITY OF THE FOREST

At the first stage of creation, Earth was stony-hearted, barren and gave no sign that it had any sympathy for any living creature.* Everywhere, there were fiery eruptions. Earth itself was constantly perturbed by quakes. It was in such a situation that the goddess of forests sent her emissaries to this courtyard, the earth. Then green, grassy areas began spreading in all directions, like the end of the goddess' sari, and Earth was able to cover its nakedness and protect itself from shame. Eventually there came trees, creepers and winding plants, bearers of life. Living creatures had not yet appeared on earth but the plant world made itself ready to nurture them when they would eventually emerge, by not only succouring them but by also providing them with shade. But their greatest contribution to life was fire. They became bearers of the heat that sunrays had brought to earth, and offered it up for human use. And till now civilization keeps advancing by making use of the heat emitted thus.

Man is intemperate in his behaviour. So long as he was a forest-dweller, he lived in harmony with the forest, and his exchanges with it were perfect, but when he took to cities he lost all feelings for his former habitat. He now turned on his first well-wishers, the beings that had first conveyed to him the blessings of the gods. He now began to cut down the trees and vines of the forest remorselessly and indiscriminately, to build houses made of bricks and wood. Ignoring the forest deity who had bestowed blessings on mankind,

* Speech delivered at the Tree Planting and Ploughing Ceremonies held in Sriniketan.

he allowed the curse to spread. Nowadays the northern parts of India have become unbearably hot in the summer months because they are so denuded of trees. And yet anyone who has read the Puranas knows very well that at one time when the region was the domain of the rishis it was full of mighty forests and was a wonderful place to live in, with its shaded groves and temperate climate. Man receives the bounty of nature greedily but not content with what he has received so easily he sets out to ravage nature mercilessly. That is why mankind now seems bent on turning earth into a desert. The gradual erosion of the earth has meant that here in the drying land of Bolpur the earth's bare bones have become visible, and soil degradation is everywhere apparent. And yet this place was once wooded and far removed from this state of things. The forests that covered the earth here had protected it, and its trees would nurture and sustain people with their fruits and berries. Because of the destruction of these forests we are in imminent danger. If we are to escape from the doom that awaits us and if we are to evade the path of self-destruction, we have to invoke again the bountiful goddess of the forest, Banalakshmi–invoke her blessings so that, once again, she preserves this land, showers on us her beneficence, and spreads on us her shade.

This is a predicament that is not unique to our part of the world; everywhere people have to contend with the problems caused when mankind's all-consuming greed threatens to do away with the treasures that the wilderness can otherwise offer them. In the United States of America large tracts of forest have been destroyed. As a consequence, swirling sandstorms have been eliminating fertile lands or burying them in sand. God had created life on earth and had provided all the essentials for that, but men are letting their greed become the source of their own destruction. It is because mankind has been ignoring God's design that we are all accursed. The avaricious human race has destroyed the forests and made itself vulnerable in the process. We have eliminated the very trees and plants whose function it was to purify the atmosphere and revitalize the soil. We have become oblivious of our own good, destroying the largesse God has bestowed on us for our welfare.

The time has now come to repent. We have vowed here that we will do whatever we can with whatever ability we have to build an altar to the deity of the woods whose concern is the welfare of mankind. The festivals we are celebrating today are therefore of two kinds. One is to celebrate ploughing—so essential to provide us with our food, with the crops that we require. It is an obligation we owe ourselves. But we must compensate earth for the way it is depleted by our ploughing. To discharge our duty towards earth and to salve its wounds we have also arranged this festival of tree plantation. I fervently hope that our celebrations will result in trees whose shade will spread everywhere and yield rich harvests that will adorn our environment and fill it with joy.

(From *Aranyadevata*, c. 1938)
Translated by Fakrul Alam

Rabindranath Tagore. Riverscape with moored boat. Pen and ink on paper, c. 1935-36

Palm trees in Santiniketan

CRISIS IN CIVILIZATION

I have completed eighty years of my life today and the whole span of my life now lies before me.* From the opposite horizon I can dispassionately see the course of life which began on the easternmost horizon and I can feel that the mental development of my life and of the entire country has suffered truncation. And there is cause for deep grief in this.

Our direct acquaintance with the great world of humanity began through the history of the British nation of those days. In our experience the identity of the character of this stranger to India was revealed from the pinnacle of a great literature. There was neither amplitude nor variety in the curriculum of our education in those days. The present day education which now emanates from a variety of institutions of education and unveils ever new aspects of the world of universal nature and its powers was, for the greater part, unknown then. There were few experts in the natural sciences. The hallmarks of a refined erudite mind lay in its ability to acquaint itself with and savour English literature through the English language. Burke's eloquence, the undulations of Macaulay's flowing prose filled our days; people often discussed Shakespeare's plays, Byron's poetry and the proclamation of the victory of man in the politics of those days. We had then begun our efforts to secure the independence of our nation, but deep inside our minds lurked a faith in the liberalism of the British. So deep-seated was this faith that at some point in those days our exponents had concluded that the magnanimity, the liberalism of the victorious nation would pave

* On 14 April 1941 (the Bengali New Year), *Sabhyatar Sankat* ('Crisis in Civilization') was read out in Santiniketan in Tagore's presence. It expressed Tagore's dark vision of man's inhumanity to man, and a stringent critique of Western civilization.

and widen the vanquished nation's path to freedom, because at that time England was the refuge of the persecuted races and unstinting in offering succour and refuge to those who had striven to their utmost to defend the dignity of their people. I found unalloyed evidence of human fraternity in the British character and hence placed the British on a pedestal in my mind, with sincere devotion. Their natural liberalism had not yet been vitiated by the arrogance of predatory imperialism.

When I was young I went to England. On several occasions I heard John Bright speak both in the parliament and outside, at certain gatherings. His speeches came alive with the eternal message of the British. The mental amplitude exhibited by those speeches transcended all narrowness of race and nationality and exerted an influence which I remember to this day and which guards my old memories even in these degraded, disgraceful times. This dependence on others was certainly not a matter of pride for us. . . . (but) we had the ability to receive it with respect and we were not inhibited. For, whatever is enduring and great in the human heritage cannot be narrowly confined to a nation or race, it does not belong to the closely guarded wealth of a miser. That is why English literature which nourished our minds reverberates in my mind to this day.

It is not easy to find an exact and proper equivalent in our language to 'civilization' which we usually translate into Bengali as 'sabhyata'. The form of this civilization which prevailed in our country has been described by Manu as sadachar which means the regime of certain social customs. The concept of these customs which was current in ancient times was also restricted to a narrow geographical entity. The word sadachar is applied to the rites, rituals and customs which traditionally prevailed in the territory which lies between the Saraswati and the Drishadvati rivers and which was well known as Brahmavarta. In other words, sadachar or achar is precisely based on customs, no matter how cruel and unjust these rituals and customs were. For this reason traditional practice laid stress on our customs and rituals and robbed us altogether of the freedom of mind. The ideal of sadachar which was established by Manu once upon a time in Brahmavarta gradually merged into popular rites, cults and liturgies or lokachar. When I began my life, a revolt against this traditional practice was already smouldering in the minds of the educated section of society owing to the impact of English education. If one reads the account of the conduct and behaviour of the educated people of those days written by Rajnarayanbabu, he will clearly understand it. We replaced sadachar with the concept of civilization, amalgamating it with the character of the British. In my family this change was entirely accepted in all spheres, be it religious faith, social intercourse or the application of the principle of justice. I was born into this atmosphere and our natural fondness for literary writings accorded a high place to English literature. This sums up the first part of my life. Then the truncation began, bringing on severe pain. I saw everyday how those who acknowledged civilization as an efflorescence from the fountainhead of their character violated it all too easily, driven by evil instincts. . . .

The terrible poverty of the Indian masses which now unfolded before my eyes was really heart-rending. Perhaps in no other country in the world which is administered in the modern way has such an acute want of food, clothing, drinking water, education, healthcare and all that is needed for sustaining the body and the mind of human beings, occurred. Yet this country has supplied England with her wealth for a long time. When I was intently absorbed in the contemplation of the greatness of the civilized world, I could never even imagine such a monstrous contortion of the human ideal bearing the name of civilization. . . .

This helpless country is deprived of the cultivation and development of scientific technology with the help of which England has maintained her world dominance. Yet right under our eyes, Japan harnessed scientific technology and became prosperous in all manner of ways. I have been to Japan and seen her prosperity with my own eyes. I have also seen how she rules her own people in a civilized manner. And I have seen awe-inspiring, truly unstinting, vast endeavours in Moscow in Russia, to educate the people and eradicate disease and as a result of these endeavours, illiteracy, poverty and self-debasement are fading away from this vast empire. This civilization did not discriminate between castes, but made the influence of pure human relationship felt everywhere. The swift and amazing success of all this has simultaneously filled me with envy and delight. When I was in Moscow, an outstanding feature of Russian administration touched my heart to the core; I saw that Muslims and non-Muslims never quarrelled over sharing state power. The true and sincere role played by the administration is evident in the reconciliation achieved of the interests of both these segments. There are now chiefly two countries–England and Soviet Russia who wield state power over a number of different races. England has decimated the prowess of the different races under her control and subdued them. Numerous Muslim Bedouin races are part of the Soviet Union. I myself can testify that the Soviet government is striving relentlessly to empower these people. I have seen evidence of the efforts made by the Soviet government to make them stake holders in all developmental schemes and also read about it. Such influence exerted by the government is by no means humiliating, nor does it do any harm to or diminish the spirit of humaneness. The administration out there is a far cry from the cruel, exploitative mechanical administration of an alien power. I have been to Persia and I have seen how this newly awakened nation which was not so long ago being crushed by two European powers has now extricated itself from the fangs of brutal European aggression and embarked on the path of achieving complete self-fulfilment. I have seen that the old fierce competition between the Zoroastrians and the Muslims has been completely resolved under the present civilized dispensation. The principal reason behind her good fortune is the fact that she was able to extricate herself from the snare of the conspiracy of European nations. I wish this Persia to prosper, with all my heart. Though our neighbouring Afghanistan is yet to achieve that all round excellence of education and societal development, her potential remains intact, the only reason of it being that no European nation, arrogantly proud of its civilization, has so far been able to overwhelm her. Everywhere these countries are now moving fast ahead to advance on the path of all round development and emancipation.

India is wallowing in helpless immobility, encumbered with the crushing burden of the civilized rule of the British. Pursuing naked self-aggrandizement, England used strong-arm methods to drive a great ancient civilized nation like the Chinese into wholesale ruinous opium addiction and in return occupied a part of China. When we had all but forgotten this past history, we saw Japan all set to swallow up north China and British statesmen considered this act of banditry a trifling matter, displaying unimaginable nonchalance and arrogance. Later, we also saw from a distance how England scuttled the Republican government in Spain. At that time we also saw that a group of Britons sacrificed their lives for imperilled Spain. Though this magnanimity and large-heartedness on the part of England had not been sufficiently awakened during the crisis in oriental China, we were once more reminded that we had once upon a time looked up to the British as friends of humanity with enormous trust and devotion when we saw some British heroes make the ultimate sacrifice to defend the freedom of a European nation. I have had to relate today the saddening history of how we gradually lost our faith in the characteristic civilization of the European nations. Under the impact of a civilized administration the gravest plight that has raised its head in India is not only the deplorable lack of food, clothing, education and health care, but also the brutal truncation of self and I have seen nothing comparable to it in the independent Muslim countries outside India. Our predicament is that our society will be held solely responsible for this plight. The shape of this plight is growing more hideous every day and such an enormously humiliating, uncivilized development could never have occurred in Indian history if it had not been abetted, indulged and fostered in a secret centre in the higher echelons of the administrative machinery in India. No one believes that Indians are in any way inferior to the Japanese in intelligence and ability. The chief difference between these two Asian countries is that India is in all respects occupied and dominated by England while Japan is absolutely free from the domination of any European nation. We know what this alien civilization—provided you call it a civilization—has appropriated from us; in return it has established with a heavy hand what it calls law and order. Or in other words, rules and regulations, which are entirely external things and amount to nothing more than policing. It has become altogether impossible to retain any respect for the European nations' pride in their civilization. They have displayed their awesome power, but not their ability to liberate. It means that the niggardliness visible in developing what is most precious and deserves to be properly called civilization, the relationship between human beings, has completely barred the way to prosperity for Indians. Yet, personally I have been fortunate enough to occasionally encounter noble-hearted Englishmen. This nobleness I have never seen in any other nation or community. Even today they keep my faith tied to the British. I can mention the name of Andrews as an example. It was my good fortune to find in him the true Englishman, the true Christian and a real friend of humanity in very close proximity. He has passed away and now placed in the setting of death, his selfless fearless nobleness appears all the more luminous. There are many reasons for my entire nation and myself to be grateful to him, but for one personal reason I am particularly grateful to him. In my old age he helped to redeem the worn out, tainted image of the British to whom in my youth I had once offered my wholehearted, unalloyed devotion in the surrounding ambience of English literature. I will ever cherish in my mind the essential nobleness of this race along with his memory. I have regarded the British as my closest friends and regard them as the closest friends of the entire human race. Their acquaintance I will cherish as one of the greatest assets of my life. The way I see it, they will be able to rescue the noble qualities of the British from shipwreck. Had I not encountered them and seen them, my pessimism about the European nations would have remained unchallenged, uncontested.

At this time everybody became aware how all over Europe barbarity was baring its teeth and claws to unleash horror. This pandemic of persecution and suffering inflicted on mankind has risen from the marrow of western civilization and humiliated the soul of humanity, polluting the air all over the world. Have we had no inkling of it in the midst of our unfortunate, helpless, utterly unrelieved poverty!

As the wheels of fate grind on, at some time or the other, further down the road, the British will have to quit the Indian empire and go. But which India will they leave behind? What god-forsaken detritus of poverty! When the rule of centuries will have dried up, the country will become an unimaginable vast morass bearing the intolerable burden of futility. In the first beginning of my life I had wholeheartedly trusted this gift of civilization–the wealth of the European mind. Now when my life is drawing to a close, my trust has been absolutely shattered. Today we are hoping that the saviour will be born in our poor, wretched hovel. We will want to see him bring the oracle of civilization and give mankind the greatest message of hope that a man can give from the same old eastern hemisphere. I have now embarked on a voyage to the far shore and how much debris left by the history of utterly insignificant pride of civilization I am leaving behind on this shore! But it is a sin to lose faith in man, I will retain my faith to the last. I shall hope that a pure epiphany of history will perhaps begin on this eastern horizon of sunrise in the clear benign sky after the armageddon. At some time in the future unvanquished man will triumphantly advance on the path to conquest, overcoming all hurdles on the way to recovering his noble dignity. I consider it a crime to conclude that the unending, irresistible defeat of humanity is the ultimate reality.

In conclusion I assert that the day has come when it will be proved that the overbearing power, vainglory, arrogance and vanity of those who are all powerful are not safe, either. It is certain that this truth will be proved–

Adharmenaidhate tabat tato bhadrain pashyati.
Tata sapatnan joyoti samoolastu vinashyati.
(Behold) the Supreme Man is coming,
Blades of grass on earth are quivering everywhere.
Conches are resounding in the abode of the gods,
Drumbeats are enacting the victory chant in the abode of humans,
The moment of the great incarnation is arriving.
All bastions of evil darkness
Are shattered today and lie in the dust.
On the eastern peaks hosannas of joy ring out
Celebrating the coming of new life—
While 'glory, glory to the coming of Man'
Soars reverberating to the vast sky.

Udayan. Santiniketan
(From *Sabhyatar Sankat*, 1941)
Translated by Subhransu Maitra

LETTERS

Rabindranath Tagore with Helen Keller

LETTER TO INDIRA DEVI

Shilaidaha
9 December, 1892

Now, ensconced at the window of that boat of mine, I have found some peace of mind at long last.* The boat is moving against the current, and to add to that, it has set full sail—in the afternoon sun, the winter day has warmed up somewhat, no boats on the Padma—the empty sandbank is a yellow stretch, the blue of the river on one side, and on the other, drawn across the blue of the sky, a sort of line—in the northern breeze the water glints ever so little and shivers, without any waves. I sit here, leaning against the open window. A slight breeze touches my head. I find it rather pleasing. After a long, acute illness, my body feels frail; at such a time, this gentle, tender care that I receive from Nature seems very sweet. Like this river, atrophied by the winter cold, my whole being seems to lie in the sun, supine, glinting, and as if half-consciously, I am scribbling my letter to you. Every time, before approaching the Padma, I fear that my Padma may have grown stale. But whenever I set forth in my boat, I feel the ripple of water, a pulsation, a shivering, a luminosity, the presence of the sky, all around me. A gentle babble, an expanse of exquisite tender blue, a fresh young line of green, announcing a daily celebration of letters, dance, music and beauty. Then, again, anew, my heart feels overwhelmed. This earth, like someone I have loved long, through many births, remains ever-new to me; the two of us share a very deep and extensive acquaintance. I can well remember that many ages ago, when the youthful earth had freshly emerged from her immersion in the sea to offer homage to the young sun of that era, I had blossomed into foliage as a tree in the new soil of this earth, in a primal life-urge that came from who knows where.

* At the beginning of the letter we find the time and place of its composition and dispatch. The place and date at the end refer to the reception of the letter by Indira Devi, as recorded in her transcription of Tagore's letters.

At that time, there were no living creatures on this earth; the vast ocean swayed, day and night, and like an unreasoning mother, sometimes enveloped its newborn offspring, this tiny earth of ours, in a mad embrace. Then I, in this world, had drunk in the sunlight with all my body, swayed like a newborn infant by a blind rapture under the blueness of the sky. Embracing this earth, my mother, I had suckled at her breast with all my roots. A dumb joy made my flowers blossom and unfurled my new leaves. When the clouds gathered and it was about to rain, the deep shade would brush all my leaves like the palm of some familiar hand. Even after that, with the advent of new eras, I have been born unto this earth. Whenever the two of us sit face to face, the earth and I seem to faintly recall that ancient relationship. My Vasundhara, my mother earth, is now in that field of grain by the riverside, clad in a sun-yellowed sari with a golden edge, and I have prostrated myself at her feet, close to her lap. Like many a mother who absently yet with a steady sympathy, doesn't seem to pay much attention to the comings and goings of her infant offspring, my earth, this afternoon, is gazing at the edge of the sky, thinking of ancient times long gone, without paying much attention to me. And I just keep on talking, without pause. So time passes, in a fashion. It is almost late afternoon. It's winter after all—before you know it, the sunshine has gone.

Solapur. 14 December, 1892.

(From *Chhinnapatrabali*)
Translated by Radha Chakravarty

Rabindranath Tagore. Landscape with lake and trees. Crayon, water colour, coloured ink, and poster colour on paper, c. 1935

LETTER TO R. G. PRADHAN
HINDU INTERCASTE MARRIAGE

Sir,

In answer to your letter dated the 8th December, I hasten to answer that Hon. Mr Patel's Bill has my heartiest support.

It is humiliating to find that some of our countrymen are opposing this Bill under the notion that it will injure Hindu Society if it passed. They do not seem to consider that those who are already willing to accept the social martyrdom should not have any further coercion, passive or active, from any governing power, to oblige them to observe against their will such conventions as are not based upon the foundation of moral laws. To say that Hindu Society cannot exist unless it has victims who are forcibly compelled to live the life of falsehood and cowardice, is tantamount to saying that it should not exist at all. Moreover, such an implication is a libel against the spirit of Hinduism, which all through its history has been accommodating differences of creeds and customs, allowing mixture of castes and making new social adjustments from the time of the Mahabharat until now when an alien Government has nearly succeeded in petrifying our social body with its rigid laws, depriving it of life's flexibleness and thus hastening its fatal stage of senility. No doubt, society everywhere looks upon with suspicion and treats with hostility those men who choose to think and act

* In response to a request from R.G. Pradhan, editor of the Marathi periodical *Bhatat Sevak*, Tagore expressed his opinion on V.B. Patel's Hindu Intercaste Marriage Validating Bill, in this letter, dated 19 December 1918. The letter was reprinted in the February 1919 issue of *The Modern Review*.

for themselves, who have an invincible love for intellectual and moral freedom. But the community, which goes beyond all limits of endurance, which takes every step to make it impossible for such men to live within its pale, the men who have the courage and honesty of their conviction and are, therefore, best fitted to fight for truth and righteousness is doomed to breed in terminable generations of slaves. Where the society is terribly effective in its weapons of persecution it is shameful to appeal to a foreign Government to stiffen by its sanction a social tyranny, to rob people of their right to the freedom of conscience and in the next moment to ask from the same Government a wider political emancipation. Those who feel no compunction in invoking the organized power of the State to compel or help by its connivance a weak minority to submit to the worst form of social slavery, can certainly not be held as fit to claim a large share of such power.

19 December 1918
Rabindranath Tagore

Rabindranath Tagore with C. F. Andrews

LETTER TO C. F. ANDREWS

Things that are stationary have no responsibility and need no law.* For death, even the tombstone is a useless luxury. But for a world, which is an ever-moving multitude advancing toward an idea, all its laws must have one principle of harmony. This is the law of creation.

Man became great when he found out this law for himself, the law of co-operation. It helped him to move together, to utilize the rhythm and impetus of the world march. He at once felt that this moving together was not mechanical, not an external regulation for the sake of some convenience. It was what the metre is in poetry—not a mere system of enclosure for keeping ideas from running away in disorder, but for vitalizing them, making them indivisible in a unity of creation.

So far this idea of co-operation has developed itself into individual communities, within the boundaries of which peace has been maintained and varied wealth of life produced. But outside these boundaries the law of co-operation has not been realized. Consequently the great world of man is suffering from ceaseless discordance. We are beginning to discover that our problem is world-

* In May 1921, *The Modern Review* published Tagore's letters to C. F. Andrews, written in 1920 in response to Gandhi's Non-Cooperation movement.

wide, and no one people of the earth can work out its salvation by detaching itself from others. Either we shall be saved together or drawn together into destruction.

This truth has ever been recognized by all the great personalities of the world. They had in themselves the perfect consciousness of the undivided spirit of man. Their teachings were against tribal exclusiveness, and thus we find that Buddha's India transcended geographical India and Christ's religion broke through the bonds of Judaism.

Today, at this critical moment of the world's history, cannot India rise above her limitations and offer the great ideal to the world that will work towards harmony and co-operation between the different peoples of the earth? Men of feeble faith will say that India requires to be strong and rich before she can raise her voice for the sake of the whole world. But I refuse to believe it. That the measure of man's greatness is in his material resources is a gigantic illusion casting its shadow over the present-day world—it is an insult to man. It lies in the power of the materially weak to save the world from this illusion; and India, in spite of her penury and humiliation, can afford to come to the rescue of humanity.

The freedom of unrestrained egoism in the individual is licence and not true freedom. For his truth is in that which is universal in him. Individual human races also attain true freedom when they have the freedom of perfect revelation of Man and not that of their aggressive racial egoism. The idea of freedom which prevails in modern civilization is superficial and materialistic. Our revolution in India will be a true one when its forces are directed against this crude idea of liberty.

The sunlight of love has the freedom that ripens the wisdom of immortal life; but passion's fire can only forge fetters for ourselves. The Spiritual Man has been struggling for its emergence into perfection, and every true cry of freedom is for this emancipation. Erecting barricades of fierce separateness, in the name of national necessity, is offering hindrance to it. Therefore in the long run it is building a prison for the nation itself. For the only path of deliverance for nations is in the ideal humanity.

Creation is an endless activity of God's freedom; it is an end in itself. Freedom is true when it is a revelation of truth. Man's freedom is for the revelation of the truth of Man, which is struggling to express itself. We have not yet fully realized it. But those people who have faith in its greatness, who acknowledge its sovereignty, and have the instinctive urging in their heart to break down obstructions, are paving the way for its coming.

India ever has nourished faith in the truth of the Spiritual Man, for whose realization she has made innumerable experiments, sacrifices and penances, some verging on the grotesque and the abnormal. But the fact is she has never ceased in her attempt to find it, even though at the tremendous cost of losing material success. Therefore I feel that the true India is an idea, and not a mere geographical fact. I have come into touch with this idea in far-away places of Europe, and my loyalty was drawn to it in persons who belonged to countries different from mine. India will be victorious when this idea wins the victory–the idea of *Purusham mahantam adityavarnam tamasah parastat*–'The Infinite Personality, whose light reveals itself through the obstruction of Darkness.' Our fight is against this Darkness. Our object is the revealment of the Light of this Infinite Personality of Man. This is not to be achieved in single individuals, but in one grand harmony of all human races. The darkness of egoism which will have to be destroyed is the egoism of the Nation. The idea of India is against the intense consciousness of the separateness of one's own people from others, which inevitably leads to ceaseless conflicts. Therefore my one prayer is, let India stand for the co-operation of all peoples of the world. The spirit of rejection finds its support in the consciousness of separateness; the spirit of acceptance finds its base in the consciousness of unity.

India has ever declared that Unity is Truth, and separateness is *maya*. This unity is not a zero; it is that which comprehends all, and therefore can never be reached through the path of negation.

Our present struggle to alienate our heart and mind from the West is an attempt at spiritual suicide. If, in the spirit of national vainglory, we shout from our housetops that the West has produced nothing that has an infinite value for man, then we only create a serious cause of doubt about the worth of any product of the Eastern mind. For it is the mind of Man, in the East and West, which is ever approaching Truth in her different aspects from different angles of vision. If it can be true that the standpoint of the West has betrayed it into an utter misdirection, then we can never be sure of the standpoint of the East. Let us be rid of all false pride and rejoice at any lamp being lit in any corner of the world, knowing that it is a part of the common illumination of our house.

The other day I was invited to the house of a distinguished art-critic of America who is a great admirer of old Italian Art. I questioned him if he knew anything of our Indian pictures, and he brusquely said that most probably he would hate them. I suspected he had seen some of them and hated them already. In retaliation I could have said something in the same language about Western art. But I am proud to say it was not possible for me. For I always try to understand Western Art and never to hate it. Whatever we understand and enjoy in human products instantly become ours, wherever they might have their origin. I am proud of my humanity, when I can acknowledge the poets and artists of other countries as my own. Let me feel with unalloyed gladness that all the great glories of man are mine.

Therefore it hurts me deeply when the cry of rejection rings loud against the West in my country with the clamour that Western education can only injure us. It cannot be true. What has caused the mischief is the fact that for a long time we have been out of touch with our own culture and therefore Western culture has not found its true perspective in our life. Very often its perspective is wrong, giving our mental eye a squint. When we have intellectual capital of our own, the commerce of thought with the outer world becomes natural and fully profitable. But to say that such commerce is inherently wrong is to encourage the worst form of provincialism, productive of nothing but intellectual indigence. The West has misunderstood the East. This is at the root of the disharmony that prevails between them. But will it mend matters if the East in her turn tries to misunderstand the West? The present age has been powerfully possessed by the West; it has only become possible because to her is given some great mission for man. We, from the East, have come to her to learn whatever she has to teach us; for by doing so we hasten the fulfilment of this age. We know that the East also has her lessons to give, and she has her own responsibility of not allowing her light to be extinguished. The time will come when the West will find leisure to realize that she has a home of hers in the East where her food is and her rest.

(London, 1920)
Rabindranath Tagore

LETTER TO MARGARET SANGER
BIRTH CONTROL MOVEMENT

Santiniketan
30 September 1925

Dear Margaret Sanger,

I am of opinion that the Birth Control movement is a great movement not only because it will save women from enforced and undesirable maternity, but because it will help the cause of peace of lessening the number of surplus population of a country, scrambling for food and space outside its own rightful limits.* In a hunger-stricken country like India it is a cruel crime thoughtlessly to bring more children to existence than could properly be taken care of, causing endless sufferings to them and imposing a degrading condition upon the whole family. It is evident that the utter helplessness of a growing poverty very rarely acts as a check controlling the burden of over-population. It proves that in this case nature's urging gets the better of the severe warning that comes from the providence of civilized social life. Therefore, I believe, that to wait till the moral sense of man becomes a great deal more powerful than it is now and till then to allow countless generations of children to suffer privations and untimely death for no fault of their own is a great social injustice which should not be tolerated. I feel grateful for the cause you have made your own and for which you have suffered.

I am eagerly waiting for the literature that has been sent to me according to your letter, and I have asked our Secretary to send you our Visva-Bharati Journal in exchange for your *Birth Control Review*.

(1925)
Rabindranath Tagore

* Tagore's letter to Margaret Sanger, editor of *Birth Control Review*, published in *Amrita Bazar Patrika* (5 January 1926). Sanger met Tagore when she visited India in 1935. According to a report in *The Madras Mail* (7 December 1935), Tagore 'promised his moral support for her movement'.

LETTER TO HEMANTABALA DEVI

Kalyaniyashu,

I enjoy reading your letters. There, I get a clear sense of the profoundest agony that troubles your woman's heart. I sense how very intense your womanly need to find anchorage in affection, love and devotion is. Where your hearts' sacred prayer offering may be completely and purely fulfilled, and your capacity for sacrifice may flow unchecked in full force–that is the direction your sadhana, your spiritual endeavour, should take. In your letters, that feminine urge for self-surrender finds expression, with unfeigned sweetness. I realize that you, too, have attracted the Vaishnava faith to which you have felt drawn–just as the earth, however tiny, still attracts the sun. You suspect, without reason, that I may not have understood your state of mind. Remember, all of us are in a sense Ardhanarishwar, the deity who is half male, half female. In some persons, the elements are evenly mixed, while in others, the proportions may vary. Had the world been divided between pure women and pure men, the two elements could never unite. Hence, though there is no difficulty in mutual understanding, it is also possible to sustain our distinctive qualities within our respective spheres. In other words, the male is predominant and the female subordinate in the composition of masculine character, while in feminine character, the reverse is true. That is what generally happens, else it would be hard for balance to prevail in this world. It is desirable that women fulfil themselves and the world through an abundance of affection, love, and devotion; this is their graceful aspect. Alongside, they have a powerful aspect, and in this dimension, their firmness of faith, patience, resolute sacrifice, displays a strength by which they shelter, nurture, sustain, improve and liberate from suffering even those who are their refuge—in other words, dependence on them does not weaken, but fulfil and gratify. But if men, too, follow that path of grace, then they would have to impose the feminine spirit upon themselves, and that would go against their nature. A man can only gain fulfilment by establishing his own nature; if he goes against the tide, he grows weak, and his attempts to attain life's goals prove futile. Using intellect, scientific knowledge, valour, and undiminished endeavour, to constantly drive creation towards excellence, defeating all obstacles, refusing to acknowledge adverse factors as the unshakeable dictates of fate—that is the way for real men to sustain health, peace, prosperity and dignity in this world, and also for women to find safe shelter and attain their glory. Otherwise, if men, too, accept that wallowing in the waves of emotion and sensuality is the ultimate goal of life, then the country, deprived of male valour, sinks in a flood of defeat, inundated in every direction. That is why, however much I might relish your letters, I cannot help reciting to you the victory call of the joyous valour, the ideal of liberty, the pursuit of creativity, the heartfelt rebellion against all forms of social malignancy, and the harshness of selfless duty, which are appropriate for the male side, to which I belong. In Bengal, for a long time, men have also been overwhelmed by the womanly ideal. That is why their creative power has grown so distorted—that is why they are mutually frustrating each other's efforts, constantly engaged in slander and envy, unable to create any major project based upon lasting foundations. . . . The roots of character are weak, the soil is too full of sensuous emotions, there is a lack of stony hardness—that is why our unity doesn't hold, our institutions have no permanence, and there is only endless argument and partisanship, only a tendency to minimize big issues and make mountains out of molehills. . . .

Yours,
Dada, your elder brother.
17 Agrahayan 1338.

(3 December 1931)
Translated by Radha Chakravarty

TRAVEL WRITING

Rabindranath Tagore. Santiniketan. 1931: Portrait by Elizabeth Brunner (1910-2001)

LETTERS FROM RUSSIA

LETTER NO. 3

I have now come to Russia.* Had I not come to Russia my life's pilgrimage would not have been complete. They have done so much here. What amazes me instantly is their incredible courage. I am not making a judgment over good or bad. We know for a fact how clinging the ancient can be. We know how attached we are to tradition, in a thousand ways, at the very core of our heart. We confine ourselves within its walls, guarded on all sides. Our accumulations pile up like mountains as if we are contributing taxes to a treasury century after century. The Russians have fearlessly got at the very root of this tangle. They have trashed the old and taken a brand new seat. We admire what the West has achieved by the strength of science. But, frankly, what has been happening here is astonishing. It would not have been so surprising had it been simply a work of destruction. Not so this time. Clearly, what they have done is to look far ahead in creating a new world. And they are in a tearing hurry to finish the job because there is opposition all round. They have to make it quick. They have to show something to prove they are doing nothing wrong. They mean to defeat the work of a thousand years by an effort that is only ten to fifteen years young. They may be weak financially but they are immensely strong in resolve.

The recent revolution was waiting to happen in Russia, for a very long time. Preparations have been going on continuously and talk of revolution has been circulating. The famous and the infamous have been giving their lives for the cause. They have suffered for it. It is only at certain moments that things come to a head like a blood-red boil erupting at some weak point on the body, as if the entire bloodstream has become polluted. Right here in Russia the

* To Prashantachandra Mahalanobis.

poor and the powerless have been subjected to immeasurable cruelty by the rich and the powerful. The extreme inequality between the two groups became stormy and moved Russia to try for a solution.

It was the oppression of inequality that had also brought about the French Revolution one day. It revealed a universal truth. That is why the call for liberty, equality, fraternity, was heard far beyond the battle lines. The reverberation however did not last. Now in Russia they too are sending out a universal message. They are putting forward the larger interest of a common humanity as national self-interest. We have no idea if this will last. But what is important is to note that the present age can recognize the common human predicament when relating to an individual country and its inherent problems.

The curtain is up in the arena of world history. As if, until now, only rehearsals were taking place, behind the scenes, in separate enclaves. Each territory maintained its own fences so that entry was not easy even if possible. Human life looked different from what it appears today. Where one could see single or individual trees, one now finds a forest. The lack of balance in one part of human society can influence the entire world and spread it from one end to the other. What human society lacked is now being exposed. Obtaining such a broad view is not a small achievement.

When I was in Tokyo I once asked a Korean youth what their sorrow was all about. He said their lives had been taken over by the profiteers. I asked what they could do to overcome the problem given their state of weakness. He replied saying that the helpless could be found all over the world today. He emphasized that the helpless are united by their sufferings. He added that the wealthy and the powerful would never be united because they themselves chose to be walled in by their iron vaults and their precious fiefdoms. He argued that Korea's strength was in her sufferings.

It is a significant change that, today, the deprived are able to see themselves as a vast common entity on the human battle-field. They could not do so in the past because they were isolated. They blamed their destinies and tolerated all the suffering. The big change today is that even the helpless are able to imagine a heaven of freedom from oppression and humiliation. That is why they, the helpless, have now stirred throughout the world.

The powerful are arrogantly trying all they can from the outside to obstruct this newly found strength of the helpless. They are trying to stop entry to their messengers and to gag their voice. They are not daunted by the sorrow of the sufferers. They consistently show only contempt for it. They do not lose even a heart-beat to drive the impoverished peasants into starvation. That is because to them profit is power. But in human society, all excesses carry their own built-in risks, which cannot be undone from without. The strong cannot forever build their strength at the cost of the weak. The rich and the powerful are not frightened by the inequality they have created because they are so intoxicated by power. Inequality is anathema to the laws of the universe.

I did not have much idea about the Bolsheviks when Moscow's invitation came. I kept hearing confusing things about them and feeling wary. That is because I knew for myself they were committed to the use of force. At the same time I did observe that Europe was no longer as hostile to them as before. Many encouraged me when told I was coming to Russia. Even the British were full of praise for them. Many said they were launched on an amazing mission.

There were also those who discouraged me. But that was mostly to do with creature comforts. I was told the food would be too coarse for me to tolerate. I was also told that a lot of what I would be shown would be false. I admit that travelling in Russia at my age and in my health is a bit daunting. But I would not have forgiven myself for not taking up an invitation from the place where the greatest historical upheaval is happening.

What is more, I kept remembering what the Korean youth told me. Russia has stood up against the powerful forces of the West to build up the strength of the poor and the weak. If I don't come to see this, who will? They want to shake up the rich and the strong. Why should that frighten us? How can that make us angry? What strength do we have? What wealth do we possess? We ourselves are among the world's starving and helpless flock.

If anyone comes forward to strengthen the weak, we cannot with any conscience put them down. They may make mistakes. So can their opponents make mistakes. The time has come to receive this truth that there will be no relief unless we build up the weak. The missiles sent out by the rich and powerful are growing deadlier by the day. They have destroyed the earth and polluted the skies. The helpless are now utterly helpless. That is because all the privileges of the world are possessed only by one section of humanity. The helplessness of the rest is unending.

I learned about the atrocities in Dhaka recently.** These stories of inhuman cruelty are deeply disturbing. Such news however is absent from the British Press. There is publicity from one end of the country to the other when their people are killed by motor cars. Our life is cheap. There can be no justice where life is cheap.

Our grievances cannot reach the world. All roads are closed to us. Yet they possess all the means for spreading negative publicity about us. This too is a disgraceful situation for the weak. In today's world the strong can use every mode of communication to destroy the weak by using defamation and malicious rumour behind the scenes. Word is rife among the world's population that Hindus and Muslims fight. But in Europe too there were communal conflicts in the past. They resolved the problem solely by means of education. That should have been the case also in our country. But in our country only five per cent of our populace got education in a whole century of British rule. That education, moreover, is something of a mockery.

Being treated with contempt without any effort to remove the cause for contempt is the penalty we pay for our weakness. Education is the one sure means with which to cure mankind's problems. But that avenue is virtually closed to us. There are no funds left in our government's budget for any other 'welfare' besides 'law and order'. So we must ourselves take charge of education in the service of our country. I have given all I possess for an education to bring

** There were Hindu Muslim riots in Dacca [Dhaka] in September 1930. The British Government apparently remained indifferent to the atrocities. Rabindranath wrote a letter to *The Spectator* as follows: '. . . At Dacca in eastern Bengal, there have been communal riots in which men of vicious character have been brought in, so as to increase the mischief, and unspeakable atrocities have occurred. While the news of a motor car in Europe causing a few casualties is circulated in all your newspapers, these crying evils, continuing from day to day in the capital city of eastern Bengal (whereby the whole neighbourhood was terrorised and all work paralysed) have hardly found any mention in English journals . . .'. Cited in *Modern Review*, October 1930, pp. 466–67.

self-reliance to my people, *atmashakti*. For this I was willing to even accept help from the government and did so. But I realized it is not to be. Our great sin is that we are weak.

That is why when I learned that Russia had brought education to her masses starting from scratch, I decided to come and see it for myself even at the cost of my broken health. They have certainly understood that the only way to make their people strong is by education. Food and health and peace all depend on that one basic factor. Mere law and order can neither feed us nor make us happy. Yet we are paying a high price for it and are losing all to it.

Being brought up in modern India I also believed that we cannot educate our thirty three crores of unlettered people, that all there is to do is blame fate for it. That is why when I was told of how rapidly education was spreading in Russia among the workers and the peasants, I timidly assumed that all they have been given is some minimum ability to read and write and do sums—that the goal was only the head count of literate people. Even that would not have been a trifling achievement. We would have gone home blessing our king had this much happened in our country. But I know better after coming to Russia. I see how solid their education is. It is an education for the growth of character, not merely for obtaining degrees by memorizing notes.

I shall write more about all this shortly. Now there is not much time left. I leave for Berlin this evening. Shall cross the Atlantic on 3 October. Not sure how long I shall be away.

I am not feeling so well nor am I feeling much enthusiasm. Still, I could not let this opportunity pass. I hope to get some rest in my last years if I can collect something of value from my current activities. Or I could simply stop, put out the lights, and bid farewell. That is not a bad plan, it is at least better than scattering a few leftovers to add to the existing filth. It is our weakness that produces ennui, malice and infighting. It is easy to be generous on a full stomach. However, it has been proven that one can harvest gold even out of a poor man's land when the attempt is genuine. It can be done if we can gather a modicum of the untiring dedication, courage and wisdom that has gone into the educational endeavour here in Russia. Finding more money becomes a necessity only if the inner will and the dedicated spirit are missing.

25 September 1930

LETTER NO. 4***

I wrote a couple of letters from Moscow. They were about the Soviet experience. Who knows when you'll get the letters, or if you will get them at all.

Two of your letters were waiting for me in Berlin. I could get from them a sense of the deepening monsoon, being letters written from an overcast Santiniketan sky spread generously over the sal trees. This is the season of sravana's bounties, of gathering clouds and outbursts of rain. You know how my heart throbs when picturing those scenes.

But on visiting Russia, this time, I have lost that excitement altogether. My mind only harps on the miseries of my country's peasants. I have known Bengal's countryside closely from my youth. There I would meet farmers every day and listen to their sorrows. I know very well that there are few on earth as helpless as them. At the social level which they occupy, submerged as they are in the lowest depths, they have not known the light of knowledge nor the breath of life.

Among the politicians of those times, there was not one who regarded the rural people as members of our own country. I said to a prominent leader at the Pabna conference that the state can progress only if we pay attention to our lowly people, if we make an effort to transform their lives. He was so dismissive of this idea that I realized instantly that he had learned his patriotism from his English school. He felt nothing for his countrymen in his heart. With such a mentality he could blame it all on the colonial government, agitate against them, and thus avoid the real issue. This class of men would rather hide behind poetry and newspaper columns. But this cannot be. The work can begin only when we take responsibility for our people.

Much time has passed since the Pabna conference. I heard echoes of what I said there about the village. Not only echoes, funds were also raised for village welfare. But all of it got spent over talks at the top. None of it reached down to the pit where our rural world has fallen.

*** To Nirmalkumari Mahalanobis.

I had anchored my boat on the river Padma for many years and pursued my writing. I was convinced I was good only for digging into my thoughts and writing them up. It is only when I failed to convince anybody that educating the neglected village was the one and only way to our self-reliance, I decided to tuck away my pen temporarily, and take on the task myself. I knew that the work must start immediately. The only person I could get to help me at the time was Kali Mohan. He was in poor health with a recurring fever. He was also under police watch.

Our road was rough, our resources meagre. My purpose was to make the peasant self-reliant and strong. There were two thoughts that drove me along. I felt strongly that the right to land had to belong to the cultivator, not to the landlord, and also that the cooperative principle had to be applied for the improvement of agriculture. The ancient mode of cultivating tiny plots of land separated by mud embankments was no better than fetching water in a leaking pot.

But accomplishing any of this is a tall order. For one thing, giving the farmer right over the land would not really help him. In times of distress the money-lender would usurp the farmer's land. As for pooling the land for farming, I have talked intimately with the farmers about this. After all I can see miles of these plots of land stretching to the distant horizon from my house in Shilaidaha. Farmers come from early morning with their bullocks to plough their little plots and return home when that's done. I have therefore seen with my own eyes how wasteful this method is and had occasion to summon the farmers and explain how much better it would be for them to join up the plots and use a tractor for ploughing the whole stretch. They agreed it would be good but asked how they could actually take on such a big task, given their ignorance? I wished I could tell them that I would take charge. But how could I have taken such a responsibility? I had neither the technical expertise nor the resource.

But the idea persisted in my mind. I hoped there would be an opportunity once again when Visva-Bharati started its cooperative. Those in charge were far younger and had more financial sense than I had. But alas our youth are school-educated, trained only in textbook learning. The system of education prevailing in our country gives us neither the courage to think nor the capacity to do the work. Our students succeed only by rote learning.

There is an even more fundamental problem besides these inherent deficiencies. We have created a class difference between those that have gone to school and those that have not, between the so-called educated and the so-called uneducated. The so-called educated have no wish to know the so-called uneducated. They are dismissed as rustic and left out of all our projects, the farmers and their kind. Yet, other societies have gained so much simply by cooperating with their masses. But all we do in our social system is to lend the needy small amounts of money to tide them over their difficulties temporarily. Giving and recovering loans is easy, even for extremely timorous minds; in fact, it is especially easy for minds that lack courage. The money lenders have nothing to lose from this age old system if they do their sums right.

It has become well nigh impossible to lift our people's miseries. We neither feel for them nor have we the will to innovate. Who can one blame for this state of things? Our education was cut out to produce clerks and thus to serve our colonial masters. Our success and salvation lay only in identifying with our employer's business. Our education meant nothing if we failed to get a job. Hence what we meant by service to our country was no more than loud proclamations of intent among the educated elite at their Congress meetings or in the newspaper articles they wrote. Those words of wisdom from our pens did nothing to help the country to grow.

I have myself grown up in this milieu. Therefore, I was neither hopeful nor confident that the burden of our missing education and related resources could be resolved. All the time I thought that we should strive at least to light an oil lamp in the lives of our hapless folk, where even sunlight is obstructed. This I believed was our minimum duty, but generally, even that small sense of responsibility does not move people's minds. It somehow does not occur to us that something can be done for those who are in darkness, deprived of the light of life.

It is with that timid hope that I went to Russia. I had heard of the progress they had made in spreading education among peasants and workers. I reckoned that the numbers educated in their rural schools had surpassed our numbers in finishing the second book of lessons. With my limited understanding I was curious to find out how many of their peasants could sign names and how many could count up to ten.

We need to remember that the revolution which destroyed the Tsars happened in 1917. Only thirteen years have gone by since. In these interim years they had to fight the strong forces arrayed against them at home and in the world. They are isolated and burdened with a shaky state system. The road left by the previous ineffective regime was difficult to cross. They were supported directly and indirectly by England and America in stepping into the new age. Their financial resources were weak and their productivity at rock bottom. They were not credit worthy in the world market. They made sacrifices by selling their own food grains to survive the beginnings of their endeavour. They spent their precious resources on their most unproductive unit, which was their army. They had no alternative but to keep their army in good shape, for all the powerful nations of today's usurious world are their enemies, and all of them have built up their stock of arms.

I remember how these very countries created a sensation among the false peace-lovers by proposing disarmament at the League of Nations. But the Soviets were not up for power. Their mission was to provide their people with education, health, food and clothing. For that what they needed most of all was peace. But as you know well the various strong arms of the League of Nations have no intention to stop aggression even when they clamour for peace. It is not surprising therefore that the production of arms has far surpassed the production of food grains in the imperial countries. To add to this, Russia was hit by a severe famine that lasted for some time. Countless people died. They faced all this squarely over the last eight years to build their new age despite their scarce external resources.

Their work is vast as is their political space which spreads over Europe and Asia. As a nation they have a great variety of races. Their racial and psychological differences are even more complicated than those in India. They are a mirror image of the world's problems on a smaller scale—the world with all its multifarious races and its multifarious ways of life.

When I first saw Moscow, it looked very dull compared to the rich cities of Europe. People on the streets wore the most ordinary clothes and never anything remotely elegant. There is no class-difference in everyday clothes; class-difference lies in stylish clothes. Here, everyone dressed the same, as is characteristic of a classless society. It was a worker's world. One saw them wherever one looked. There is no need to search in a library or to visit villages and slums to study the changes that have come over the peasant and the worker here. If anything one would have to search for those whom we call the 'bhadra-lok' in Bengal, its white collared class.

The common people here are no longer overshadowed by the gentlefolk. They have struck out on their own. It is obvious they have been transformed into human beings just in these few years, that they are not merely struggling with the pages of the school primer.

My mind went back to our own peasants and farmers. The Russian experience felt like the work of a magician from the Arabian Tales. Even ten years ago they were as illiterate and helpless and famished as the workers in our country, just as superstitious and bigoted as them. Our peasants still bang their foreheads on temple gates when in trouble. They dread life after death and invest their faith wholly in the wisdom of the priests. In day to day affairs they live at the mercy of the landlords and the moneylenders. They are content to clean the boots with which they are beaten. Nothing of this has changed for a thousand years. The tools they use are from the time of their great grandfathers. They refuse to modify these. It used to be like this in Russia. They too were browbeaten by a ghost from the past. How could they shake up such a stupendous mountain of inertia and stupidity? What baffles me as an Indian, like nothing else, is that during those years of change in Russia there was none of our celebrated law-and-order business . . . .

28 September 1930

EPILOGUE

I went to Russia at a time when my mind was in deep despair over the greed for power and intolerable indifference that characterized my country. I saw the tremendous wealth accumulated by some of the European nations I visited, and I also saw how they displayed it. The poor nations could not even afford to be jealous of that state of things. But in Russia such ostentation was completely absent. It was therefore possible to look into her soul.

I witnessed what Russia had done where India was so utterly deprived. It is true that I looked at things from an intense hunger for change. It is not therefore possible for me to judge how somebody from the fortunate West would see Russia's work. It is not my intention to argue about how much wealth was siphoned off from India to the British Isles in the past, nor dwell on what is being drained away now. But what is absolutely clear, and what many British writers also say, is that India has turned anaemic, that we live inwardly and outwardly in a moribund state. I cannot agree with the canard that the root cause of this lies only with our people, that it is beyond the power of any government to change this state of affairs.

I have always known that India's relationship with its alien government is founded on the government's self-interest and not on any affection for us or between us. I know also that the government is concerned only about taking strong measures to retain the power to rule over us, but is totally indifferent to rejuvenating our people. . . . At the same time they have taken complete charge over us. We have no means by which we can stop our destruction.

If indeed it is true that the way to halt our destruction is by obtaining education, that too is in the hands of our rulers. The countrywide disaster over education cannot be solved by the advice of a Commission. A government has to take measures for this purpose as this government would have done had the problem struck its own land, the British Isles. Our question to the Simon Commission therefore is that if ignorance and the absence of education have dealt death blows to India, why has not the British Government done anything about it in the hundred and sixty years of its rule? Has the Commission collected the numbers that would reveal how much was spent on police *lathi* charges compared to what could have been spent on education? The *lathi* charges matter to the alien government's survival. But not those on whom the *lathis* fall. Their education can be shelved for centuries.

The first thing I notice on coming to Russia is the transformation of their peasants and workers in the last eight years. They were in the same dire straits as our masses in India. What they have now achieved in education is better than what the upper echelons of our society have in these hundred and fifty years. What we did not dare to even imagine for the education of the poor is what the Russians have done from one end to the other.

I asked myself time and again how was this possible? The answer in my heart is that it happened because they were not obstructed by greed. They really believed that education could transform one and all. They were thus not afraid to take this mission to the far reaches of Asia's Turkmenistan. Leave alone being afraid, they were most keen to make this happen. . . .

Everyone will have heard rumours of the atrocities practiced in Russia presently—they may not be that far-fetched. This may not also easily change as they have always been oppressive rulers. Yet the Soviet government is forever propagating the misdeeds and injustices of their previous regime through paintings and films as well as the pages of their history books. It seems strange and misguided that they are spreading hate about activities which they are themselves perpetuating. . . .

What remains now is for me to address a question that people keep asking. What do I think about the Bolshevik economy? Given how submissive our people are to the diktats of the priests, I fear they could get too easily charmed by the foreign import policies without a question. What also worries me is our people's inclination to imitate all things foreign. It is crucial for us to snap out of the spell of the guru mantra, no matter whether the guru is homebred or foreign. We have to learn to judge for ourselves how a theory is working out on the ground, what the outcome of its application is. The test is not over. It will take some time to know and judge. Every theory about human beings is founded on human nature. What is most important is to determine the right balance between the two. We have to wait to see whether the theory will prove to be compatible with human nature before we accept it. But we can keep the discussion going, not just by logic but by keeping human nature in view.

There are always two elements in human nature. Man is an independent being at one level. Man is also related to all of humanity. What remains after dismissing one or the other is hardly real. The balance is therefore spoiled by taking sides, and in a crisis the tendency is to do just that. When the balance is upset due to extreme individualism and selfishness, our advisors counsel us to completely cut out one element or the other. That may reduce our troubles, but it could also halt our progress altogether. . . .

(From *Russiar Chithi*, *c.* 1931)
Translated by Uma Das Gupta

Rabindranath Tagore. Dancer. Coloured ink, watercolour and pastel on paper. May 1932. Teheran

IN PERSIA

The next day, we had to be up at three in the morning, to travel at four. We arrived at Bushire at half past eight on the morning of 13 April.

The governor of Bushire has offered us his hospitality. There is no limit to his concern about our comfort.

Now that this man of the soil has come into intimate contact with the sky, let me take this opportunity to record my responses.

Since childhood, all the creatures of the sky I have seen are notable for their felicity of speed, and the exquisite friendship between their wings and the breeze. From the room on the terrace, I remember gazing, at the flight of the kite in the afternoon sunshine. It seemed to be flying, not out of necessity, but to revel in its right to unrestricted movement in the breeze. That joy expressed itself not only in its graceful motion, but also in the beauty of its form. The sail of a boat must adjust to the temperament of the breeze; it is the need for this rhythm that the sail looks so beautiful. Likewise, the wings of a bird move in consonance with the wind, hence their exquisite grace. And then there is such harmony of colour in those wings. So much for living creatures. Beyond that, there is the play of clouds—distilling such a variety of hues from the sunlight, to conjure up a fantasy playroom in the sky! Movement on land is a struggle; gravity holds sway, and we must deal with weighty burdens. Through the ages, what has captivated our minds about the realm of air is the absence of weight, the grace of easy movement.

At long last, humans have dragged the burden of weight from earth to sky. Hence, their flight has the appearance of forced motion. The movement of the human disturbs the wind, instead of harmonizing with it. This disturbance has now travelled from the earthly realm to the heavenly sphere. In this painful struggle, there is no birdsong; the roar of the beast is heard instead. Having conquered the sky, the land today is shouting out its triumph.

The sun rose above the horizon. The arrogant machine had not made the slightest effort to adapt to the red hue of the sun. Its difference from the blueness of the sky struck a discordant note, and in the colour-palace of space, its disharmony with the clouds remained unchanged. A messenger of the modern age, the airplane has no truck with sentiment; it despises grace, elbowing aside all things that are unnecessary. When the eastern horizon grew rosy and the sky at its western edge acquired a pearly white glow above the tender blue, that machine flew through it all, droning like a giant cockroach.

The higher the air-vessel climbed, the more tenuous and remote became our sensory connection with the land, the play of senses shrinking to just one—the sense of sight. The world we had known in its concreteness and variety through the combined evidence of different senses, gradually faded away; a three-dimensional reality became a two-dimensional image. It is within unified structures of time and place that the forms of Creation can be apprehended. The vaguer those contours become, the more sharply our awareness of the created world seems to decline. With our senses in that state of decline, the world appeared insubstantial, and its hold on our hearts became weaker. It seemed to me that in such a condition, when humans set forth to rain down deadly missiles from airplanes, they might turn brutally violent, for they would act without hesitation, having lost their sense of proportion in calculating the extent of their victims' guilt. With the blurring of that real world which evokes human love, the ground for sympathy vanishes as well. The philosophical advice offered by the Gita is a flying machine of the same kind, carrying the guilt-ridden heart of Arjuna to a realm so remote that distinctions between killer and victim, friend and enemy, cease to matter when viewed from that perspective. The human armoury has many such flying machines produced by philosophy, which obfuscate reality; they are to be found in the man-made ideas of imperialism, social law and religious dogma.

There is a British air-force contingent stationed in Baghdad. Their Christian priest informed me that they have been daily bombarding a local village inhabited by the Sheikhs. There, all those who die, young, old, male or female, are assailed from above by the British empire; it is because this force of imperialism blurs the individuality of particular persons that such violence comes so easy. Christ acknowledged all these people as children of God the Father, but to the Christian priest, the Father and his offspring have become unreal, unrecognizable when viewed from the flying machine of imperialism. Hence, all over the Empire today, violence rains down upon the heart of Christ himself. Besides, it is very easy to destroy all these desert nomads from the flying machine; the fear of retaliation is so negligible that the reality of the violence also diminishes correspondingly. Those who can be destroyed with utter absence of risk, are not real enough to their destroyers. For this reason, to the eyes of the western military, the humanity of those unversed in the western art of destruction is growing progressively blurred.

On behalf of their contingent, the priest of the Iraq-based air-force requested me for a statement. Let us share the message I sent them:

> From the beginning of our days man has imagined the seat of divinity in the upper air from which comes light and blows the breath of life for all creatures on this earth. The peace of its dawn, the splendour of its sunset, the voice of eternity in this starry silence have inspired countless generations of men with an ineffable presence of the infinite urging their minds away from the sordid interests of daily life. Man has accepted this dust-laden earth for his dwelling place, for the enacting of the drama of his tangled life ever waiting for a call of perfection from the boundless depth of purity surrounding him in a translucent atmosphere. If in an evil moment man's cruel history should spread its black wings to invade that realm of divine dreams with its cannibalistic greed and fratricidal ferocity then God's curse will certainly descend upon us for that hideous desecration and the last curtain will be rung down upon the world of Man for whom God feels ashamed.

The perspective from far above offers a much more extensive view of the land than what we normally see when we are on the ground, gazing into the distance. Hence, when the airborne vessel races ahead at a speed of almost two miles a minute, it does not seem, looking down, that we are moving so fast. Because many remote distances have shrunk and merged before our eyes, even our measures of time have lost their accuracy. Due to these combined factors, the perception of reality that takes shape now is far removed from our natural sense of time and space. If this mechanical measure of the airplane was also the natural measure of our lives, we would be living in a different world. That is why I have been thinking that Creation, the world we know, is the play of rhythm. The tempo of our apprehension of this world, if altered to a faster or slower one, would yield a different Creation. We are encompassed by countless invisible rays of light. Because the rhythm of our pulse does not match theirs, they are beyond our ken. How can we assert that at this very moment there do not exist countless similar worlds all around us, each imperceptible to all the others? What the minds there apprehend, know and perceive, according to their respective forms of consciousness, is utterly unknowable for us. Through the play of different minds, like the instruments in a great symphony, the outpourings of different worlds are simultaneously emerging, rolling forth towards an infinite unknown.

(From *Parasye*, c.1936)
Translated by Radha Chakravarty

CONVERSATIONS

Rabindranath Tagore and George Bernard Shaw

Rabindranath Tagore and Romain Rolland

TAGORE AND ROMAIN ROLLAND

TAGORE: Do you think that Geneva is likely to play an important role in the world of international relationship?*

ROLLAND: It may, but a good deal depends on factors over which Geneva has no control.

TAGORE: The League of Nations seems to me to be but one of the various forces which are at work here. At the present moment it is by no means the most instrumental for the readjustment of international relationships. It may or may not develop into a power for bringing greater harmony in the political world. I have much faith in the various international groups and societies and the individuals working in this place, and my hope is that they will eventually create in Geneva a genuine centre of international activities which will shape the politics of the future.

ROLLAND: We find a large number of people eagerly looking for a message from the East. India, they think–and I may add, rightly–is the country that can, in this epoch, give that message to the world.

TAGORE: It is curious to note how India has furnished probably the first internationally minded man of the nineteenth century. I mean Raja Rammohan Roy; he had a passion for truth. He came from an orthodox Brahmin family, but he broke all bonds of superstition and formalism. He wanted to understand Buddhism, went to Tibet, studied Hebrew, Greek, Arabic, Persian, English,

* This conversation took place in August, 1930, in Geneva. A report of this conversation was first published in *Asia* (March, 1937).

French; he travelled widely in Europe, and died in Bristol. Spiritual truth for him did not mean a kind of ecclesiasticism confined within sectarian sanctuaries; nor did he think that it could be inflicted upon people outside the sect by men who have professional rights to preach it as a doctrine. He realized that a bond of spiritual unity links the whole of mankind and that it is the purpose of religion to reach down to that fundamental unity of human relationship, of human efforts and achievements.

ROLLAND: I have often wondered at the spirit of religious toleration in India; it is unlike anything we have known in the West. The cosmic nature of your religion and the composite character of your civilization make this possible. India has allowed all kinds of religious faith and practice to flourish side by side.

TAGORE: Perhaps that has also been our weakness, and it is due to an indiscriminate spirit of toleration that all forms of religious creeds and crudities have run riot in India, making it difficult for us to realize the true foundation of our spiritual faith. The practice of animal sacrifice, for instance, has nothing to do with our religion, yet many people sanction it on the grounds of tradition. Similar aberrations of religion can be found in every country. Our concern in India today is to remove them and intensify the larger beliefs which are our true spiritual heritage.

ROLLAND: In Christian scriptures too, this theme of animal sacrifice dominates. Take the opening chapters: God gave preference to Abel because he had offered a lamb for sacrifice.

TAGORE: I have never been able to love the God of the Old Testament.

ROLLAND: . . . The emphasis is wrongly placed, and the attitude is not spiritual in the larger sense.

TAGORE: We should stress always the 'larger sense'. Truth cannot afford to be tolerant where it faces positive evil; it is like sunlight, which makes the existence of evil germs impossible. As a matter of fact, Indian religious life suffers today from the lack of a wholesome spirit of intolerance, which is characteristic of a creative religion. Even a vogue of atheism may do good to India today, even though my country will never accept atheism as her permanent faith. It will sweep away all noxious undergrowths in the forest, and the tall trees will remain intact. At the present moment, even a gift of negation from the West will be of value to a large section of the Indian people.

ROLLAND: I believe that scientific rationalism will help to solve India's question.

TAGORE: I know that India can never believe in mere intellectual determination for any long period of time; balance and harmony will certainly be restored. That is why a temporary swing in one direction may help us arrive at the central adjustment of spiritual life. Science should come to our aid to be humanized by us at the end.

ROLLAND: Science is probably the most international element in the modern world; that is, the spirit of cooperation in scientific research. But we have today poison gas at the disposal of politicians. It is tragic that scientists are at the disposal of military powers who are not in the least interested in the progress of human thought and culture . . . The problem today is not so much the antagonism of nations as the clash between different classes in the body of a nation itself. This does not, of course, justify or minimize to any degree the real curse of aggressive nationalism and the spirit of war.

TAGORE: Words are too conscious; lines are not. Ideas have their form and colour, which wait for their incarnation in pictorial art. Just now painting has become a mania with me. My morning began with songs and poems; now, in the evening of my life, my mind is filled with forms and colours.

(Geneva, 1930)

Rabindranath Tagore and Albert Einstein

TAGORE AND ALBERT EINSTEIN

EINSTEIN: Do you believe in the Divine as isolated from the world?
TAGORE: Not isolated.* The infinite personality of Man comprehends the Universe. There cannot be anything that cannot be subsumed by the human personality, and this proves that the truth of the Universe is human truth. I have taken a scientific fact to illustrate this. Matter is composed of protons and electrons, with gaps between them; but matter may seem to be solid. Similarly humanity is composed of individuals, yet they have their inter-connection of human relationship, which gives living solidarity to man's world. The entire universe is linked up with us in a similar manner, it is a human universe. I have pursued this thought through art, literature and the religious consciousness of man.

EINSTEIN: There are two different conceptions about the nature of the universe: (i) The world as a unity dependent on humanity. (ii) The world as a reality independent of the human factor.

TAGORE: When our universe is in harmony with Man, the eternal, we know it as truth, we feel it as beauty.

EINSTEIN: This is a purely human conception of the universe.

TAGORE: There can be no other conception. This world is a human world–the scientific view of it is also that of the scientific man. There is some standard of reason and enjoyment which gives it truth, the standard of the Eternal Man whose experiences are through our experiences.

*This conversation took place in Kaputh on 14 July 1930.

EINSTEIN: This is a realization of the human entity.

TAGORE: Yes, one eternal entity. We have to realize it through our emotions and activities. We realize the Supreme Man who has no individual limitations through our limitations. Science is concerned with that which is not confined to individuals; it is the impersonal human world of truths. Religion realizes these truths and links them up with our deeper needs; our individual consciousness of truth gains universal significance. Religion applies values to truth, and we know truth as good through our own harmony with it.

EINSTEIN: Truth, then, or Beauty, is not independent of man?

TAGORE: No.

EINSTEIN: If there would be no human beings any more, the Apollo of Belvedere would no longer be beautiful.

TAGORE: No.

EINSTEIN: I agree with regard to this conception of Beauty, but not with regard to Truth.

TAGORE: Why not? Truth is realized through man.

EINSTEIN: I cannot prove that my conception is right, but that is my religion.

TAGORE: Beauty is in the ideal of perfect harmony which is in the Universal Being; Truth the perfect comprehension of the Universal Mind. We individuals approach it through our own mistakes and blunders, through our accumulated experience, through our illumined consciousness how, otherwise, can we know Truth?

EINSTEIN: I cannot prove scientifically that truth must be conceived as a truth that is valid independent of humanity; but I believe it firmly. I believe, for instance, that the Pythagorean theorem in geometry states something that is approximately true, independent of the existence of man. Anyway, if there is a reality independent of man there is also a truth relative to this reality; and in the same way the negation of the first engenders a negation of the existence of the latter.

TAGORE: Truth, which is one with the Universal Being, must essentially be human, otherwise whatever we individuals realize as true can never be called truth at least the truth which is described as scientific and can only be reached through the process of logic, in other words, by an organ of thoughts which is human. According to Indian Philosophy there is Brahman the absolute Truth, which cannot be conceived by the isolation of the individual mind or described by words, but can only be realised by completely merging the individual in its infinity. But such a truth cannot belong to Science. The nature of truth which we are discussing is an appearance that is to say what appears to be true to the human mind and therefore is human, and may be called *maya*, or illusion,

EINSTEIN: So according to your conception, which may be the Indian conception, it is not the illusion of the individual, but of humanity as a whole.

TAGORE: In science we go through the discipline of eliminating the personal limitations of our individual minds and thus reach that comprehension of truth which is in the mind of the Universal Man.

EINSTEIN: The problem begins whether Truth is independent of our consciousness.

TAGORE: What we call truth lies in the rational harmony between the subjective and objective aspects of reality, both of which belong to the superpersonal man.

EINSTEIN: Even in our everyday life we feel compelled to ascribe a reality independent of man to the objects we use. We do this to connect the experiences of our senses in a reasonable way. For instance, if nobody is in this house, yet that table remains where it is.

TAGORE: Yes, it remains outside the individual mind, but not outside the universal mind. The table which I perceive is perceptible by the same kind of consciousness which I possess.

EINSTEIN: Our natural point of view in regard to the existence of truth apart from humanity cannot be explained or proved, but it is a belief which nobody can lack, no primitive beings even. We attribute to Truth a super-human objectivity; it is indispensable for us, this reality which is independent of our existence and our experience and our mind though we cannot say what it means.

TAGORE: Science has proved that the table as a solid object is an appearance, and therefore that which the human mind perceives as a table would not exist if that mind were naught. At the same time it must be admitted that the fact, that the ultimate physical reality of the table is nothing but a multitude of separate revolving centres of electric forces, also belongs to the human mind.

In the apprehension of truth there is an eternal conflict between the universal human mind and the same mind confined in the individual. The perpetual process of reconciliation is being carried on in our science and philosophy, and in our ethics. In any case, if there be any truth absolutely unrelated to humanity then for us it is absolutely nonexisting.

It is not difficult to imagine a mind to which the sequence of things happens not in space, but only in time like the sequence of notes in music. For such a mind its conception of reality is akin to the musical reality in which Pythagorean geometry can have no meaning. There is the reality of paper, infinitely different from the reality of literature. For the kind of mind possessed by the moth, which eats that paper, literature is absolutely non-existent, yet for Man's mind literature has a greater value of truth than the paper itself, In a similar manner, if there be some truth which has no sensuous or rational relation to the human mind it will ever remain as nothing so long as we remain human beings.

EINSTEIN: Then I am more religious than you are !

TAGORE: My religion is in the reconciliation of the Super-personal Man, the Universal human spirit in my own individual being. This has been the subject of my Hibbert Lectures, which I have called 'The Religion of Man'.

(From *The Religion of Man*, 1931).

POEMS

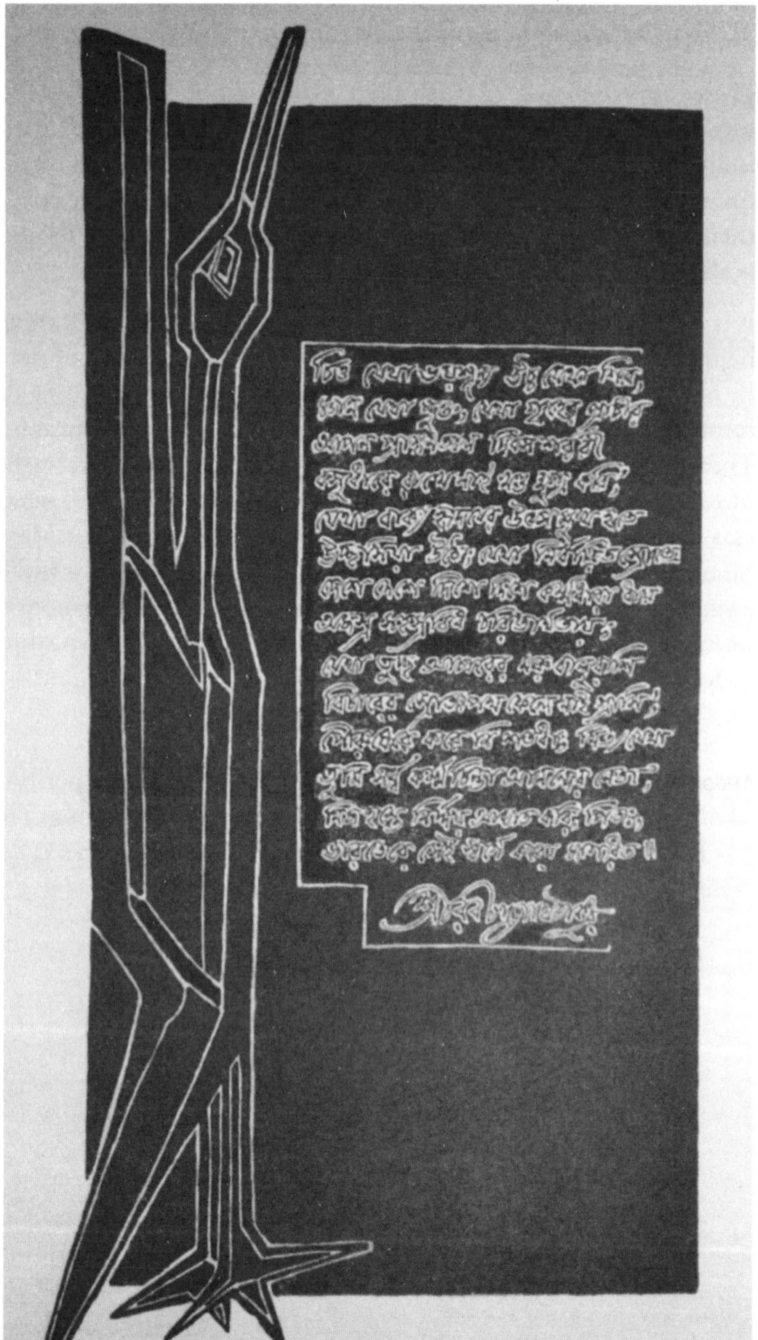

Manuscript page of the Bengali original of the poem 'Where the mind is without fear' in the English Gitanjali

From *GITANJALI* (1912)

11

Leave this chanting and singing and telling of beads! Whom dost thou worship in this lonely dark corner of a temple with doors all shut? Open thine eyes and see thy God is not before thee!*

He is there where the tiller is tilling the hard ground and where the pathmaker is breaking stones. He is with them in sun and in shower, and his garment is covered with dust. Put off thy holy mantle and even like him come down on the dusty soil!

Deliverance? Where is this deliverance to be found? Our master himself has joyfully taken upon him the bonds of creation; he is bound with us all for ever.

Come out of thy meditations and leave aside thy flowers and incense! What harm is there if thy clothes become tattered and stained? Meet him and stand by him in toil and in sweat of thy brow.

(*Bhajan pujan sadhan aradhana*)

* In a letter to Edward Thompson, Tagore wrote, 'So I went to Shelidaha and simply to while away time I translated the *Gitanjali* songs. I felt sure my translations were only schoolboy exercises'–(*Gitanjali*, Rabindra-Bhavana: 7).

Published by the India Society, London, in 1912, the English *Gitanjali* is a combination of poems from the Bengali volumes *Chaitali* (1896), *Kalpana* (1900), *Naibedya* (1901), *Smaran* (1903), *Kheya* (1906), *Shishu* (1903), *Gitanjali* (1910), *Gitimalya* (1914), *Utsarga* (1914) and *Achalayatan* (1918). William Rothenstein, W.B. Yeats and Ezra Pound were deeply impressed with these poems. Macmillan later published the book in March 1913.

27

Light, oh where is the light? Kindle it with the burning fire of desire!

There is the lamp but never a flicker of a flame—is such thy fate, my heart? Ah, death were better by far for thee!

Misery knocks at thy door, and her message is that thy lord is wakeful, and he calls thee to the love-tryst through the darkness of night.

The sky is overcast with clouds and the rain is ceaseless. I know not what this is that stirs in me—I know not its meaning.

A moment's flash of lightning drags down a deeper gloom on my sight, and my heart gropes for the path to where the music of the night calls me.

Light, oh where is the light! Kindle it with the burning fire of desire! It thunders and the wind rushes screaming through the void. The night is black as a black stone. Let not the hours pass by in the dark. Kindle the lamp of love with thy life.

(*Kothai alo kothai o re alo*)

35

Where the mind is without fear and the head is held high;

Where knowledge is free;

Where the world has not been broken up into fragments by narrow domestic walls;

Where words come out from the depth of truth;

Where tireless striving stretches its arms towards perfection;

Where the clear stream of reason has not lost its way into the dreary desert sand of dead habit;

Where the mind is led forward by thee into ever-widening thought and action–

Into that heaven of freedom, my Father, let my country awake.

[*Chitta jetha bhaishunya*]

39

When the heart is hard and parched up, come upon me with a shower of mercy.

When grace is lost from life, come with a burst of song.

When tumultuous work raises its din on all sides shutting me out from beyond, come to me, my lord of silence, with thy peace and rest.

When my beggarly heart sits crouched, shut up in a corner, break open the door, my king, and come with the ceremony of a king.

When desire blinds the mind with delusion and dust, O thou holy one, thou wakeful, come with thy light and thy thunder.

(*Jiban jakhan shukaye jai*)

44

This is my delight, thus to wait and watch at the wayside where shadow chases light and the rain comes in the wake of the summer.

Messengers, with tidings from unknown skies, greet me and speed along the road. My heart is glad within, and the breath of the passing breeze is sweet.

From dawn till dusk I sit here before my door, and I know that of a sudden the happy moment will arrive when I shall see.

In the meanwhile I smile and I sing all alone. In the meanwhile the air is filling with the perfume of promise.

(*Amaar ei path chaoatei ananda*)

69

The same stream of life that runs through my veins night and day runs through the world and dances in rhythmic measures.

It is the same life that shoots in joy through the dust of the earth in numberless blades of grass and breaks into tumultuous waves of leaves and flowers.

It is the same life that is rocked in the ocean-cradle of birth and of death, in ebb and in flow.

I feel my limbs are made glorious by the touch of this world of life. And my pride is from the life-throb of ages dancing in my blood this moment.

(*E amaar sharirer shiraye shiraye*)

73

Deliverance is not for me in renunciation. I feel the embrace of freedom in a thousand bonds of delight.

Thou ever pourest for me the fresh draught of thy wine of various colours and fragrance, filling this earthen vessel to the brim.

My world will light its hundred different lamps with thy flame and place them before the altar of thy temple.

No, I will never shut the doors of my senses. The delights of sight and hearing and touch will bear thy delight.

Yes, all my illusions will burn into illumination of joy, and all my desires ripen into fruits of love.

(*Bairagya sadhaney mukti*)

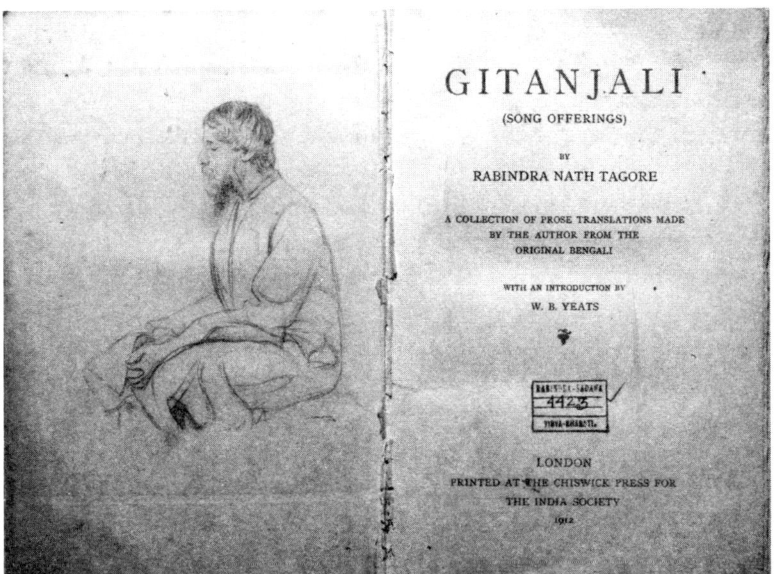

First edition of the English Gitanjali

From *THE GARDENER* (1913)

The tame bird was in a cage, the free bird was in the forest.*
They met when the time came, it was a decree of fate.
The free bird cries, 'O my love, let us fly to the wood.'
The cage bird whispers, 'Come hither, let us both live in the cage.'
Says the free bird, 'Among bars, where is there room to spread
 one's wings?'
'Alas', cries the caged bird, 'I should not know where to sit perched
 in the sky.'

The free bird cries, 'My darling, sing the songs of the woodlands.'
The cage bird sings, 'Sit by my side, I'll teach you the speech of
 the learned.'
The forest bird cries, 'No, ah no! songs can never be taught.'
The cage bird says, 'Alas for me, I know not the songs of the
 woodlands.'

Their love is intense with longing, but they never can fly wing to
 wing.
Through the bars of the cage they look, and vain is their wish to
 know each other.
They flutter their wings in yearning, and sing, 'Come closer, my love!'
The free bird cries, 'It cannot be, I fear the closed doors of the cage.'
The cage bird whispers, 'Alas, my wings are powerless and dead.'

(*Dui pakhi*)

* *The Gardener*, published by Macmillan in 1913, is dedicated to W.B. Yeats. It has prose translations of Bengali poems from fifteen different works, composed over almost three decades.

O woman, you are not merely the handiwork
of God, but also of
men; these are ever endowing you with
beauty from their hearts.
Poets are weaving for you a web with
threads of golden imagery;
painters are giving your form ever new
immortality.
The sea gives its pearls, the mines their
gold, the summer
gardens their flowers to deck you, to cover
you, to make you
more precious.
The desire of men's hearts has shed its glory
over your youth.
You are one half woman and one half dream.

Infinite wealth is not yours, my patient and dusky mother dust!
You toil to fill the mouths of your children, but food is scarce.
The gift of gladness that you have for us is never perfect.
The toys that you make for your children are fragile.
You cannot satisfy all our hungry hopes, but should I desert you
for that?
Your smile which is shadowed with pain is sweet to my eyes.
Your love which knows not fulfilment is dear to my heart.
From your breast you have fed us with life but not immortality,
that is why your eyes are ever wakeful.
For ages you are working with colour and song, yet your heaven is
not built, but only its sad suggestion.
Over your creations of beauty there is the mist of tears.
I will pour my songs into your mute heart, and my love into your
love.
I will worship you with labour.
I have seen your tender face and I love your mournful dust,
Mother Earth.

(*Manasi*)

SONGS OF KABIR

(mo ko kahân dhûnro bande)

O servant, where dost thou seek Me?
Lo! I am beside thee.
I am neither in temple nor in mosque: I am neither in Kaaba nor in Kailash:
Neither am I in rites and ceremonies, nor in Yoga and renunciation.
If thou art a true seeker, thou shalt at once see Me: thou shalt meet Me in a moment of time.
Kabîr says, 'O Sadhu! God is the breath of all breath.'

(Santan jât na pûcho nirguniyân)

It is needless to ask of a saint the caste to which he belongs;
For the priest, the warrior. the tradesman, and all the thirty-six castes, alike are seeking for God.
It is but folly to ask what the caste of a saint may be;
The barber has sought God, the washerwoman, and the carpenter—
Even Raidas was a seeker after God.
The Rishi Swapacha was a tanner by caste.
Hindus and Moslems alike have achieved that End, where remains no mark of distinction.

(*Bago na ja re na ja*)

Do not go to the garden of flowers!
O friend! go not there;
In your body is the garden of flowers.
Take your seat on the thousand petals of the lotus, and there gaze on the Infinite Beauty.

(*Nacho re mero man, matta hoy*)

Dance, my heart! dance to-day with joy.

The strains of love fill the days and the nights with music, and the world is listening to its melodies:

Mad with joy, life and death dance to the rhythm of this music. The hills and the sea and the earth dance. The world of man dances in laughter and tears.

Why put on the robe of the monk, and live aloof from the world in lonely pride?

Behold! my heart dances in the delight of a hundred arts; and the Creator is well pleased.

(1914)
Translated by Rabindranath Tagore

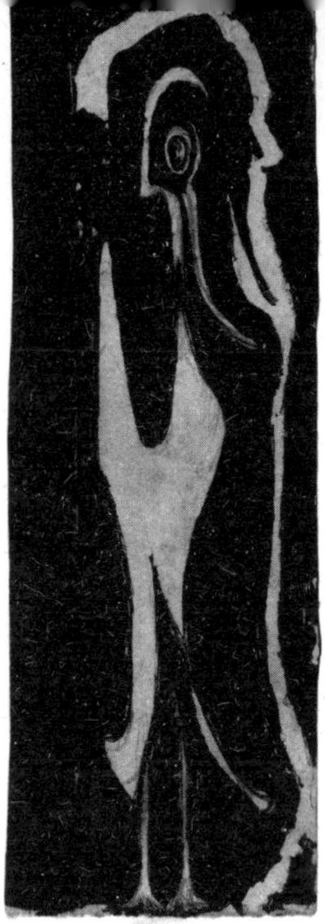

Rabindranath Tagore.
Bird-Man. Ink on paper.
November 1928

From *STRAY BIRDS* (1916)

'What language is thine, O sea?'*
'The language of eternal question.'
'What language is thy answer, O sky?'
'The language of eternal silence.'

ꕥ ꕥ ꕥ

He has made his weapons his gods. When his weapons win he is defeated himself.

ꕥ ꕥ ꕥ

I thank thee that I am none of the wheels of power but I am one with the living creatures that are crushed by it.

ꕥ ꕥ ꕥ

We come nearest to the great when we are great in humility.

ꕥ ꕥ ꕥ

God grows weary of great kingdoms, but never of little flowers.

* *Stray Birds* (1916) is dedicated to T. Hara of Yokohama, Tagore's host during his Japan visit in 1916. While some of the poems are from the Bengali *Kanika* (1899), some others reappeared in the bilingual *Lekhan* (1926) and were probably written in Japan. Krishna Kripalani argues that these poems were influenced by Japanese Haiku (*Rabindranath Tagore: A Biography*, London: Oxford University Press, 1962; p.255). In the Preface to *Lekhan*, Tagore writes: 'The lines in the following pages had their origin in China and Japan where the author was asked for his writings on fans or pieces of silk'.

ଔ ଔ ଔ

What is this unseen flame of darkness whose sparks are the stars?

ଔ ଔ ଔ

Let life be beautiful like summer flowers and death like autumn leaves.

ଔ ଔ ଔ

In death the many becomes one; in life the one becomes many.
Religion will be one when God is dead.

ଔ ଔ ଔ

Power said to the world, 'You are mine'.
The world kept it prisoner on her throne.
Love said to the world, 'I am thine'.
The world gave it the freedom of her house.

ଔ ଔ ଔ

The night kisses the fading day whispering to his ear, 'I am death, your mother. I am to give you fresh birth'.

ଔ ଔ ଔ

'I am ashamed of my emptiness,' said the Word to the Work.
'I know how poor I am when I see you,' said the Work to the Word.

☙❧☙

The world has kissed my soul with its pain, asking for its return in songs.

☙❧☙

Woman, thou hast encircled the world's heart with the depth of thy tears as the sea has the earth.

☙❧☙

Woman, in your laughter you have the music of the fountain of life.

☙❧☙

A mind all logic is like a knife all blade.
It makes the hand bleed that uses it.

☙❧☙

When the sun goes down to the West, the East of his morning stands before him in silence.

☙❧☙

Life has become richer by the love that has been lost.

☙❧☙

The fountain of death makes the still water of life play.

☙❧☙

The movement of life has its rest in its own music.

Man is worse than an animal when he is an animal.

Truth seems to come with its final word; and the final word gives birth to its next.

The smell of the wet earth in the rain rises like a great chant of praise from the voiceless multitude of the insignificant.

Man's history is waiting in patience for the triumph of the insulted man.

Rabindranath Tagore. Landscape with huts. Coloured ink on paper. 1932

From FRUIT-GATHERING

The sun had set on the western margin of the river among the tangle of the forest.*

The hermit boys had brought the cattle home, and sat round the fire to listen to the master, Gautama, when a strange boy came, and greeted him with fruits and flowers, and, bowing low at his feet, spoke in a bird-like voice—

'Lord, I have come to thee to
be taken into the path of the supreme Truth.

'My name is Satyakâma.'

'Blessings be on thy head,' said the master.

'Of what clan art thou, my child? It is only fitting for a Brahmin to aspire to the highest wisdom.'

'Master', answered the boy, 'I know not of what clan I am. I shall go and ask my mother.'

Thus saying, Satyakâma took leave, and wading across the shallow stream, came back to his mother's hut, which stood at the end of the sandy waste at the edge of the sleeping village.

The lamp burnt dimly in the room, and the mother stood at the door in the dark waiting for her son's return.

* *Fruit Gathering* was published by Macmillan in 1916. A later edition, *Gitanjali and Fruit Gathering* (Macmillan, 1918) carried illustrations by Surendranath Kar, Nandalal Bose, Abanindranath Tagore and Nabendranath Tagore.

She clasped him to her bosom, kissed him on his hair, and asked him of his errand to the master.

'What is the name of my father, dear mother?' asked the boy.

'It is only fitting for a Brahmin to aspire to the highest wisdom, said Lord Gautama to me.'

The woman lowered her eyes, and spoke in a whisper.

'In my youth I was poor and had many masters. Thou didst come to thy mother Jabâlâ's arms, my darling, who had no husband.'

The early rays of the sun glistened on the tree-tops of the forest hermitage.

The students, with their tangled hair still wet with their morning bath, sat under the ancient tree, before the master.

There came Satyakâma.

He bowed low at the feet of the sage, and stood silent.

'Tell me', the great teacher asked him, 'of what clan art thou?'

'My lord', he answered, 'I know it not. My mother said when I asked her, "I had served many masters in my youth, and thou hadst come to thy mother Jabâlâ's arms, who had no husband."'

There rose a murmur like the angry hum of bees disturbed in their hive; and the students muttered at the shameless insolence of that outcast.

Master Gautama rose from his seat, stretched out his arms, took the boy to his bosom, and said, 'Best of all Brahmins art thou, my child. Thou hast the noblest heritage of truth.'

[*Brahman*, 1916]

Over the relic of Lord Buddha King Bimbisâr built a shrine, a salutation in white marble.*

There in the evening would come all the brides and daughters of the King's house to offer flowers and light lamps.

When the son became king in his time he washed his father's creed away with blood, and lit sacrificial fires with its sacred books.

The autumn day was dying. The evening hour of worship was near.

Shrimati, the queen's maid, devoted to Lord Buddha, having bathed in holy water, and decked the golden tray with lamps and fresh white blossoms, silently raised her dark eyes to the queen's face.

The queen shuddered in fear and said, 'Do you not know, foolish girl, that death is the penalty for whoever brings worship to Buddha's shrine?

'Such is the king's will.'

Shrimati bowed to the queen, and turning away from her door came and stood before Amitâ, the newly wed bride of the king's son.

A mirror of burnished gold on her lap, the newly wed bride was braiding her dark long tresses and painting the red spot of good luck at the parting of her hair.

Her hands trembled when she saw the young maid, and she cried, 'What fearful peril would you bring me! Leave me this instant.'

Princess Shuklâ sat at the window reading her book of romance by the light of the setting sun.

* The Bengali poem *Pujarini* provided the inspiration for Tagore's play *Natir Puja* (translated by Tagore as *The Dancing Girl's Worship*.)

She started when she saw at her door the maid with the sacred offerings.

Her book fell down from her lap, and she whispered in Shrimati's ears, 'Rush not to death, daring woman!'

Shrimati walked from door to door. She raised her head and cried, 'O women of the king's house, hasten!

'The time for our Lord's worship is come!'

Some shut their doors in her face and some reviled her.

The last gleam of daylight faded from the bronze dome of the palace tower.
Deep shadows settled in street corners: the bustle of the city was hushed: the gong at the temple of Shiva announced the time of the evening prayer.

In the dark of the autumn evening, deep as a limpid lake, stars throbbed with light, when the guards of the palace garden were startled to see through the trees a row of lamps burning at the shrine of Buddha.

They ran with their swords unsheathed, crying, 'Who are you, foolish one, reckless of death?'

'I am Shrimati', replied a sweet voice, 'the servant of Lord Buddha.'

The next moment her heart's blood coloured the cold marble with its red.

And in the still hour of stars died the light of the last lamp of worship at the foot of the shrine.

(*Pujarini*, 1916)

THANKSGIVING

Those who walk on the path of pride crushing the lowly life under their tread, covering the tender green of the earth with their footprints in blood;

Let them rejoice, and thank thee, Lord, for the day is theirs.

But I am thankful that my lot lies with the humble who suffer and bear the burden of power, and hide their faces and stifle their sobs in the dark.

For every throb of their pain has pulsed in the secret depth of thy night, and every insult has been gathered into thy great silence. And the morrow is theirs.

O Sun, rise upon the bleeding hearts blossoming in flowers of the morning, and the torchlight revelry of pride shrunken to ashes.

From *THE FUGITIVE* (1921)

Neither mother nor daughter are you, nor bride, Urvashi.* Woman you are, to ravish the soul of Paradise.

When weary-footed evening comes down to the folds whither the cattle have returned, you never trim the house lamps nor walk to the bridal bed with a tremulous heart and a wavering smile on your lips, glad that the dark hours are so secret.

Like the dawn you are without veil, Urvashi, and without shame.

Who can imagine that aching overflow of splendour which created you!

You rose from the churned ocean on the first day of the first spring, with the cup of life in your right hand and poison in your left. The monster sea, lulled like an enchanted snake, laid down its thousand hoods at your feet.

Your unblemished radiance rose from the foam, white and naked as a jasmine.

Were you ever small, timid or in bud, Urvashi, O Youth everlasting?

Did you sleep, cradled in the deep blue night where the strange light of gems plays over coral, shells and moving creatures of dreamlike form, till day revealed your awful fullness of bloom?

Adored are you of all men in all ages, Urvashi, O endless wonder!

* In *The Fugitive* (1921), published by Macmillan in New York, Tagore combines translations of his Bengali poems with religious lyrics translated from the works of others, in the sections on 'Vaishnava Songs' 'Baul Songs' and 'Hindi Songs of Jnanadas'. Urvashi was the dancing girl of Paradise who rose from the sea.

The world throbs with youthful pain at the glance of your eyes, the ascetic lays the fruit of his austerities at your feet, the songs of poets hum and swarm round the perfume of your presence. Your feet, as in careless joy they flit on, wound even the heart of the hollow wind with the tinkle of golden bells.

When you dance before the gods, flinging orbits of novel rhythm into space, Urvashi, the earth shivers, leaf and grass, and autumn fields heave and sway; the sea surges into a frenzy of rhyming waves; the stars drop into the sky—beads from the chain that leaps till it breaks on your breast; and the blood dances in men's hearts with sudden turmoil.

You are the first break on the crest of heaven's slumber, Urvashi, you thrill the air with unrest. The world bathes your limbs in her tears; with colour of her heart's blood are your feet red; lightly you poise on the wave-tossed lotus of desire, Urvashi; you play forever in that limitless mind wherein labours God's tumultuous dream.

(*Urvashi*, 1921)

I have donned this new robe to-day because my body feels like singing.

It is not enough that I am given to my love once and for ever, but out of that I must fashion new gifts every day; and shall I not seem a fresh offering, dressed in a new robe?

My heart, like the evening sky, has its endless passion for colour, and therefore I change my veils, which have now the green of the cool young grass and now that of the winter rice.

Today my robe is tinted with the rain-rimmed blue of the sky. It brings to my limbs the colour of the boundless, the colour of the oversea hills; and it carries in its folds the delight of summer clouds flying in the wind.

(*Sarba deher byakulata*, 1921)

You, like a rivulet swift and sinuous, laugh and dance, and your steps sing as you trip along.

I, like a bank rugged and steep, stand speechless and stock-still and darkly gaze at you.

I, like a big, foolish storm, of a sudden come rushing on and try to rend my being and scatter it parcelled in a whirl of passion.

You, like the lightning's flash slender and keen, pierce the heart of the turbulent darkness, to disappear in a vivid streak of laughter.

(*Tomra o amra*, 1921)

If the ragged villager, trudging home from the market, could suddenly be lifted to the crest of a distant age, men would stop in their work and shout and run to him in delight.

For they would no longer whittle down the man into the peasant, but find him full of the mystery and spirit of his age.

Even his poverty and pain would grow great, released from the shallow insult of the present, and the paltry things in his basket would acquire pathetic dignity.

(*Samanya lok*, 1921)

How often, great Earth, have I felt my being yearn to flow over you, sharing in the happiness of each green blade that raises its signal banner in answer to the beckoning blue of the sky!

I feel as if I had belonged to you ages before I was born. That is why, in the days when the autumn light shimmers on the mellowing ears of rice, I seem to remember a past when my mind was everywhere, and even to hear voices as of playfellows echoing from the remote and deeply veiled past,

When, in the evening, the cattle return to their folds, raising dust from the meadow paths, as the moon rises higher than the smoke ascending from the village huts, I feel sad as for some great separation that happened in the first morning of existence.

(*Basundhara*, 1921)

Rabindranath Tagore.
Woman on a chair
and a poem.
Coloured ink on wood.
15 March 1929

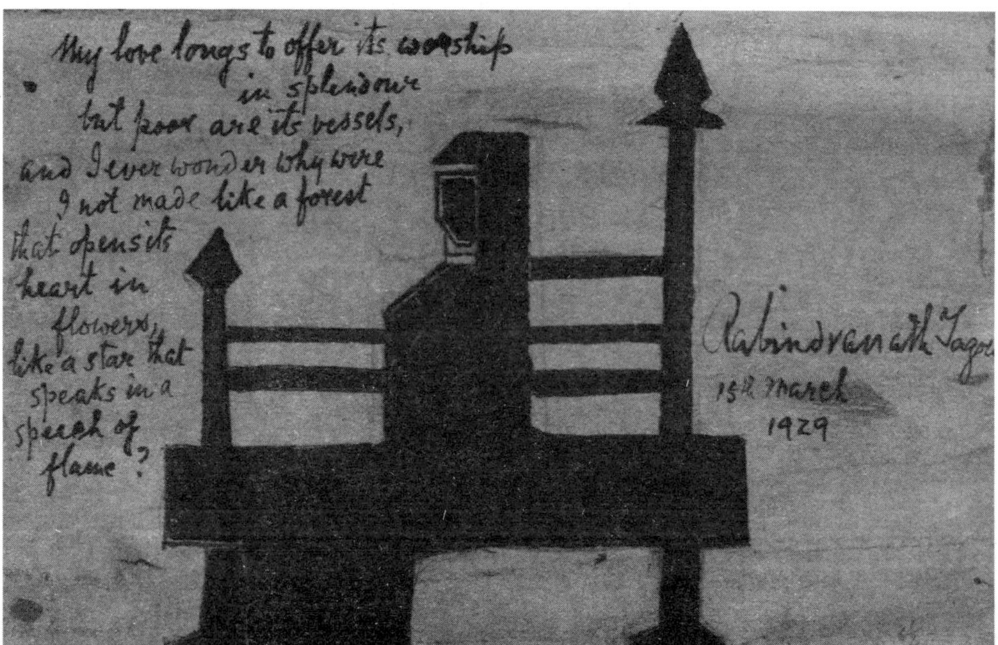

Karna and Kunti

The Pandava Queen Kunti before marriage had a son, Karna, who, in manhood, became the commander of the Kaurava host. To hide her shame she abandoned him at birth, and a charioteer, Adhiratha, brought him up as his son.*

Karna
I am Karna, the son of the charioteer, Adhiratha, and I sit here by the bank of holy Ganges to worship the setting sun. Tell me who you are.

Kunti
I am the woman who first made you acquainted with that light you are worshipping.

Karna
I do not understand: but your eyes melt my heart as the kiss of the morning sun melts the snow on a mountain-top, and your voice rouses a blind sadness within me of which the cause may well lie beyond the reach of my earliest memory. Tell me, strange woman, what mystery binds my birth to you?

Kunti
Patience, my son. I will answer when the lids of darkness come down over the prying eyes of day. In the meanwhile, know that I am Kunti.

Karna
Kunti! The mother of Arjuna?

Kunti
Yes, indeed, the mother of Arjuna, your antagonist. But do not, therefore, hate me. I still remember the day of the trial of arms in Hastina when you, an unknown boy, boldly stepped into the arena, like the first ray of dawn among the stars of night. Ah! who was that unhappy woman whose eyes kissed your bare, slim body

* In the *Mahabharata*, Kunti, queen of the Pandavas, had a son Karna, born before her marriage. She abandoned him at birth, and he was brought up by charioteer Adhiratha. Later, Karna became commander of the Kaurava army.

through tears that blessed you, where she sat among the women of the royal household behind the arras? Why, the mother of Arjuna! Then the Brahmin, master of arms, stepped forth and said, 'No youth of mean birth may challenge Arjuna to a trial of strength.' You stood speechless, like a thunder-cloud at sunset flashing with an agony of suppressed light. But who was the woman whose heart caught fire from your shame and anger, and flared up in silence? The mother of Arjuna! Praised be Duryodhana, who perceived your worth, and then and there crowned you King of Anga, thus winning the Kauravas a champion. Overwhelmed at this good fortune, Adhiratha, the charioteer, broke through the crowd; you instantly rushed to him and laid your crown at his feet amid the jeering laughter of the Pandavas and their friends. But there was one woman of the Pandava house whose heart glowed with joy at the heroic pride of such humility;—even the mother of Arjuna!

Karna
But what brings you here alone, Mother of kings?

Kunti
I have a boon to crave.

Karna
Command me, and whatever manhood and my honour as a Kshatriya permit shall be offered at your feet.

Kunti
I have come to take you.

Karna
Where?

Kunti
To my breast thirsting for your love, my son.

Karna
Fortunate mother of five brave kings, where can you find place for me, a small chieftain of lowly descent?

Kunti
Your place is before all my other sons.

Karna
But what right have I to take it?

Kunti
Your own God-given right to your mother's love.

Karna
The gloom of evening spreads over the earth, silence rests on the water, and your voice leads me back to some primal world of infancy lost in twilit consciousness. However, whether this be dream, or fragment of forgotten reality, come near and place your right hand on my forehead. Rumour runs that I was deserted by my mother. Many a night she has come to me in my slumber, but when I cried: 'Open your veil, show me your face!' her figure always vanished. Has this same dream come this evening while I wake? See, yonder the lamps are lighted in your son's tents across the river; and on this side behold the tent-domes of my Kauravas, like the suspended waves of a spell-arrested storm at sea. Before the din of tomorrow's battle, in the awful hush of this field where it must be fought, why should the voice of the mother of my opponent, Arjuna, bring me a message of forgotten motherhood? and why should my name take such music from her tongue as to draw my heart out to him and his brothers?

Kunti
Then delay not, my son, come with me!

Karna
Yes, I will come and never ask question, never doubt. My soul responds to your call; and the struggle for victory and fame and the rage of hatred have suddenly become untrue to me, as the delirious dream of a night in the serenity of the dawn. Tell me whither you mean to lead?

Kunti
To the other bank of the river, where those lamps burn across the ghastly pallor of the sands.

Karna
Am I there to find my lost mother for ever?

Kunti
O my son!

Karna
Then why did you banish me—a castaway uprooted from my ancestral

soil, adrift in a homeless current of indignity? Why set a bottomless chasm between Arjuna and myself, turning the natural attachment of kinship to the dread attraction of hate? You remain speechless. Your shame permeates the vast darkness and sends invisible shivers through my limbs. Leave my question unanswered! Never explain to me what made you rob your son of his mother's love! Only tell me why you have come to-day to call me back to the ruins of a heaven wrecked by your own hands?

Kunti
I am dogged by a curse more deadly than your reproaches: for, though surrounded by five sons, my heart shrivels like that of a woman deprived of her children. Through the great rent that yawned for my deserted first-born, all my life's pleasures have run to waste. On that accursed day when I belied my motherhood you could not utter a word; to-day your recreant mother implores you for generous words. Let your forgiveness burn her heart like fire and consume its sin.

Karna
Mother, accept my tears!

Kunti
I did not come with the hope of winning you back to my arms, but with that of restoring your rights to you. Come and receive, as a king's son, your due among your brothers.

Karna
I am more truly the son of a charioteer, and do not covet the glory of greater parentage.

Kunti
Be that as it may, come and win back the kingdom, which is yours by right!

Karna
Must you, who once refused me a mother's love, tempt me with a kingdom? The quick bond of kindred which you severed at its root is dead, and can never grow again. Shame were mine should I hasten to call the mother of kings mother, and abandon my mother in the charioteer's house!

Kunti
You are great, my son! How God's punishment invisibly grows

from a tiny seed to a giant life! The helpless babe disowned by his mother comes back a man through the dark maze of events to smite his brothers!

Karna

Mother, have no fear! I know for certain that victory awaits the Pandavas. Peaceful and still though this night be, my heart is full of the music of a hopeless venture and baffled end. Ask me not to leave those who are doomed to defeat. Let the Pandavas win the throne, since they must: I remain with the desperate and forlorn. On the night of my birth you left me naked and unnamed to disgrace: leave me once again without pity to the calm expectation of defeat and death!

(*Karna Kunti Samvad*, 1921)

Rabindranath Tagore

Rabindranath Tagore. Male nude with one arm akimbo. Ink and opaque white on paper, c. 1930-31.

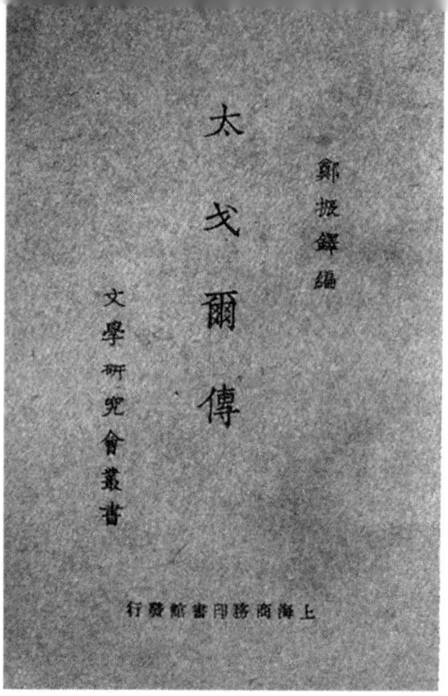

Chinese edition of Fireflies

From *FIREFLIES* (1928)

My fancies are fireflies, –
Specks of living light
twinkling in the dark.*

In the mountain, stillness surges up
to explore its own height;
in the lake, movement stands still
to contemplate its own depth.

Bigotry tries to keep truth safe in its hand
with a grip that kills it.
Wishing to hearten a timid lam
great night lights all her stars.

Clouds are hills in vapour,
hills are clouds in stone, –
a phantasy in time's dream.

The sea of danger, doubt and denial
around man's little island of certainty
challenges him to dare the unknown.

* *Fireflies* (1928) was an illustrated edition published in New York by Macmillan. Of the 256 verses and epigrams, some are written in English and others are translations from the Bengali. See also the bilingual text *Lekhan* (1926) and Note on *Stray Birds* (1916) on p. 268.

The world speaks to me in pictures,
my soul answers in music.

Beauty knows to say, 'Enough,'
barbarism clamours for still more.

An unknown flower in a strange land
speaks to the poet:
'Are we not of the same soil, my lover?'

As the tree its leaves, I shed my words on the earth,
let my thoughts unuttered flower in thy silence.

My offerings are not for the temple at the end of the road,
but for the wayside shrines
that surprise me at every bend.

The tree is a winged spirit
released from the bondage of seed,
pursuing its adventure of life
across the unknown.

My life like the reed with its stops,
has its play of colours
through the gaps in its hopes and gains.

I miss the meaning of my own part
in the play of life
because I know not of the parts
that others play.

When death comes and whispers to me,
'Thy days are ended,'
let me say to him, 'I have lived in love
and not in mere time.'
He will ask, 'Will thy songs remain?'
I shall say, 'I know not, but this I know
that often when I sang I found my eternity.'

Before the end of my journey
may I reach within myself
the one which is the all,
leaving the outer shell
to float away with the drifting multitude
upon the current of chance and change.

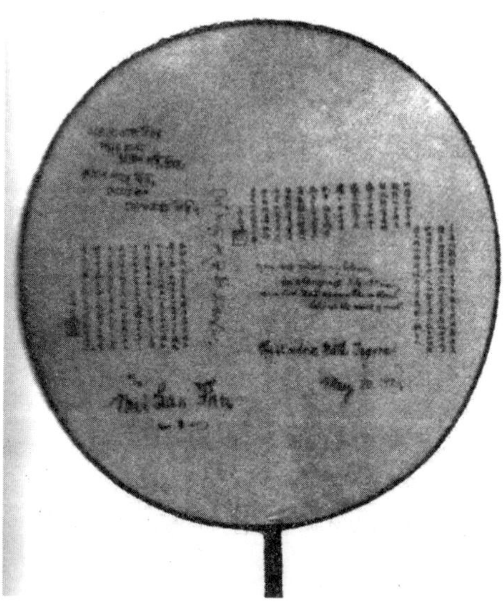

Chinese fan with Haiku by Rabindranath Tagore

From *POEMS* (1942)

RAIDAS, THE SWEEPER

Raidas, the sweeper, sat still, lost in the solitude of his soul, and some songs born of his silent vision found their way to the Rani's heart,the Rani Jhali of Chitore.*

Tears flowed from her eyes, her thoughts wandered away from her daily duties, till she met Raidas who guided her to God's presence.

The old Brahmin priest of the King's house rebuked her for her desecration of sacred law by offering homage as a disciple to an outcaste.

'Brahmin', the Rani answered, 'while you were busy tying your purse-strings of custom ever tighter, love's gold slipped unnoticed to the earth, and my Master in his divine humility has picked it up from the dust.

'Revel in your pride of the unmeaning knots without number, harden your miserly heart, but I, a beggar woman, am glad to receive love's wealth, the gift of the lowly dust, from my Master, the sweeper.'

(*Premer Sona*, 1942)

If they answer not to thy call walk alone,
If they are afraid and cower mutely facing the wall,
O thou of evil luck,
open thy mind and speak out alone.

* *Poems* (1942) consists of poems translated by Rabindranath and edited by Krishna Kripalani, with Amiya Chakravarty, Nirmal Chandra Chattopadhyay and Pulinbehari Sen. The collection was published posthumously, soon after Tagore's death. It also has 12 poems translated by Amiya Chakravarty.

If they turn away, and desert you when crossing the wilderness,
O thou of evil luck,
trample the thorns under thy tread,
and along the blood-lined track travel alone.

If they do not hold up the light
when the night is troubled with storm,
O thou of evil luck,
with the thunder flame of pain ignite thine own heart
and let it burn alone.

(*Jadi tor dak suney*)

**The world today is wild with the delirium of hatred,
the conflicts are cruel and unceasing in anguish,
crooked are its paths, tangled its bonds of greed.
All creatures are crying for a new birth of thine,
O Thou of boundless life,
save them, rouse thine eternal voice of hope,
Let Love's lotus with its inexhaustible treasure of honey
open its petals in thy light.

O Serene, O Free,
in thine immeasurable mercy and goodness
wipe away all dark stains from the heart of this earth.

Thou giver of immortal gifts
give us the power of renunciation
and claim from us our pride.
In the splendour of a new sunrise of wisdom
let the blind gain their sight
and let life come to the souls that are dead.

** The Bengali original was composed in 1927, published in *Natir Puja* 2nd edition (1932). The poem is addressed to the Buddha.

O Serene, O Free,
in thine immeasurable mercy and goodness
wipe away all dark stains from the heart of this earth.
Man's heart is anguished with the fever of unrest,
with the poison of self-seeking,
with a thirst that knows no end.
Countries far and wide flaunt on their foreheads
the blood-red mark of hatred.
Touch them with thy right hand,
make them one in spirit,
bring harmony into their life,
bring rhythm of beauty.

O Serene, O Free,
in thine immeasurable mercy and goodness
wipe away all dark stains from the heart of this earth.

(*Himsaye unmatta prithibi*, 1942)

KABIR AND THE WOMAN

The rumour spread all around the country that Kabir was a man of God.

People flocked to his door.

The sick asked him for cures; the barren women begged for the blessing of children; some challenged him to show mystic power; some wanted him to prove that God is.

Kabir raised his hands to his God and cried, 'By your mercy I was born a weaver in a humble home. But what game is this you are playing; gathering all the crowd at my door to leave me yourself!'

When Brahmins saw the people worshipping him, a man of low birth and occupation, they burned with rage.

With a woman of evil repute they took counsel, and they bought her over to their plan.

It was the market day. Kabir came to sell his cloths.

The woman rushed to him, and caught his hand. She cried, with tears in her eyes-'Faithless one, why desert me and break my heart?'

'Out with you, impostor!' exclaimed the jeering crowd of Brahmins. 'You play the saint to delude men and leave this poor woman to starve!'

'Yes' said Kabir, 'I am to blame. Why should she go without food when there is enough for me?'

He welcomed the woman to his home and said 'Surely, my lord has heard my prayer.'

A sudden fear possessed the woman.

She fell upon her knees and cried, 'I have sinned against you. Your curse will be my death.'

'You are forgiven,' said Kabir, 'live with me without fear.'

Days passed and her heart became sweet and her thoughts pure. Her voice rang in praise of her dear lord. And Kabir was forsaken by men.

One day the king, in a fit of idle fancy, said he must hear Kabir sing.

The poet shook his head, and said to the men from the court, 'I am not fit for a king's audience.'

'I dare not go back without you', said the royal servant.

The king sat on the throne, and his nobles and courtiers sat around him.

Kabir entered the hall, the woman following him.

Some smiled and others frowned. The king thought, 'What shamelessness to come before me with a woman!'

At his signal the guard took them out.

He was hailed with loud laughter from the Brahmins, who were waiting in the street.

It pierced the woman's heart. She fell at Kabir's feet, and said weeping', You lifted me out of the mud to besmirch your own fair name!'

'You are the gift of my lord', said Kabir, 'My crown of humiliation'.

(*Apaman bar*, 1899)
Rabindranath Tagore

Rabindranath Tagore with daughter Madhurilata and son Rathindranath

A section of Rabindranath Tagore's house at Jorasanko, Kolkata, where he was born

First floor veranda of No.6
Jorasanko House, Kolkata
Courtesy - Samit Das